PRAISE FOR
THE ECONOMIC CASE FOR LGBT EQUALITY

"The denial of LGBT equality is morally wrong. Lee Badgett's superbly researched book also shows the immense economic losses that result from this inhumanity. Eye-opening in its global scope, *The Economic Case for LGBT Equality* is a must-read for all business leaders and policymakers."

—JANET YELLEN, Distinguished Fellow, Brookings Institution

"Lee Badgett is the premier economist working on LGBT issues today—and perhaps ever. In this tough-minded, far-ranging, and accessible volume, she crisply articulates the benefits of LGBT inclusion across multiple domains, including education, employment, and health. Along the way, she illuminates why advocates of LGBT rights should embrace economic arguments, which support rather than supplant their moral claims."

—KENJI YOSHINO, Chief Justice Earl Warren Professor of Constitutional Law, New York University School of Law

"One of the world's leading authorities on the economics of the LGBT experience, Lee Badgett articulates the importance of granting LGBT community members full and equal participation in basic economic, education, health, social, and political settings. This well-written and impactful resource offers business leaders an in-depth analysis on the significance of driving LGBT inclusion in the workplace and marketplace."

—TONY TENICELA, Global Leader, Marketplace Diversity and Workforce Engagement Services, IBM

"I wish people would support LGBTQI rights because it is the moral and just thing to do, but if not, *The Economic Case for LGBT Equality* provides the evidence to confirm what many of us know firsthand: homophobia, transphobia, and patriarchy not only keep LGBTQI people in poverty or compensated less compared with their straight or cisgender counterparts, but they also cause entire nations to lose. When LGBTQI people can't bring their full selves into the workforce, creativity is stifled and opportunity lost. No employer can afford to lose talent, no nation can afford to lose revenue, and no person should be marginalized economically because of their sexual orientation, gender identity, or gender expression. This book has the potential to persuade even the most ambivalent that LGBTQI rights matter for everyone, and every person with power should read it."

—JESSICA STERN, executive director,
OutRight Action International

"*The Economic Case for LGBT Equality* deserves to be a best seller. LGBTQI people in Uganda and around the world are often conceived as a high business risk since employers are unwilling to address cases of harassment and discrimination. As a result, not only do LGBTQI individuals lose out on important employment opportunities, but M. V. Lee Badgett shows that companies' bottom lines are adversely affected as well. This articulate and convincing book for why fairness truly benefits us all should be read by all organizations, activists, and governments."

—KASHA JACQUELINE NABAGESERA, queer radical feminist
and founder of Freedom & Roam Uganda

THE ECONOMIC CASE FOR LGBT EQUALITY

QUEER ACTION/QUEER IDEAS
A UNIQUE SERIES ADDRESSING PIVOTAL ISSUES
WITHIN THE LGBTQ MOVEMENT

THE
ECONOMIC
CASE FOR
LGBT
EQUALITY

WHY FAIR AND EQUAL TREATMENT
BENEFITS US ALL

M. V. LEE BADGETT

QUEER ACTION/QUEER IDEAS
A Series Edited by Michael Bronski

BEACON PRESS
BOSTON

BEACON PRESS
Boston, Massachusetts
www.beacon.org

Beacon Press books
are published under the auspices of
the Unitarian Universalist Association of Congregations.

23 22 21 20   8 7 6 5 4 3 2 1

QUEER ACTION/QUEER IDEAS a series edited by Michael Bronski

Many names and identifying characteristics of people mentioned in this work
have been changed to protect their identities.

This book is printed on acid-free paper that meets the uncoated paper
ANSI/NISO specifications for permanence as revised in 1992.

Text design and composition by Kim Arney

Library of Congress Cataloging-in-Publication Data

Names: Badgett, M. V. Lee (Mary Virginia Lee), author.
Title: The economic case for LGBT equality : why fair and equal treatment
   benefits us all / M.V. Lee Badgett.
Description: Boston : Beacon Press, [2020] | Series: Queer action/queer
   ideas | Includes bibliographical references and index.
Identifiers: LCCN 2019026850 (print) | LCCN 2019026851 (ebook) |
   ISBN 9780807035603 (hardcover) | ISBN 9780807035610 (ebook)
Subjects: LCSH: Homophobia—Economic aspects. | Transphobia—Economic
   aspects. | Gay rights—Economic aspects. | Transaction costs. | Opportunity costs.
Classification: LCC HQ76.4 .B33 2020 (print) | LCC HQ76.4 (ebook) |
   DDC 306.76/6—dc23
LC record available at https://lccn.loc.gov/2019026850
LC ebook record available at https://lccn.loc.gov/2019026851

To Mr. X and Mr. Y,
and to all the other Salzburg Global
LGBT Fellows who are bearing
these costs and working to
change them for us all.

CONTENTS

AUTHOR'S NOTE ON LANGUAGE AND TERMS

THIS BOOK USES some important terms in ways that might be unfamiliar to some readers, so here is a brief guide. When we talk about *lesbian, gay, bisexual,* and *transgender* people, we usually mean people who have a particular identity—they think of themselves as belonging to one of those four groups. Sometimes they are also called *sexual and gender minorities* as a group, since most surveys find LGBT people to constitute somewhere around 3–6 percent of the population in places with high quality statistics. Another umbrella term preferred by some activists is *queer*, which I sometimes use to refer to LGBT people broadly.

Here's another way to think about it: lesbian, gay, and bisexual people are those with a particular *sexual orientation*, which can also be thought of as having a romantic or sexual attraction to people of the same sex or having sex partners of the same sex. Bisexuals are attracted to or have had sexual partners from more than one gender group. Heterosexuals are attracted to and are partners with different-sex people. So sexual orientation can refer to a self-identity, an attraction, or a behavior.

Gender identity captures whether someone thinks of themselves as male or female, nonbinary, or something else. Transgender people include those who live as and think of themselves as a gender that is not the same as the sex they were assigned when they were born. Someone born male who lives as a woman would be a transgender woman. Someone born female who lives as a man would be a transgender man. Some transgender people would prefer not to use what they see as restrictive binary male-female gender labels and might call themselves genderqueer, nonbinary, third gender, or some other label. Not all nonbinary people identify as transgender, though. And transgender and nonbinary people also have sexual orientations, sometimes thinking of themselves as lesbian, gay, bisexual, or heterosexual, just as nontransgender—or cisgender—people do.

It's important to note that identity labels will continue to evolve over time. They also don't always line up with attraction or sex partners, especially outside the Western contexts that generated these terms and identities. Some cultures define sexual minorities with local terms that combine someone's sexual partners and gender identity. For example, in India, *hijra* are people born as male who think of themselves as a third gender, and they generally have sex with men. In Indonesia, *waria* is the term used for some transgender women.

Just as there are different ways to think of LGBT people, there are also different ways of describing their inequality. Psychologist Gregory M. Herek defines *stigma* as society's negative view of LGBT people that assigns them an inferior social status. *Sexual prejudice* is the negative view of LGBT people held by individuals who have internalized that social stigma.

Discrimination is more active and happens when LGBT people are treated poorly compared to non-LGBT people, such as in hiring or in an educational setting, even when they have the same abilities or qualifications. *Violence* refers to actions that directly generate physical, psychological, or sexual harm to LGBT people. We could think of *rights* as legal or moral claims that allow LGBT people to insist on equal treatment if they face discrimination or violence.

Inequality is one general term that captures the potentially measurable differences in social, legal, and economic outcomes. For example, worse health outcomes or lower incomes for LGBT people (compared with non-LGBT people) are inequalities that might result from stigma, violence, and discrimination.

The terms *inclusion* and *exclusion* go beyond inequality, rights, or discrimination to define whether LGBT people are able to fully participate in all social institutions like the job market, educational system, healthcare system, and political process. The United Nations Development Programme defines inclusion as "access to opportunities and achievement of outcomes" that are consistent with human dignity. Exclusion flips the definition in situations in which LGBT do *not* have such opportunities or outcomes.

Finally, two LGBT-specific terms also refer to the big picture of the unfair and harmful situation of LGBT people, encompassing actions as well as the negative social or individual view of LGBT people: *homophobia* and *transphobia*. They don't have the precision of academic concepts and typically mean something broader than a literal phobia or fear of homosexual or transgender people. They are very useful, though, for focusing attention on LGBT people and implying the links between stigma and prejudice with the treatment that an inferior status generates: violence, discrimination, lack of rights, and inequality. In short: exclusion.

The broad terms like inclusion, exclusion, inequality, homophobia, and transphobia are useful for thinking about the general situation faced by LGBT people, and I use those somewhat interchangeably. I try to use the more specific terms more precisely. Although these concepts are distinct—and potentially confusing in their similarities and differences—they all reflect the fact that LGBT people may be targeted for harmful treatment.

Thinking about the situation faced by LGBT people also helps to better define the people this book talks about. Despite its complexity and origins in particular countries, I use *LGBT* as an umbrella term, because those groups of sexual and gender minorities—however they are labeled in different places—face similar issues of stigma, violence, and discrimination, although sometimes in varying forms and intensity. While those terms are not always used to describe sexual and gender minorities in the world's range of cultures, human rights, development and governmental bodies increasingly use the LGBT framework, so that umbrella is a familiar one for thinking about local identities and terms. However, sometimes research and ideas specifically point to lesbian, gay, or bisexual people and *not* to transgender people; in those cases I deliberately designate the relevant group as LGB.

Finally, international human rights institutions have begun to add an "I" for *intersex* to the LGBT label. Intersex people have variations in sex characteristics that might not fit into social understandings of what it means to be male or female. Their issues and concerns often overlap with LGBT people in some cases, particularly because intersex people experience stigma and discrimination, and they are sometimes even assumed to be gay or transgender. But in many other ways, intersex people face different concerns about bodily integrity and consent for surgery, for example. Because currently there is very little research about inequality in employment, health, or education related to being intersex, it's not possible to directly discuss intersex issues in this book using a strong evidence base, so the first five chapters are limited to a discussion of research on LGBT people. However, given anecdotal evidence on the treatment of intersex people and emerging research on discrimination and other challenges, I have little doubt that the social inclusion of intersex people would also benefit the economy. For that reason, and because the global debate and social movements increasingly include intersex people, in chapters 6 and 7, I add intersex people into the discussion under the expanded LGBTI umbrella.

PREFACE

WHEN I WAS IN HIGH SCHOOL, I got my first real job in the toy section of a local department store. Through the Christmas rush and beyond, many other young women and I waited on customers and kept the shelves well stocked with Sesame Street stuffed animals and Star Wars paraphernalia. Our other main duty was to ring up purchases, both from toys and from the neighboring sporting goods department.

One slow day a guy from my high school who worked in sporting goods brought over a customer with some goods to pay for. After the customer left, I chatted with my classmate and had a chance to ask him something I'd been wondering about: Why did we have to type in a clerk's identification number for sporting goods purchases?

To my shock, he said, "We get a commission on sales," something not paid to us in the toy department. That was a blow, but I had to ask another question: What was his hourly wage? A good fifteen cents an hour more than mine!

As a high school athlete in two sports, I knew I had at least as much knowledge about sports as my classmate. So off I went to our mutual manager to ask for a transfer. He stalled, explaining, "Well, we once had a girl in sporting goods, and she didn't work out too well. But I'll think about it." I heard nothing. Shortly after that, I found a better paying job with more hours and left the store.

That experience was the first step on my path to becoming a labor economist who studies employment discrimination and economic inequality.

I've thought about that job from many angles since then. Did the person who hired me put me in the lower-paying toy department just because I was female? Wouldn't my firsthand knowledge of athletics and ability to relate to female customers have been assets to be sought after in sporting goods? I've also never forgotten what discrimination feels like: disbelief, outrage, and frustration, along with shame for being the wrong kind of person—wrong as others with power saw it.

Later, as I trained to be an economist, I learned the theories and methods that are relevant for answering those questions. I studied employment discrimination based on race and sex, along with affirmative action and other policy remedies. A few years into my first job as an economist, I found a way to apply those theories and methods to new questions that have animated my career since then: How does being lesbian, gay, bisexual, or transgender (LGBT) affect people's economic well-being? Thus began my journey to open the economics profession to the study of sexual orientation and gender identity so I could better answer questions for which we otherwise had only stereotypes.

For the last three decades, I've explored many data sources to see how LGBT people fare economically. I've analyzed wages, discrimination charges, employment, occupational attainment, poverty, compensation, and public policies, finding that LGBT people experience unequal outcomes compared with heterosexual and cisgender (that is, nontransgender) people. I've studied how inequality in family policies hurt same-sex couples, making them less economically secure because they could not marry, and how marriage equality would help government budgets and local businesses.

Over those decades, it's been wonderful to be part of an emerging international scholarly community studying LGBT issues within the social and health sciences. We now have access to much more data than when I started my career, and journals regularly publish excellent research on LGBT-related topics. In this book, I draw on that body of academic research as well as my own to show the harm of inequality and exclusion on LGBT people's education, health, and economic well-being. Given the many studies that have been conducted, it's not possible to be comprehensive even in one discipline or for one country. Thus the studies I refer to in this book are better thought of as examples, giving a sense of the experience of LGBT people across a wide range of countries. Certainly there will be many more in print by the time this book is published.

In many ways this book brings me back to the questions from my toy department days, exploring both the personal economic and health costs of discrimination along with the larger cost to economies and businesses. These are not just academic questions. The last three decades have also seen the emergence of strong LGBT political movements in the US and many other countries that have generated intense public debates over issues like decriminalization of homosexuality (which happened in 2003 in the US), the right to determine one's own gender, employment discrimination, and marriage equality. These developments gave me the opportunity to contribute my research to some of those debates in the US through op-ed pieces, policy analysis, public speaking, and expert testimony in courts and legislatures. I saw firsthand how ideas and data matter in public policy debates, and also how important it is to provide credible information on the effect of inequality on people and the economy.

Then in 2013 at more or less the same time, Claire Lucas at USAID and Fabrice Houdart at the World Bank convinced me to take on two projects that would take some of that analysis to a new level. Could I estimate the cost of homophobia and transphobia on national economies outside of the US? Those two projects led me to new collaborations on publications, and those publications led to new audiences of LGBT advocates outside the US: economic development agencies, human rights activists, and multinational businesses. My interactions with those groups taught me that we are all working together toward similar goals in our different countries: dignity, fairness, and freedom for LGBT people.

Many people in those audiences saw the idea that LGBT inclusion is good for economies as a useful door opener and conversation starter in locations that are not persuaded by pure human rights arguments. I've been talking about this idea in many places ever since, particularly on extended speaking tours in Peru, the Philippines, Hong Kong, and Australia, and shorter visits to Vietnam, South Korea, China, OECD, USAID, Asian Development Bank, and the Inter-American Development Bank, along with talks at many global conferences of LGBT advocates, diplomats, development professionals, human rights practitioners, researchers, businesspeople, and economists. Many people I've met in these contexts generously offered to speak with me on the record for use in this book about why this idea matters.

In all of those places, I have heard heartrending stories from LGBT people, impassioned pleas for respecting human rights, and about historical-cultural roots for respecting LGBT people in particular countries. Those are all excellent reasons to end stigma, violence, and discrimination against LGBT people. The economic case is another reason that connects one good with another—dignity and rights for LGBT people can help to make our societies and all people more prosperous. I offer this contribution to the larger realm of ideas that can expand freedom and equality.

INTRODUCTION

Vancouver, 2018

O N A GLORIOUS SUMMER DAY IN VANCOUVER, Chrystia Freeland, Canada's foreign affairs minister and real-life "Madam Secretary,"[1] strode to the stage to officially welcome a ballroom full of delegates from seventy-five countries to the Equal Rights Coalition conference on rights for people who are lesbian, gay, bisexual, transgender, and intersex (LGBTI).* Young, charismatic, and articulate, Freeland opened the meeting with a frank admission of the dark chapters in Canada's own history with regard to LGBT and intersex people. Less than a year earlier, Prime Minister Justin Trudeau offered a tearful apology to LGBT Canadians for decades of persecution in the military and public service. Freeland also noted some of Canada's modern-day LGBT issues: high rates of homelessness and suicide attempts for LGBT youth and rates of violence twice as high as for other Canadians.

Those of us in the ballroom also came from countries with equally alarming statistics about the social and health challenges

---

* In the global arena, intersex people are now rightfully included as a sexual and gender minority facing stigma and discrimination in important institutions. Because of the lack of research on inequality for intersex people, as I discuss in the author's note, I focus in this book on LGBT people. In some cases, though, because of the organizations being discussed, I will use "LGBTI" to capture the focus of an organization. In some cases, I use "LGB" to refer to an organization, issue, or study that focuses on sexual orientation but not on gender-identity issues.

faced by LGBT people. In the US, where I live and work, policy attention ebbs and flows with the political tides when it comes to stark realities like these: transgender people are almost ten times more likely to attempt suicide than cisgender people, and one in five LGBT people have experienced employment discrimination.[2] And yet public acceptance is at an all-time high. Nine out of ten Americans know someone who is gay or lesbian, and increasing numbers know a transgender person.[3] Same-sex marriage became law in 2015, an achievement supported now by two-thirds of Americans.[4]

Behind every statistic are many real people, and some in the ballroom were living the challenging lives we were about to discuss. One lesbian panelist from Central America spoke about her recent detainment by police and the death threats she would soon be returning to face down. A transgender activist from Africa described their organization's struggle to survive financially. Lesbians from South Asia worried about the tension between increasing visibility of LGBT people and the resulting increase in their vulnerability to violence. Not everyone in the room was LGBT, but we were all there because of our commitment to improving the quality of LGBT and intersex lives globally.

The theme of the meeting was "Leave No One Behind," tracking the aspiration at the heart of the United Nations Sustainable Development Goals (SDG) to extend human rights and inclusive development to LGBT and intersex people. This was the fifth meeting since 2010 of a little-known and evolving group of diplomats and global leaders from foundations, advocacy groups, governments, international human rights agencies, development banks, and academia. Their efforts had spawned the formal Equal Rights Coalition at a 2016 meeting in Uruguay. By 2018 the governments of the US, Canada, Chile, and Germany, along with thirty-six other countries on five continents, had signed on to the coalition's pledge to cooperate, coordinate, and share information about how to advance the human rights of LGBT and intersex people and to make sure they were included in economic development efforts.[5]

The low visibility of this group of countries and delegates is not because it's a hidden global cabal, but because many of the world's 195 or so governments have little knowledge of or interest in queer people. Many reject the very premise of human rights for LGBT people, with sixty-nine countries criminalizing homosexuality and eleven allowing the death penalty to punish people who have sex with someone of the same sex; at least fifty-seven countries criminalize or prosecute transgender people.[6] Other countries aren't convinced that the rights of such a small group matter in the face of pressing issues like poverty, violence, and war. Even delegates from LGBT-supportive countries reported how hard it was to convince their economic ministries and development offices that they should care about LGBT issues.

My attendance in Vancouver was as a member of the World Bank's delegation, and we were there to share with delegates an excellent reason for all countries to care about LGBT rights: simply put, they are good for our economies. Five years earlier I'd received a call at my University of Massachusetts Amherst office from a professional acquaintance at the bank. He was starting a new project on LGBT people in India and wanted to know if I would be interested in developing a way to estimate the economic cost of homophobia there. I was intrigued by the idea, and after gathering all the data I could find on queer people there, I estimated that India lost as much as 1 percent of its gross domestic product (GDP) because of homophobia and transphobia.[7]

A PERMANENT RECESSION?

Consider this: if production in factories, shops, hospitals, restaurants, and other service companies suddenly fell by 1 percent, government, business, and academia would all leap into action, deeply invested in seeking remedies. If the downturn lasted long enough, economists would call it a recession, and policymakers would jump into action to correct the economy's course.[8]

But what happens when the global economy is dragged down for decades not by a financial crisis or oil shock but because of society's prejudices against lesbian, gay, bisexual, and transgender people? Not much.

That inaction is at least as costly as any economic downturn, however, and that's why continuing to communicate the cost of homophobia and transphobia was so crucially important for us in Vancouver. Excluding LGBT people through discrimination and violence means not only unfairly limiting their individual prospects but also robbing communities of the skills, knowledge, and abilities that are available to run and improve economies and societies. Even though LGBT people are a relatively small and often invisible minority, about 3–5 percent of the population, according to studies in the US (where 8.1 percent of millennials identify as LGBT) and Europe,[9] the India study and later research prove that their exclusion from the economy can generate a meaningful drop in income and jobs for a nation's people, especially in an era of slower growth. While there has been progressive movement in some countries toward ending discrimination against LGBT people, I argue in this book that realizing the full effect of bias on global economies merits an urgent and unified response, for both human rights and economic reasons.

LIVES BEHIND THE STATISTICS

As an economist, I appreciate that sometimes numbers can be numbing, so it's important to hear the stories of individuals whose lives are reflected in economic statistics. Later chapters include many stories of people I have encountered who shared what homophobia has cost them, but a good place to start is an innovative study published a few years ago. A team of researchers asked fifty-seven lesbian, gay, and bisexual people in New York City what their lives would be like without homophobia.[10] Their responses reveal how profoundly their lives have been affected by homophobia—what has been lost or ruptured, and perhaps also what could be regained in a more accepting world. (And although transgender people were not included in this study, we can imagine similar stories.)

They spoke of the pain and necessity of leaving home to escape the violence of homophobia; they spoke in anguish about lost family and community ties. Without homophobia, one man concluded his life would be completely different from what it actually is because, as he put it, "I would probably be at home." Another man shared that he left Lebanon, his home, because the unwelcoming culture made it impossible for him to be honest about his identity: "So maybe if there was no homophobia, I would still be in Lebanon, and I would be gay there."

Many people reported they had lost the opportunity for a quality education because of homophobic violence and discrimination. Some could not hold a partner's hand in public or demonstrate love or care for them for fear of violence. Others, to avoid discrimination, stayed hidden at work, carefully monitoring their language to prevent anyone guessing or gossiping about their sexual orientation.

These LGBT people did not put these effects of homophobia in monetary terms, but the costs are clear: countries lose people. And those people lose education, time, social support, energy, and possibly much more. From an economic perspective, it adds up, as we will see.

Interestingly, homophobia and transphobia have served one useful purpose in these people's lives: encouraging the creation of a community based on LGBT identities and a social movement to change the harsh realities. The resilience of LGBT people makes it possible to challenge exclusion and to consider what a world without homophobia and transphobia could look like.

I read hope and potential in those wistful and yet resilient responses. If homophobia and transphobia could be reduced, the lives of millions of sexual and gender minorities (whether they call themselves LGBT or not) would improve. At a minimum, they would have more educational opportunities, more safety, and, broadly, a sense of belonging in the world. LGBT people would be better off, and I would argue, we would *all* be better off in that world by reducing the economic costs of homophobia and transphobia.

ECONOMICS AND HUMAN RIGHTS

Most of us are not used to thinking about LGBT rights in the context of business and the economy. Instead, we understandably see pain and injustice in stories like the ones from the study of New Yorkers; we feel outrage and grief. Sadly, it's not uncommon in the US to see stories in our social media feeds about young transgender kids who have died by suicide, or to hear news about a lesbian being fired after marrying her female partner. We hear horrific accounts of gay men tortured and detained in concentration camps in Chechnya. We read about violent religious fundamentalists hacking two Bangladeshi LGBT activists to death. These are classic cases of human rights violations that, thankfully, have been met by at least some global concern.

Putting those traumatic human stories next to the calculating logic of business makes us wonder: Why would we try to understand the impact of those events on our economy and not on our very souls? Depriving some humans of dignity and even their lives seems like the kind of harm that should keep us awake at night trying to figure out how to eliminate hatred and prejudice, not calculating what it costs.

Even as an economist, I agree that harm to LGBT people is first and foremost a human rights issue. The human rights perspective gives us an essential tool with which to work, and the UN Universal Declaration of Human Rights rightly states, "All human beings are born free and equal in dignity and rights." Education and activism at the United Nations and by other human rights and civil rights enforcement organizations over the decades have tried to provide some recourse to the suffering of LGBT individuals. In addition to those official bodies, many nongovernmental organizations (NGOs) apply public pressure and provide education to reduce the incidence of human rights violations. These processes bring moral condemnation to the perpetrators of violations and sometimes generate meaningful change.

The truth is that in practice economics and human rights are deeply intertwined. The Universal Declaration of Human Rights includes economic rights such as the right to work, equal pay for equal work, social security, education, and an adequate standard of living. People will be able to achieve those economic rights in their country only through "national effort and international co-operation and *in accordance with the organization and resources of each State.*"[11] In other words, expanding countries' economic capacity is essential to realizing some human rights.

By themselves, human rights declarations and compliance processes have not been enough to stop discrimination and violence against LGBT people. For one thing, human rights enforcement has only partially incorporated LGBT issues into its mandates in many locations. More glaringly, officials in many countries ignore LGBT people's claims about violations and bigotry and fail to see the link with human rights when their countries have laws that make LGBT people criminals. These countries and others often have no protective policies to prevent or discourage discrimination against LGBT people.

It's important to point out that there are indicators of a disadvantaged social position for LGBT people everywhere—including Europe, North and South America, Africa, Asia, and the Pacific. My research indicates that *every* country is a "developing country" when it comes to enacting rights for LGBT people and in taking action to make LGBT people's lives better. For those who assume that the United States is in another category, the fact remains that protections against discrimination vary greatly across states and are fragile in an era of political polarization.

So, in addition to the efforts that are already being made, we need some new ways of thinking to convert the many people who use their power to hurt LGBT people, whether in passing discriminatory laws, firing them from jobs, harassing them in school, beating them in the streets, witnessing but failing to protect them from beatings, putting them in jail, kicking them out of families, or depriving them of appropriate healthcare—in short, excluding them from the core institutions that make it possible to live a healthy and good life. If such people can't be convinced that LGBT people should be fully and fairly included in these areas because it's the morally right thing to do, a basic human rights argument, then we need other arguments to catalyze desperately needed social change.

The economic cost of homophobia and transphobia is one of those arguments, and I met some people in Vancouver who were already deploying that argument with success. With a cold, calculating lens, we may yet make our societies more civil and humane. Because the exclusion of LGBT people from full and equal participation in basic economic, education, health, social, and political settings doesn't just hurt them—it hurts everyone. In short, when LGBT people are fully included, we'll all be better off. Just as human rights have economic foundations, an economic argument can help achieve the goal of human rights.

THE HEART OF THE ECONOMIC CASE: THE POWER OF PEOPLE

While the economic cost of stigma and exclusion against LGBT people is a new idea, it's based on a simple and obvious point: economies are composed of individuals. To survive, we produce food, shelter, and clothing, along with the things that human ingenuity can dream up to collectively make our lives easier and healthier. We make social connections and take care of each other to sustain and reproduce human beings in families and communities. These fundamental tasks require not only natural resources like land, water, and air but also people's time, focus, and skills. Learning to use and add to human abilities has always been central to expanding economies' capacity to produce what humans need.

Who gets what and why—the other big question at the heart of economies—varies greatly over time and place. Although some of us like to think skill and talent determine who gets what, power and prejudice have been, and continue to be, at least as or sometimes more important. Women and girls get less to eat than men and boys in some places, for example, and women globally are still often paid less than men for the same work. People in certain castes or races are assigned difficult jobs that pay little, such as Indigenous people or African Americans in the US, while in India, the Dalit caste, once known as untouchables, are still discriminated against. We will see how LGBT people are kept out of some jobs and constrained in almost all jobs. But are these practices fixed and natural in some sense, or can these cultural constraints be changed?

The twentieth century saw many efforts to make the distribution of what economies produce fairer. The US civil rights and women's movements led to new laws preventing the use of race and sex to limit access to well-paid jobs. Many northern European countries pooled public resources to create health and income insurance programs for their citizens. The Soviet Union used state ownership to try to equalize access to the means of production for all workers. In each case, some worried that increased equity came at the cost of impeding economic efficiency and capacity, seemingly posing a dilemma for nations trying to achieve both goals.

But then economists began to see that discrimination might be bad for the economy. In the 1950s, Nobel Prize–winning economist Gary Becker showed how racial discrimination is financially costly for employers. Other American economists argued that racial discrimination in the US was holding back our economy. For example, in 1965 the President's Council of Economic Advisers estimated that employment and education discrimination based on race cost the US economy as much as $20 billion a year. A 1971 study by economist Barbara Bergmann showed that opening up more jobs to African Americans would allow for a more efficient allocation of workers and would increase national income.

Partly because of those well-known economists, the presumed relationship between equity and efficiency has reversed in the twenty-first century. Now many economists worry that it's *inequality* that threatens our economic capacity.[12] Rising levels of wealth and income inequality within many countries, like the US, the UK, South Africa, and China, pose both political and productive threats. Wealthy individuals can use their money to generate political decisions in their favor, even when those decisions are not in the larger economic interest. The dismantling of safety nets and publicly provided goods takes away important supports for creating the next generation of entrepreneurs and an educated population. Economic inequalities persist despite some efforts to reduce discrimination and to distribute income more equally, demonstrating that our economies are not fully using the people and skills available.

Reports come out frequently making an economic argument for gender equality all over the world: increasing women's education, health, political engagement, and access to employment would provide new ideas and new participants in nations' economies. And this argument has been made for the Roma people in Eastern Europe and other ethnic minorities. And for people with disabilities. And for immigrants. And all for excellent reasons—forcing a group of people to the side, no matter how large or small the group, means limiting the skills, knowledge, and abilities that are available to improve economies and societies.[13]

It's time to turn the economic spotlight on LGBT people because much is at stake. Imagine the tangible losses to the world's economies and cultures if LGBT people are excluded from creative work. We might miss out on the inventions of the next Alan Turing, the father of the modern computer. We might lose the musical delights of the next Aaron Copland or Elton John, the literature of the next James Baldwin or Virginia Woolf, or the entrepreneurial imagination of Martine Rothblatt. But the point isn't fame—it's that every LGBT person contributes something, whether they are teachers, cashiers, nurses, custodians, in the beauty industry, unpaid caregivers, and truck drivers or whether they are in the underground or informal economy. Their individual human losses from being unfairly targeted turn into our collective social losses as we miss out on the full benefit of their skills, experience, and creativity.

THE POWER OF A NEW IDEA

The potential power of this idea will depend on the evidence that supports it, and the ability to get it to decision makers who will use it. Obviously, we can't run an experiment to compare the size of one economy that we make inclusive of LGBT people to a second identical economy that is not. Fortunately, we have other options. Data on LGBT people's lives has improved greatly in the US, the UK, and Canada, and it's starting to come in from many other countries, too, such as China, India, and Ecuador. What we can see so far provides clear evidence supporting the economic case for LGBT equality by showing how exclusion diminishes the capacity of LGBT people within the economy.

The next three chapters show how LGBT people are treated differently from non-LGBT people in important economic contexts—education, employment, and health. Education plays a crucial role in getting good jobs and in economic growth, so what happens to LGBT people in schools and universities matters a lot for their economic contributions. When Pema Dorji, now a young gay activist, was growing up in Bhutan, his school experience was brutal, in his words, "like going to a war." Data from many parts of the world shows he was not alone in his battle, with similarly high rates of bullying of LGBT students in countries as different as the US and Thailand. Bullying takes a toll on academic performance and persistence in schools, so queer students aren't receiving the education they need and are capable of. That deficit, in turn, puts them at economic risk and also reduces the knowledge and skills available in a country.

In every country that's been studied, there is also evidence of significant discrimination against queer people in the workplace, whether it's harassment, getting fired, or being forced to stay in the closet. A mapping of workplaces shows that LGBT people sometimes face barriers, keeping them out of certain jobs. When they do get jobs, they have to carefully avoid stepping outside the boundaries of coworkers' acceptance. Unfortunately, being too open about being gay can get them in trouble, even in relatively accepting workplaces. Stereotypes funnel LGBT people into some jobs and away from others. Given these risks, it's not surprising that they often choose to stay in the closet at work. Taken as a whole, the workplace constraints that LGBT people face keep them out of jobs they're qualified for, while simultaneously preventing them from performing their jobs at the levels they're capable of—and that's inefficient.

Employment and education are also closely connected to the challenges LGBT people face regarding health, the subject of chapter 3. Violence, bullying, discrimination, and being forced to hide take their toll on the mental and physical health of LGBT people, as a growing number of studies show. LGBT people might think they're doing fairly well in their jobs, but the hidden effects of exclusion manifested in antigay or antitransgender campaigns and repressive public policies can affect health in numerous ways for even the most resilient LGBT people. Getting treatment for health issues is also a challenge. Poorer health makes it harder to get and keep a job, adding to the economic consequences of homophobia and transphobia.

LGBT activists don't take these educational, employment, and health disparities for granted, of course. Instead, they take these stories of their friends and comrades to the court of public opinion, and sometimes to actual courts of human rights or legislative bodies to improve the status and treatment of LGBT people. These advocates think that new arguments like the economic case will help them, and chapters 1, 2, and 3 show examples of how it's been used. At international meetings, in emails, and in one-on-one conversations, activists from countries in Africa, Central America, and Asia show how the economic case for LGBT rights will help their cause.[14] To be sure, they aren't giving up the human rights argument—but they see the need to work with a broader toolkit.

In chapter 4, we will see how economic arguments have already made a difference for LGBT people in some parts of the world. "The business case" for LGBT equality, a subset of the economic case, has circulated widely across corporations in the United States and Europe. Businesses are convinced that their employees will be more productive, creative, loyal, and engaged when they are treated fairly, and a growing body of research backs them up. LGBT employees are healthier and more productive when they work for supportive employers. Businesses can recruit and retain a more skilled workforce when their policies are equal. And businesses that have equal policies outperform those companies that don't.

The evidence is behind the decision of many multinational firms, including almost every Fortune 500 firm in the US, to *voluntarily* add sexual orientation to their company nondiscrimination policy, and more and more companies are adding gender identity too. It's likely that millions of LGBT people in the US and Europe have been protected by company nondiscrimination policies that were motivated by the business case.

The business case has also led companies to advocate for LGBT equality well beyond the company walls. Hundreds of businesses with global brands, like Apple, Amazon, and Microsoft, told the US Supreme Court that they supported marriage equality because they wanted the law to make it possible for businesses to treat their LGBT employees equally. Many US businesses have put their money where their mouths are when LGBT rights are threatened by new legislation, moving events and investments to more tolerant states. The business case seems to be gaining momentum in other parts of the world now, too, both in company policies and in how multinationals engage with national governments, although there is still a long way to go.

Chapter 5 puts the pieces together to estimate the overall losses to countries' economies from excluding LGBT people. First I take what would be a ten-thousand-foot view from a plane. Here I focus on estimates of several different kinds of inequality in jobs, health, and education and add up the effects on all LGBT people in a country. To get the detailed data that is necessary for the estimates, I use examples from the US, Canada, India, the Philippines, Kenya, and South Africa. In each case, the costs stack up to a meaningful amount for those countries, on the order of 1 percent of GDP. In other words, the benefits to LGBT inclusion would be large.

Next I take more of a thirty-five-thousand-foot view, looking across borders to see the costs of LGBT inequality and the benefits of inclusion. The idea is straightforward. If LGBT inclusion is good for economies, we should see that countries with better policies and attitudes toward LGBT people also have stronger economies. And we do: national output of goods and services is significantly higher in countries that grant more rights to LGBT people. Of course, one reasonable question is whether that correlation implies causation. Does inclusion increase economic output, or do richer countries have more room for recognition of the rights of LGBT people? It is a difficult question, and one that's hard to answer definitively—probably both dynamics are at work.

In the final two chapters, I look at the way forward if we are to make the economic case for LGBT equality. One challenge is to address the objections and questions that have been raised. Interestingly, the most fervent objections come from some people invested in seeing LGBT inclusion as a human rights issue. Even though they seek the same equality, they doggedly argue that human rights belong to everyone, and they are not for sale. They argue that the economic case appears to put a price tag on rights and to only value people who make measurable economic contributions in a heartless capitalist economy. But in my view, the cost of homophobia and transphobia argument is a complement and extension to the human rights argument, not a replacement for it. Even though human rights advocates don't speak the same language as economists, the goals are the same when it comes to LGBT rights and inclusion.

The bigger challenge comes from those in power who are blinded by anti-LGBT arguments. This book is part of the answer to that problem. Getting this new idea—along with stories, examples, data, and studies—into the hands of activists, development agencies, government officials, and businesspeople makes possible a new conversation about a controversial issue that is growing in visibility. By opening up fresh discussions in new locations, we can unlock substantial potential for economic growth for all and improve the lives of LGBT people worldwide.

I close the book with ideas for actions that the economic cost argument should unlock. If homophobia and transphobia are costly, then we can and must make changes that will reduce those costs and more fully include LGBT people in our economies and societies. As the Vancouver meeting suggests, the economic case is now attracting some attention from influential agencies and organizations that work on economic development globally, like the World Bank, the United Nations Development Programme (UNDP), and the US Agency for International Development (USAID). As these agencies hear that LGBT inclusion matters for their core work—economic development—they put LGBT people on their agendas too. International organizations and national governments need tools to start reducing the cost of homophobia and transphobia by fully including LGBT people in every aspect of their work.

The need to send this new idea far and wide is clear. This book presents the economic case for LGBT equality to all who have something at stake: investors, community organizations, businesses, government agencies, universities, schools, hospitals, development agencies, and human rights agencies. More importantly, perhaps, it presents this case to citizens who can give the argument legs and make it more urgent to those organizations. Over time, more and more people around the world are being asked to make a choice about LGBT issues, whether in their votes for anti-gay politicians, their acceptance of family members, or their hiring decisions. They need to know the consequences of their decisions for us all, including for LGBT people.

CHAPTER 1

STIGMA AND SCHOOLS

WHEN PEMA DORJI, now a young gay activist, was growing up in Bhutan, attending school was "like going to a war."[1] Growing up was traumatizing because his peers, in his words, "never failed to make me realize that I don't belong with them, that I was an abnormal anomaly around them." Pema recalls that they refused to use his name, taunting him by using "a word that roughly translates to 'not a male, nor a female.'"

Teachers not only failed to protect him but also informed him that he was the problem. After a student poured a bucket of freezing water over Pema, the bully justified his action to their teacher exclaiming, "He behaves like a girl!" The teacher reproached Pema saying, "You need to change if you want this to stop."

Over time, these experiences were profoundly damaging, and Pema became severely depressed and attempted suicide twice. Years later, he still feels despair and sadness when he reflects on those days. "Whenever I have alone time, whenever I am going to bed, these thoughts come across my mind saying that if I hadn't been through this experience I might be a really different person; better or worse, but still a different person."

Pema decided that "no child deserves to go through the same situation that I went through" and today he works to ensure that all students have a better and more positive school environment in Bhutan. But Pema's story is still a common one.

All over the world, children are sent to school to learn important lessons. Students learn practical skills in primary school for everyday life, like learning to read and do basic math. Schools connect students to their cultures, teaching a country's history and exposing young people to art, music, and literature that convey values and traditions. As children get older, they learn about political systems and how they can and should participate. The skills and knowledge young people learn in school are useful in the marketplace when they become consumers, entrepreneurs, employees, or investors. But often students who think of themselves as LGBT, along with those who don't look or act in mainstream gendered ways, also learn something else: they are potential targets.

That lesson is reinforced by bullying and violence as well as outright discrimination by teachers and school administrators. And that's a big problem—not just for those students, who face horrendous treatment in school, but also when they take what they've learned into jobs or their own businesses. The connection to the economy makes the treatment of LGBT students, and the barriers that bullying and discrimination pose to their success, something for us all to be concerned about.

The connection between education and economic growth is widely accepted among economists. The knowledge and basic skills that students acquire in school make them more productive in the workforce later in life. Economists see education as so important to what people can accomplish in the economy that they call knowledge and skills "human capital." It's like machinery, computers, buildings, or other kinds of physical capital because it doesn't get used up after a day's work.

The evidence has accumulated over the years that education leads to greater productivity for individuals and for countries.[2] People with more education earn more, with the financial returns to education reflecting higher productivity. Countries with higher levels of education produce more. Countries whose students have higher test scores grow faster than countries with lower test scores. As a result of those strong connections, many global economic development programs focus on education. One of the Millennium Development Goals, a late-twentieth-century effort led by the United Nations to funnel resources and energy into reducing global poverty, was to eliminate differences between girls and boys in primary and secondary education. By 2015 almost two-thirds of developing countries had reached gender parity in primary education, and many countries had also reached gender parity in secondary education.[3]

Given the economic importance of education, if many other LGBT people have had experiences like Pema Dorji, we should be very worried, not just for their personal well-being but also for our collective economic well-being. For most countries, statistics don't exist right now that allow tracking of how many years of education LGBT people receive or how much LGBT young people learn in school. But researchers all over the world are using surveys and interviews to find out more about what happens to queer students. The stories they tell to researchers of their time in school paint a troubling picture.

BULLYING AND VIOLENCE ARE COMMON

Bullying is a potential problem for students just about everywhere. The kind of bullying tracked by education experts includes hitting or kicking, as well as other physical violence. Psychological bullying includes name-calling, unwanted teasing, spreading rumors, exclusion, public humiliation, or cyberbullying. Bullying often happens repeatedly and usually involves asserting power over another young person, who as a result experiences distress.

On a broad level, bullying is a global problem for all students, not just LGBT people. That's why the Organization for Economic Cooperation and Development (OECD), an international organization led by ambassadors from the US and thirty-four other countries, follows educational experiences closely. In 2015 the OECD surveyed fifteen-year-olds from fifty-three countries about their bullying. In these relatively high-income countries, 19 percent reported they were bullied at school in some way at least a few times a month, and 9 percent were frequently bullied. For all fifty-three countries, frequent bullying ranged from 2 percent in Korea to 19 percent in Qatar.[4]

The international data found that one in ten American high school students experience frequent bullying, and almost one in five (19 percent) experience it several times a month. That's bad enough. But it's even worse for LGBT students.

In a 2015 survey in the US, an appalling 85 percent of LGBT students, age thirteen to twenty-one, reported that they had experienced verbal harassment, mostly because of their sexual orientation or gender expression.[5] They are often targeted because they are LGBT or because people assume they are. The importance of perceptions means that non-LGBT students can also face violence if they don't conform to traditional ideas about how boys or girls should look and act. In addition, 27 percent faced physical harassment and 13 percent were physically assaulted because of their sexual orientation; 20 percent were physically harassed and 9 percent assaulted because of their gender expression.[6]

Anti-LGBT bullying is not just an American issue, since similar evidence can be seen all over the world. Unfortunately, the big international surveys of students don't yet allow students to report their sexual orientation or gender identity, so cross-national comparisons aren't possible. The United Nations agency that focuses on education, UNESCO, helped to fill the gaps in knowledge by scanning the globe for existing research on LGBT young people in schools. In 2016, UNESCO gathered studies of LGBT students that were conducted by NGOs or academics in ninety-four countries from every continent.[7]

Examples from these studies tell the familiar story of vulnerability and violence. Let's start with Asia. In Hong Kong, 10 percent of LGB students (transgender students were not included) reported physical and sexual violence, and 40 percent reported verbal harassment and social exclusion. In Mongolia, 7 percent of LGBT students in one survey had faced physical violence, one of the lowest rates found in UNESCO's study. But more than half—55 percent—of Thai students had experienced physical, psychological, or sexual violence in the month before they were surveyed. European countries have been in the vanguard of nations enacting laws giving equal rights to LGBT people, but bullying still finds its way into schools. In one survey, 23 percent of Dutch LGBT students reported being bullied; in Belgium, 56 percent of queer students had faced violence at school related to being LGBT; 36 percent of LGBT students experienced bullying in Finland. Studies from the UK find rates ranging from 20 to 55 percent of LGBT students reporting some kind of violence related to being LGBT. Studies in Norway find that 15 percent of lesbians, 24 percent of bisexuals, and 48 percent of gay male students were bullied. They were two to seven times more likely to be bullied than heterosexual students.

Latin American countries have also made rapid gains in LGBT equality legislation, but again schools remain problematic. A 2012 survey in Mexico showed that bullying was common against gay boys (75 percent), lesbian girls (50 percent), and transgender students (66 percent). In Ecuador, 26 percent of LGB students reported experiences of physical violence.

In Africa, researchers used a different approach in a survey of sixteen- to seventeen-year-olds, asking about students with varying gender expression rather than LGBT identities. They uncovered a high level of "diversity-related violence" against students seen as being different in their gender, "such as boys who look or act like girls and girls who look or act like boys." The percentage of students reporting diversity-related violence in their schools ranged from 18 percent in Swaziland to 41 percent in Namibia, and 44 percent in Lesotho and Botswana.[8]

The sometimes violent policing of sexual and gender nonconformity seen in schools from these studies also harms heterosexual students who are perceived as queer. So are young people who don't appear to conform to mainstream ideas about masculinity (for boys) or femininity (for girls). A study in Thailand found that 24 percent of heterosexual students were bullied because they were seen as gender nonconforming. A third of all Canadian male students in grades nine through eleven were verbally harassed because of their actual or perceived sexual orientation or gender identity, even though many of them did not identify as gay or bisexual.

These statistics about bullying are overwhelming—it's a serious and increasingly visible problem, so researchers in many countries are studying it. It's also important to point out that the differences in rates of bullying across countries are hard to interpret. Countries with low levels of bullying could be more accepting of LGBT students, but they might also be worse. In less accepting countries, students might be less likely to perceive the violence as something notable or to report it on a survey, and students might be disguising their LGBT status more effectively to avoid violence. Regardless of the reported level, though, these and many other surveys indicate that LGBT students face a serious problem in their schools in every country studied.

BULLYING AS A BARRIER TO EDUCATION

The impact of bullying extends well beyond a particular incident for one student. Those experiences reduce the quality of education for bullied students when they can't concentrate as well on their classes. The big international study by the OECD showed the toll bullying takes on academic performance all over the world. Students who were bullied had lower science scores on tests, for example. The impact scales up to schools too. Schools with high levels of bullying have lower average test scores (even after controlling for differences in socioeconomic levels of students).

Not surprisingly, LGBT students who've been bullied report similar effects. They report lower grades in studies from England, El Salvador, Australia, and Europe.[9] A 2016 study in the United States compared LGBT students who reported some kind of victimization related to their sexual orientation or gender expression to those that had not been victims. The extended harm was clear: those who were bullied had lower grades.[10]

This treatment also means that LGBT people are missing out on the crucial experiences they need in school, sometimes very directly. In the US, LGBT students who've been bullied are three times more likely to skip school than others. LGBT students also drop out because of bullying and are less likely to plan to attend college.

Violence additionally takes a toll on their health, and because bullying increases anxiety, depression, and risky health behaviors, it also reduces self-esteem. Studies from Thailand and Mexico indicate a link between bullying and suicidal thoughts or attempts.

Will these experiences reduce how much education LGBT people get over their lifetimes? If bullying leads to skipping school and dropping out, one would think LGBT students would end up with less education as adults than non-LGBT young people. That pattern holds for transgender people in the US: only 10 percent of transgender men, 12 percent of transgender women, and 18 percent of gender nonconforming people have a college degree compared with 25 percent of cisgender men and 29 percent of cisgender women.[11] However, some data from the US, Canada, Australia, and several European countries appear to suggest the opposite for LGB people (those studies did not focus on transgender people).[12] Many studies of adult LGB people across a wide age range find they have higher levels of education than do heterosexual people on the same surveys. For example, US National Health Interview Survey data from 2013 through 2016 indicates that 40 percent of lesbians and 44 percent of gay men had a college or graduate degree, but only 31 percent of heterosexual women and men did.[13] Of course, some of those LGB people grew up at a very different time, so it's difficult to know what those differences in average levels of education mean.

Fortunately, in the US it's possible to focus on one particular cohort of young people that has been surveyed several times since they were fourteen to eighteen years old in 1994 (the so-called Add

Health survey). Several researchers have found differences in the high school experiences between heterosexual young people and sexual minorities (those with some kind of same-sex behavior or attraction or a nonheterosexual identity).[14] The patterns are consistent with poor treatment in high school: Women with some kind of same-sex behavior, attraction, or nonheterosexual identity had more emotional distress and poorer school performance and less school engagement than heterosexual women. The men with adolescent same-sex sexual experiences also had more distress and interpersonal problems than men without same-sex contact.

With this tighter focus on a recent group of young adults, the educational outcome picture looks markedly different. When researchers measured educational attainment for these young people in 2008, they found attainment is affected by high school experiences and sexual orientation. In contrast to the broad studies of all adults, young sexual minority women had *lower* levels of education than heterosexual women, including being less likely to graduate from high school or to enroll in and complete college. However, most men with same-sex attraction, identity, or behavior had similar educational levels as heterosexual men in their age group, with the exception of one group. Late bloomers, whose same-sex attractions or behavior first occurred in adulthood, were more likely to finish high school and college than heterosexual men. Researchers think that the late-blooming men might have been able to avoid some of the harsh high school experiences that the women and some men had experienced. A study of more than 2,200 gay and bisexual men in the late 1990s supports that conclusion: those who decided they were gay or had their first same-sex sexual experience before they were eighteen were less likely to get a bachelor's degree than those coming out later.[15]

Data from other countries isn't available to make similar comparisons. But what is available suggests that the experiences of LGBT students in schools hurts students while they are there *and* in the future. The amount of actual education they receive may be lower because of experiences like bullying and discrimination, and the quality of that education is likely to be poorer as well. The effects of school bullying can also follow people into the labor market. A study of Greek adults found that those who'd been bullied in school—whether homosexual or heterosexual—were less likely to be employed and had lower wages. But those effects were even stronger for gay men, adding to the wage gap they experienced compared to heterosexual men.[16] Add to that the health effects that we'll see in chapter 3, and it's evident that schools are, in fact, potentially perilous places for LGBT students' human rights and future economic contributions.

OTHER BARRIERS TO EDUCATION FOR LGBT PEOPLE

As harmful as it is, bullying by one's peers is only one of the reasons that LGBT young people do not have equal access to educational systems. Teachers like Pema Dorji's can make the problem exponentially worse, failing to support their LGBT students against bullies. Less than half of the queer students who were harassed or assaulted at school in the US reported those incidents to school officials.[17] They didn't expect teachers or staff to do anything useful, and their instincts were correct. Of the students who did report the incidents, 64 percent—almost two-thirds—said the school staff either did nothing or advised them to ignore the abuse.

Teachers themselves are sometimes part of the problem, harassing students directly or creating an unwelcome environment. Less research on this question exists, but there are many examples from around the world. Nick, a gay university student in Burundi, shared that his professor "was talking in class one day about the [antigay] law that was proposed, and he said, 'If I had a homosexual child, I would banish him from my family.' Normally I participate in class a lot, but since he said that, I am afraid to raise my hand."[18] Certainly the obverse is also true, because teachers can be part of the solution. When LGBT students have positive relationships with their teachers, those students are less likely to have problems with other students, paying attention in school, and getting homework done.[19]

Teachers and other school officials also sometimes discriminate against LGBT students, denying them admission, giving them
lower grades, or expelling them because of their sexual orientation
or gender identity. A Kenyan lesbian, who asked to remain anony-
mous, experienced this in high school:

> I was found making out with another girl in the dining hall. . . .
> We were both expelled. . . . The administration never even gave
> us a hearing. They said they could not risk us "infecting" other
> girls. They made us feel diseased. Due to the disruption in my
> studies I performed below average [on a national exam] and had
> to repeat form four in another school the following year.[20]

Transgender students have a particularly hard time getting
into educational institutions. In Guatemala, a transgender student
applied to attend the main technical training center. The director
barred her from admission even though she had passed the quali-
fying exam, telling her that the institute's rules said that "only men
and women" could be admitted, not students like her.[21] Similarly,
Arina Alam, a transgender woman in rural India, also encountered
problems getting into a university. She reported, "The principal
at a renowned college posed some uncomfortable questions like:
'Where would we place you: in girls' or boys' hostels?' The principal told me that my presence in a hostel could bother other students."[22] Finally, getting the official documents needed to apply
and enroll is often an issue for transgender students.

A unique experiment by World Bank researchers shows how
clear the disadvantages for gender nonconforming students can
be. Women posing as mothers called 184 public primary schools in
Serbia to ask about enrollment of their fictional fourteen-year-old
son. Half of the time, the "mother" mentioned that her son was
feminine, and the other half of the time, that characteristic was not
mentioned. A small number (5 percent) of nonfeminine boys were
refused enrollment because the school was full. But the feminine
boys were three times as likely to be refused enrollment: 15 percent

versus 5 percent. The reason given by administrators was often startlingly honest: "Given that the child has such a profile, and the children of that age in our school are cruel, I would kindly ask you to try with another school. . . . I know what our children are like. They tolerate differences with lots of difficulties. They actually can't stand any differences."[23]

Schools also often have rules or informal practices that discriminate against LGBT students. Most LGBT students in the US have experienced one form or another of discrimination.[24] Some schools ban clothing that's considered inappropriate for a student's sex assigned at birth and won't allow students to use their preferred name or pronouns. Students are sometimes not allowed to discuss LGBT topics in class assignments, or they get in trouble for public displays of affection with a same-sex partner or for going to a dance together.

For many LGBT students in other parts of the world, families also control access to education, providing—or withholding—fees and living expenses. For example, a Ugandan lesbian who asked to be referred to as "KAB" was outed to her mother when her brothers found messages on her phone indicating she was a lesbian.[25] They beat her and kicked her out of her home. Her family also stopped paying for her university fees until she agreed to see a counselor who would "straighten [her] out."

KAB writes about her experience with counseling: "I fully understood that my sexuality was not something I could switch on and off like a light bulb but I obliged because I needed the educational support." She gave up on the counselor when he suggested that they have sex to cure her lesbianism. Other LGBT students rejected by their families have had to drop out of school while they work and try to save money to pay for further education.

TRYING TO MAKE IT BETTER

LGBT students and their allies have not given up hope of change. Pema Dorji turned his difficult education experience into activism, modeling one important strategy. Fortunately, numerous efforts are underway to improve the situation for LGBT students. The UNESCO study pointed to many ideas that education systems could adopt, and some are already doing so: policies and programs to prevent bullying, training for staff on how to respond to violence and to support queer students, inclusion of LGBT people in curricula, and collecting data to monitor violence in schools.

Some evidence suggests that these efforts are working in the United States. The Gay, Lesbian, and Straight Education Network (GLSEN) has been conducting its studies of LGBT students' experiences since 2001, and it has been following the trends to see if the situation has improved. GLSEN's answer to the question about change in US schools is a qualified yes: rates of discrimination and bullying against LGBT students appear to have declined; however, a substantial amount of work remains to be done. For example, the percentage of students reporting verbal harassment based on sexual orientation was cut in half, falling from more than 40 percent in 2001 to 20 percent in 2015.[26] Schools with gay-straight alliances, antibullying policies, and more supportive peers, teachers, and staff were safer for LGBT students. Those schools had less bullying of LGBT students and fewer reports of anti-LGBT remarks. Other research has seen similar positive effects of policies and programs on the experiences of LGBT students.[27]

Activists and policymakers are on the right path in many countries, but the pace and resolve needs to be intensified. Given the evidence from people's stories and from multiple, credible global studies, Pema Dorji's metaphor of school as "like going to a war" is an apt one for describing the situation of LGBT young people around the world. They wear the scars of the battles on their hearts and bodies, with depression and lower self-esteem and—most likely—with a worse education, in both quality and quantity.

As a result of discrimination, violence, and rejection, LGBT students will carry those wounds when they leave school and go to work to support themselves and their families. They will have lower incomes if they must end school early, and the poorer quality of their education is likely to result in a smaller gain from having more years of schooling. Without the bullying, stigma, and discrimination that is common in schools, they would fare better, and the economy would benefit from their expanded skills.

So, whether the larger society realizes it or not, we will continue to lose out until we fully appreciate the reason behind their lower levels of skills and knowledge, how profoundly that affects the economy, and what needs to change.

CHAPTER 2

EMPLOYMENT

Funnels, Fences, and Walls

D RESSED IN A TWEEDY SUIT AND TIE, Jason Thorne looks like the professional he is, with a graduate degree, decades of experience,
and expertise in a highly technical field.[1] Jason is openly gay in
his workplace, a large private nonprofit organization in the United
States. Initially Jason reported no "overt forms of harassment or
discrimination such as name calling or physical assault" that many
LGBT individuals must endure.

When people at work learned that he was married to a man,
though, things changed. A group of colleagues—one in particular—began to shun him, ducking out of the corridor or changing
direction when they saw Jason headed their way. They walked out
if they saw him in the break room or other common areas and
ignored Jason when he greeted them directly. Jason has overheard
them making negative comments about queer people in general.

Even though it's a relatively small group of coworkers, Jason
says they make his work environment uncomfortable. Additionally, it's not just a social issue. "I've also noticed that I'm not included in work teams that they control, even though I could make
a useful contribution to the project," Jason notes.

When economists examine this kind of workplace discrimination, the harm to Jason is obvious. He could be fired or demoted if his homophobic colleagues prevent him from doing his job successfully or if one becomes his boss. Jason is upset by this treatment and isn't sure how to respond. The personal stress he is under is evident—the "minority stress" that results from experiencing stigma in the workplace and that health researchers know is harmful to physical and mental health. As the next chapter details, workplaces are also connected to health. LGBT people are more likely to be depressed or anxious, and are at least twice as likely as non-LGBT people to think about or attempt suicide, and discrimination plays a part in creating those health disparities.

Since his expertise relates to many parts of the organization's work, the problems with his coworkers aren't simply a personal financial or health issue for Jason—the shunning is a problem for his employer, too, and in several ways. First, the organization isn't getting the full benefit of Jason's knowledge and skills, since he's cut out of work teams. Without him, his employer is missing the chance to get more done for the people and issues the organization serves.

The harm to his employer could get worse. If Jason's employer were a for-profit business, we would expect financial effects of discrimination, since Jason's coworkers are keeping him from doing his job at the level he's capable of. In short, without him on their teams, the coworkers are not as productive as they could be. On top of those losses, in many places antigay discrimination is illegal, including the state where Jason works, so an employer that condones discrimination is setting itself up for expensive legal problems if he files a discrimination complaint or a lawsuit.

In countries that have become more accepting of LGBT people, Jason is the modern face of discrimination against LGBT people. This picture surprises some people. Jason fits the stereotype of the well-educated gay man with a good job, but his workplace experience shows that even relatively privileged LGBT people can face difficult situations. What looks like an open, tolerant workplace turns out to have invisible boundaries that have tripped Jason up. The situation faced by other LGBT people, including queer people of color and trans individuals, is likely to be much worse, either because they don't have Jason's advantages or because they face more challenging workplace situations. Transgender people face unwarranted hurdles when they transition in the workplace, such as getting access to gender-segregated spaces (like bathrooms) or obtaining documents that allow them to specify their gender identity. Employers and governments are not moving as quickly as they should to dismantle those barriers.

Economist Gary Becker long ago predicted that discrimination would hurt the profitability of businesses, since turning away highly qualified, productive employees will weaken a company's competitiveness compared to less discriminatory competitors.[2] The stories and data in this chapter reveal how that process works, presenting the experiences of LGBT people in workplaces in the US and other parts of the world, including personal and painful evidence of stigma and discrimination. We will see that LGBT people end up in work situations that do not fully use their talents and skills. They are capable of doing more, but something—perhaps obvious barriers and explicit discrimination—stops them or slows them down. Or it might be the stereotypes and other barriers that funnel them into jobs for which they are overqualified or jobs where they have to hide their identity. All of these forms of prejudice diminish the capacity of LGBT people to engage and contribute fully.

The people who are worried about these violations of human rights, whether activists, policymakers, or social scientists, already know how this treatment hurts LGBT people. What is often missed is how it hurts the economy too. This chapter focuses on how stigma diminishes an economy's most important resource: the contributions of people to the economy.

At the outset, it's important to note that considerably more is known about what happens in US workplaces than in those of most other countries, mainly because researchers in the US have more data and more professional acceptance to study LGBT people. I include knowledge about other countries wherever possible, and that body of knowledge continues to grow.

EXPLICIT BARRIERS: BUILDING WALLS AROUND JOBS TO KEEP LGBT PEOPLE OUT

HISTORICAL BANS ON GOVERNMENT JOBS

The most blatant kind of discrimination happens when an employer explicitly states that LGBT people are not allowed to hold certain jobs. The ban on transgender people serving in the US military—a paid federal job that is often a pathway to training, education, and a good civilian career—is one ongoing example. These bans used to be much more common, and they show very clearly how much discrimination can hurt economically. In the situations described in this section, discrimination undermines the economic foundations of public sector budgets.

The twentieth century saw many efforts to construct barriers around particular kinds of jobs to keep LGBT people out. The most infamous effort in the United States started in the 1950s when some of Senator Joseph McCarthy's colleagues who hated homosexuals as much as McCarthy hated Communists began a purge of homosexuals in government jobs. Historian David Johnson termed this the "Lavender Scare." The federal government, along with many cities and states, responded by banning lesbian and gay people through civil service rules in this era, with President Dwight D. Eisenhower's 1953 executive order leading the way.[3] Similar bans existed in other countries in that era, such as Canada, and they are likely to still exist in countries that criminalize homosexuality, as lawyers in India argued when challenging that nation's law against same-sex sexual activity.[4]

The Lavender Scare set off witch hunts to identify and investigate many federal employees.[5] At first the government justified the firings by pointing to the immorality of homosexuality, a rather dubious job disqualification. Eventually government officials concocted a work-related justification: homosexuals were a security risk. They might relinquish government secrets if blackmailers threatened to reveal their homosexuality.[6] That set up a catch-22, since federal workers could neither be openly homosexual nor quietly homosexual without being fired. It's important to point out that there were no reported cases of security breaches resulting from that kind of blackmail in the US. But the spurious claim served its purpose: thousands of people were unjustly fired or denied jobs for being homosexual.

Inspired by the federal purge, California, Massachusetts, Iowa, North Carolina, Oklahoma, Texas, and other states also targeted lesbian and gay state employees in the 1950s.[7] Teachers and university professors were prominent targets given the stereotype of homosexuals as sexual predators of children. For example, in 1960, Professor Newton Arvin (once a lover of Truman Capote) was arrested by state police and later fired by Smith College for possessing and sharing "obscene" photos of men.[8] Gay law enforcement employees were also sought out for firing.

State laws that criminalized homosexual acts helped to justify employment bans. Arrests for those "crimes" also gave employers an easy way to investigate whether an employee or applicant was gay.[9] Even after arrests became much less common, the so-called sodomy laws justified another method of singling out LGBT people for discrimination. Occupational licensing requirements for many public and private sector jobs included "moral fitness," potentially making it harder for open LGBT people to hold such jobs as doctors, dentists, lawyers, realtors, or hairdressers.

As attitudes about homosexuality became more liberal over the years, the Civil Service Commission started in 1975 to unwind the explicit forms of discrimination in federal employment—but it took four long decades to finish the job. President Bill Clinton issued an executive order ending the use of sexual orientation as a barrier to security clearances in 1997 and forbade sexual orientation discrimination in federal employment in 1998. Sodomy laws were finally struck down by the US Supreme Court in 2003. President Barack Obama took the final step in 2014 when he banned gender identity discrimination in federal employment.

WALLS AROUND MILITARY JOBS

Hotly contested bans on LGBT people have also been present in one of the nation's largest employers: the US military, with more than two million active duty and reserve troops.[10] The military bans are particularly interesting because they show in dollars and cents how costly discrimination can be for employers and taxpayers, a question we'll return to in chapter 5. Over time, evidence has accumulated showing discharges of lesbian, gay, and bisexual service members cost the US government an extraordinary amount—between $290 million and $500 million from 1993 to 2010 alone.[11]

One reason the military bans were so expensive is that the armed services threw out people with highly valued and unique skills who had to be replaced. Notably, the military was aware of this all along. In fact, its own data from decades ago showed that the people discharged for homosexuality (the term used by the military) had higher scores on cognitive ability tests than new military recruits.[12] Later, discharges of highly trained—and exceedingly scarce—fighter pilots and Arab linguists further highlighted how the ban hurt military preparedness and added to the expense of training replacements.

At the same time, the main justification for the ban had evolved from homosexuals being security risks to the claim that openly homosexual people would undermine morale and cohesion. The presence of homosexual soldiers was said to undermine the effectiveness of the military, mainly because heterosexuals would have a hard time working well with openly homosexual people. But that argument also flew in the face of evidence. Extensive research showed that militaries in the UK, Canada, and many other countries reported positive experiences and no harm to morale and cohesion when openly LGBT people were allowed to serve.[13]

Over time, both the rationale for the ban and the political support for its continuation collapsed under the weight of the evidence. The US Congress finally repealed the ban on lesbian, gay, and bisexual service members in 2011.

However, as noted earlier, transgender people are still not allowed to serve in the US, even though many other countries do allow them, including Australia, Austria, Bolivia, Canada, Germany, Israel, and New Zealand.[14] The trans ban also defies economic logic. If every transgender service member were discharged and replaced, the military would have to spend almost $1 billion to recruit and train replacements.[15]

Advocates of the ban ask a different economic question, though: What about the added costs to the military of retaining transgender people, particularly their unique transition-related healthcare costs? Careful studies, along with the military's own experience, have found that the added health costs would be the proverbial drop in the bucket on the order of $2–$8 million per year or less, mainly because such a small number of people are likely to need those services.[16] This evidence about the low financial costs of allowing transgender people to serve has been used in lawsuits to show that the Trump administration's reinstatement of the ban in 2017 served no legitimate government purpose, an important test of the constitutionality of that ban.

The transgender military bans show that some explicit policies of discrimination are still in place today in high-income countries like the US and UK as well as many other countries. The impact of discrimination against LGBT people isn't just historical, even when the policies have been changed. Being investigated or discharged as a young person from the 1970s on would have affected the skills and health of people alive and working today.

The recentness of this treatment can be jarring. In 2017, Canadian prime minister Justin Trudeau apologized to the public servants, members of the military, and Royal Canadian Mounted Police officers who had been investigated, fired, or pressured to resign from the 1950s through the 1990s. Indeed, many were in the audience to hear the apology.

> To those who were fired, to those who resigned, and to those who stayed at a great personal and professional cost; to those who wanted to serve, but never got the chance to because of who you are—you should have been permitted to serve your country, and you were stripped of that option. We are sorry. We were wrong. Indeed, all Canadians missed out on the important contributions you could have made to our society.[17]

His government also settled a lawsuit by agreeing to provide $85 million in US dollars to those who had been harmed by that treatment. A mere $85 million could never fully compensate for the pain and economic losses that many of the purge victims experienced. But it's at least an acknowledgement of the direct financial and emotional costs that people bore as a result of discrimination, as well as the loss to Canadian society.

INVISIBLE FENCES

Today, not all barriers are so obvious as a wall around military jobs. The remaining walls are more like the invisible fence that my neighbors use to keep their dog in the yard. The dog wears a collar that shocks her if she gets too close to the electric wires ringing the yard. She can't see the fence, but through repeated shocks she learns its location and respects the border.

Similarly, LGBT people might feel some freedom to work and socialize in their workplaces or to come out to coworkers and supervisors. But if they get too close to the edge of a boss's or coworker's comfort zone with LGBT people, they get zapped, just like Jason Thorne did when his marriage to another man became known. So, through painful experiences, they learn where those limits are and how to avoid them.

MANY LGBT PEOPLE REPORT DISCRIMINATION EXPERIENCES

LGBT people report the shock of discrimination surprisingly often. Recent surveys show that about one in five LGBT Americans have experienced discrimination at some point in their lives when applying for jobs, seeking promotions, or in their wages.[18] For transgender people, in particular, discrimination is common in the US, with 30 percent of those employed reporting being fired, denied a promotion, or other kind of mistreatment in the past year.[19] Almost one in four (23 percent) experienced mistreatment likely related to transitioning or outness, including restrictions on restroom use or gender presentation in the workplace.

LGBT people of color face a double disadvantage: they are twice as likely as white LGBTs to report experiences of employment discrimination: 32 percent versus 13 percent.[20] One highly publicized lawsuit in the US showed the vulnerability of people of color. Jameka Evans is an African American gay female who worked as a security guard at a hospital in Savannah, Georgia. Her short haircut and masculine attire did not sit well with her boss, Evans reported in her discrimination lawsuit. She said her boss harassed her and hired someone less qualified to be her supervisor. "I remember on breaks just going into work closets and crying because I was so stressed out," she recalled to her attorneys. Eventually she left her job, but her court challenge was dismissed because protections against sexual orientation discrimination are not explicit under current US law.[21]

Because of differences across countries in how surveys are conducted, it's hard to gauge if the problem is better or worse in other countries, but it's clear that discrimination against LGBT people is a global phenomenon.[22] A 2014 survey of ninety thousand LGBT people in the European Union (EU) also found about one in five (19 percent) reported discrimination at work in the prior year. Rates ranged widely across EU countries. In countries that are known for being LGBT-friendly, rates were lower: 11 percent of Danish LGBT people and 12 percent of Dutch LGBT people reported workplace discrimination compared with 27 percent in

Lithuania and 29 percent in Cyprus. A separate survey in the Western Balkans countries also found that 20 percent of respondents had experienced discrimination in the workplace in the last year. Studies in Asian countries reveal a similar pattern of discrimination. In Vietnam, 20 percent of lesbian, gay, and bisexual people and 60 percent of transgender people have experienced discrimination in applying for jobs.[23] A survey of eighteen thousand Chinese LGBT people found that 21 percent reported workplace discrimination.[24] World Bank researchers surveyed more than 2,300 LGBT people in Thailand, a country seen as relatively accepting. Even so, 29 percent of lesbians, 19 percent of gay men, and a shocking 60 percent of transgender people reported workplace discrimination and harassment.[25] These surveys also show that in countries like Thailand and China, transgender people have a difficult time getting identity documents that include their correct gender identity, which makes getting jobs and government services particularly difficult.

In Latin America, Ecuador's official National Institute of Statistics and Census was a pioneer in studying LGBT people with a survey of 2,805 LGBT Ecuadorians.[26] Overall, 44 percent reported experiencing workplace discrimination. Violence in the workplace was also strikingly common, reported by 22 percent of the LGBT survey participants.

WHAT HAPPENS WHEN LGBT PEOPLE ARE OPEN?

Some discrimination is undoubtedly related to the disclosure of being LGBT. If coworkers or bosses suddenly discover or are told that an employee is LGBT, it puts that employee in a vulnerable position. In fact, this process can be seen in action when LGBT workers apply for jobs, thanks to some clever experiments in fourteen countries, including the US, UK, Sweden, Belgium, Italy, Greece, Cypress, Germany, Austria, Canada, Malaysia, Singapore, Thailand, and Vietnam.

The experiment is simple. The researchers send out a job application for an LGBT applicant and a heterosexual (or cisgender) applicant and see if they're treated differently by employers. Researchers create their own fictional applicants who have the same level of education, experience, and other job requirements. They mark one applicant as nonheterosexual primarily by adding a line to one résumé about being an officer or volunteer in an LGBT organization. The other applicant lists job-related volunteer service with a different organization that's not LGBT. To indicate a transgender identity, résumés typically noted a difference in birth name versus preferred name for an applicant or listed a transgender identity for gender (which is reported on a résumé in many countries). Once both have applied, the researchers then wait to see who gets invited for an interview, the main outcome in these experiments.

Out of twenty studies, seventeen have found that the LGBT candidate was significantly less likely to be invited for a job interview.[27] The difference is often large. To get one job interview in the United States, for example, a gay male applicant would need to apply to fourteen jobs, but a heterosexual man would only need to apply to nine.[28] A similar study in New York City sent pairs of real people— one transgender applicant and one cisgender (nontransgender) applicant—to apply for retail sales jobs. Employers' treatment of the transgender applicants was clearly discriminatory. In about half of the stores, the cisgender applicant got a job offer but the transgender person did not; in only one case was that pattern reversed.[29] In a four-country comparison of transgender and cisgender applicants in Malaysia, Singapore, Thailand, and Vietnam, pairs of résumés were sent to three thousand entry-level jobs. Transgender men and women were much less likely to be invited for an interview in every country, even in competitive fields like computer science, but the biggest discrepancies were in Singapore, where the transgender applicants were half as likely to get an interview.[30]

If an employer is prejudiced against LGBT people, these experiments suggest that putting one's social orientation and gender identity (SOGI) on a résumé is the equivalent of running through the invisible fence while wearing a shock collar. That's the risk of being open about being LGBT. It might be fine in some places but not others, and it's very hard and sometimes impossible to tell the difference from the outside of an office or factory.

LGBT-FRIENDLY WORKPLACES COME WITH STRINGS

What about people who get jobs in more LGBT-friendly workplaces? Given the growing acceptance of LGBT people in many countries, one would think that there are more spaces like that. LGBT employees tell researchers that they like working in those situations where they can be more open and where they feel they're treated as normal.

At the same time, though, they describe the invisible fences they avoid so they can remain "normal."[31] Coworkers might be more comfortable hearing about a lesbian's kids than about her female partner, so some people don't talk about their partners much. That means photos of same-sex partners on the desk might also be seen as flaunting one's sexual orientation. Leaving sexuality aside, these openly LGBT employees feel the need to conform to traditional ideas of how men (for gay men and trans men) and women (for lesbians and trans women) should dress or act. The act of marrying has also become a moment of truth, revealing the invisible fence for Jason Thorne, as well as others in the US who've married same-sex partners and then lost their jobs.

Legal scholar Kenji Yoshino uses the term *covering* for these sorts of pressures on LGBT people to assimilate into versions of themselves that are palatable to non-LGBT people.[32] He sees the demand to "straighten up" (as some LGBT people would put it) one's appearance or to stay quiet about friends and activism as just another form of discrimination. Covering is something demanded only of LGBT people, not heterosexual or cisgender people, and not covering makes one vulnerable to being fired or not hired. It's a lose-lose situation and can take a toll on LGBT people in the workplace.

More generally, sociologists call these challenges "managing a stigmatized identity," and like any kind of management, it takes time and energy. In the case of LGBT people managing how they disclose their sexual orientation and deal with the aftermath, the issue is less about time and more about the energy and uncertainty that management involves.

CLOSET WALLS BUILT TO PROTECT LGBT PEOPLE

Not all people are open about their sexual orientation or gender identity, partly because they fear discrimination. The other strategy for managing a stigmatized identity is for LGBT people to build their own fortresses well inside the borders of the invisible fence. Knowing why people are "in the closet," or trying to keep people from knowing that they are LGBT, is another piece to understanding the economic cost of homophobia and transphobia in the workplace.

Building and maintaining those walls might seem easy, since it's not always apparent just from looking that someone is lesbian, gay, bisexual, or transgender. If someone doesn't say explicitly that they are LGBT, would anyone know? Some people wonder why LGBT people don't just keep that information to themselves to avoid stigma and discrimination in the first place.

LGBT people sometimes justify their secrecy with professional-sounding rationalizations: "It's nobody's business." Almost two-thirds of LGBT people reported that reason in a survey by the Human Rights Campaign, an LGBT advocacy group.[33] But often their underlying reason for the closet is to manage the potential damage from rejection, harassment, or discrimination. In fact, many of those arguing "it's nobody's business" had experienced harassment or heard anti-LGBT comments in their workplaces. It's not surprising, then, that they justify the closet, given these worries about the impact on workplace relationships and work opportunities.

However, keeping this secret in the workplace is hard when people try to figure out their coworkers' sexual orientation or gender identity anyway. Gender nonconformity is a signal that coworkers often use to infer that someone is LGBT.[34] A woman who wears tailored pantsuits and flat heels and doesn't carry a purse or use makeup might be sending a signal to the world that she's a lesbian—or possibly a trans man in transition. A man wearing bright clothes and speaking in an expressive voice could be suspected of being gay. In a survey of lesbian and gay professional actors—people who obviously have some control of their self-presentation when they want to—half of them report that their coworkers can tell that they are gay without being told.[35] Almost half of transgender people report that people can tell they're transgender without being told.[36]

Other subtle signs of being LGBT are gaps in one's public biography. If you're in the closet, you're probably not putting a picture of your same-sex partner on your desk or talking about former partners. You're probably not talking about who you went on vacation with or who you hung out with last Saturday night. The point is that the closet walls are not very good protection in the workplace if coworkers are curious.

THE COST OF THE CLOSET

Worse yet, the closet takes a toll on LGBT people's happiness and health (see chapter 3). John Browne rose to the very top of BP, a global oil giant, but stayed firmly in the closet to avoid the drag of homophobia on his career. This strategy for moving up the corporate ladder came at a great personal cost, as he recounts in his memoir: "But inside I concealed deep unease and had to deal with inner turmoil almost daily. It is difficult to feel good about yourself when you are embarrassed to show who you actually are."[37]

Eventually outside forces shattered his "glass closet," as he calls it, when word leaked to the press about his three-year relationship with a male escort. Browne resigned as CEO of BP in 2007. Today the cost of the closet is clear to him, for both individuals and their employers:

> [A] decision to conduct your life in the closet is not a neutral one. It involves straddling two worlds. You will be sapped of mental energy as you switch from one to the other, even if you are

well practiced. This energy could be used far more productively, whether in business to solve problems, or in private life to build a stable relationship with a partner.[38]

As Browne's rise and fall suggest, the closet is often not helpful for one's professional future. Deflecting workplace conversations away from personal information in the course of idle social chit-chat is harder and more stressful than most heterosexual cisgender people realize. Counterfeiting a heterosexual identity, a more extreme closet strategy used by some, can involve weaving a web of fictitious people, places, and events that can unravel.[39] The social needs of many workplaces include a level of trust and engagement that put someone maintaining a secret in an impossible position. In other words, keeping one's sexual orientation or gender identity hidden requires action, not just silence. And keeping secrets like that is likely to harm workplace relationships.

Some research suggests that closeted LGBT people might even hurt their heterosexual coworkers' productivity. In an intriguing experiment, undergraduate students at the University of California at Los Angeles were asked to work with a male student from San Francisco who was majoring in interior design and liked to cook and dance—stereotypical qualities pointing to the possibility that the student was gay.[40] The participants in the study got lower scores on a math test and a shooting game when they worked with this "ambiguously gay" man than when they knew that he had a boyfriend named Josh. The study participants had very low levels of homophobia, so the performance deficit didn't seem to be related to bias against their colleague. The researchers suggest instead that the study participants might have wanted to resolve the ambiguity, and that extra cognitive work made them less effective in the two tasks. Obviously, more research is needed to understand what's going on, but this study should at least make us worry that the closet is bad for everybody.

It's especially worrying because the closet is a more powerful influence on LGBT people's work lives than most of us can see without the help of some data. Studies show that LGBT people tend to avoid occupations that are likely to have coworkers who are prejudiced against LGBT people, possibly because it's harder to be open in those jobs.[41] Homophobic and transphobic coworkers make the closet look protective, and avoiding such people makes the prospect of being open less costly and stressful.

Instead, at least some LGBT people gravitate toward jobs that allow them to work relatively independently from coworkers and bosses, like web developers, occupational therapists, or psychologists.[42] Not having to rely so much on coworkers or supervisors might make it easier to control information about one's life. Plus, if LGBT workers face negative reactions when they come out voluntarily or are "outed" by someone else, then not having to rely on others can protect them. They can keep doing their jobs in spite of the backlash, much as Jason Thorne is trying to do, but his example reminds us that few employees work completely on their own. The strategy of working independently seems to provide some protection, judging from the fact that the wage gap between the earnings of gay men and heterosexual men is smaller in jobs with more independence.[43]

Ironically, the closet is also a training ground for certain useful skills. LGBT people must learn how to read social cues so they can predict reactions of other people to their presence and identity if it is disclosed. Is a group of kids on a playground potentially threatening? Is it safe to come out as LGBT to this person? Grappling with those vital questions leads LGBT people to develop a sense of social perceptiveness and sensitivity to other people that's a generally valuable skill in dealing with customers, students, or patients.[44] While it's tempting to see this sensitivity as a silver lining, the vigilance required for that learning process is also a predictor of mental health challenges, as we will see in chapter 3.

THE PERSISTENCE OF WORKPLACE CLOSETS

The expectation of secrecy is starting to change outside of workplaces, fortunately. One sign of the increasing space for LGBT people to be open in many countries is due to high profile celebrities, from Hollywood to Manila to London, who are queer and out. We might know about openly LGBT national leaders who have served as governors of states in the US (Kate Brown of Oregon and Jared Polis of Colorado), mayors of big cities (Annise Parker in Houston and Lori Lightfoot in Chicago), or prime ministers in Belgium (Elio DiRupo), Ireland (Leo Varadkar), Iceland (Jóhanna Sigurdardóttir), Luxembourg (Xavier Bettel), and Serbia (Ana Brnabić).[45] Openly transgender people are being elected to office, too, including Danica Roem, a representative to the Virginia state legislature in the US.

We are also more likely to know when our friends and family members are LGBT. In 1985, only one in four Americans reported that a friend, relative, or coworker had come out to them as gay or lesbian.[46] By 2013, that number had tripled to three out of four people. Almost everyone in the US—88 percent of people—now knows someone gay or lesbian, and most know more than one or two gay people.[47]

Transgender people are still less widely known, though, probably because there are fewer trans people than lesbian, gay, or bisexual people. In the US, a Pew Research Center survey found that only 37 percent of Americans personally know someone who is transgender.[48] Most of those people are acquaintances, though, not friends or family members.

In spite of this evidence of broader cultural openness of LGBT people, the workplace is still seen as riskier territory for coming out than with family and friends. About half of LGBT people are open to most or all of their coworkers in the US, so half of LGBT people are still mostly in the closet in the workplace.[49]

Data from other countries also show that openness in the workplace is not common. In a survey of eighteen thousand Chinese LGBT people, three-quarters were not out at all in their workplaces.[50] Only 5 percent were fully out, and the remaining 20 percent were selectively open. Contrast this workplace experience with being more open to families and in schools. Almost 15 percent were fully open to their families, and half of these LGBT people were at least selectively out in their families and educational settings. Another study of highly educated workers in Chinese companies found similar low levels of openness, with almost half completely not open, another near half open only to close friends and colleagues, and 6 percent saying they were completely open.[51] In Vietnam, 47 percent of LGBTs surveyed said there were not out to their colleagues.[52]

Two surveys across several countries provide an interesting comparison across countries in outness even though the samples weren't randomly chosen. The first focused on college-educated people, finding that in some countries people are more likely to be closeted in their workplace than in others: 77 percent in Japan were *not* out, as well as 55 percent in India, 47 percent in the US, and 34 percent in the UK.[53] The second sample had more countries and broader levels of education, so their figures were quite different. Australia was the most open country, with only 12 percent saying they were out to no one, and Brazil, India, and Italy were the least open, ranging from 32–35 percent not open. Canada, France, Germany, Mexico, the UK, and the US were in the middle in the 16–21 percent range.[54]

These figures, while not necessarily representative of the level of openness in those countries, help to explain why some employers, government officials, and economic development agencies seem to think that LGBT issues aren't much of a problem: they simply cannot see the LGBT people in the workplaces around them. But this is a classic chicken and egg problem. If workplaces (and other social settings) aren't accepting of LGBT people, then most of the LGBT people there will try to hide who they are. If society shows it is more accepting, then more LGBT people will seem to magically appear, because they were there all along.

That's the theory, anyway. In practice, what it takes to pull down closet walls is a multifaceted problem that LGBT people and their employers are only beginning to understand.

A few years ago I was invited to speak about the cost of homophobia in Peru. My US State Department hosts asked me to meet with the human resources staff at the embassy, who wanted to make it a more LGBT-welcoming workplace for their local employees. After a long conversation about a checklist of policies that good workplaces have—nondiscrimination policies, partner benefits, and the like—it was clear the embassy had the basics. But they kept pumping me for more ideas. Finally I asked them what their LGBT employees had told them they want and need. A long awkward silence ensued. It turned out that *none* of their Peruvian employees were openly LGBT, so the HR staff had no one to consult.

And the problem wasn't just because the workplace was the US Embassy. I also met officials from several local and multinational firms at another event in Lima. One from IBM said that she knew of only five openly LGBT employees among the thousand or so IBM employees in Peru. That's striking for a company that's considered one of the best places in the world for LGBT people to work! Whether it was the local culture, the strength of Catholicism, or fear of families finding out, LGBT Peruvians appeared to be largely closeted about their sexual orientation and gender identities at work. An employee survey in China mentioned earlier asked participants who weren't out whether they would be more open if their companies had antidiscrimination policies and encouraged them to come out, but even then, 40 percent would still not tell others beyond close friends and colleagues. Plus, 43 percent of the employees who weren't open said that was because they worried that their families would find out. So the decision to be open or not is affected by a complex set of influences beyond the workplace itself.

It looks like supportive employer polices are not enough to guarantee that all LGBT people will be out, but surely they help. Should the goal be that 100 percent of LGBT people are open? In countries that are very unaccepting—or even dangerous—being open might not be a good strategy for most people. And maybe workplaces will always have some shy or very private LGBT people who prefer not to share any personal information. I would argue, though, that 100 percent of LGBT people should be able to make that choice without fear of discrimination or violence, and where that is the case, I predict many more than half of LGBT people will come out at work.

FUNNELS: STEERING WITH STEREOTYPES INSTEAD OF TALENT

Explicit walls, invisible prejudices, and the closet are not the only forces generating inequality and inefficiency in the workplace and labor market. We still hold harmful stereotypes about who LGBT people are and how they live that shape the attitudes and expectations of non-LGBT people: Gay men are creative . . . and they will harm children. Lesbians hate men . . . and they love sports. Bisexual people are promiscuous. Transgender people are mentally ill. The myths and contradictions behind the stereotypes are easy to spot, and they're also easy to refute, not surprisingly.[55] And yet these stereotypes shape LGBT people's lives and shut off opportunities, shaping their lives in ways that aren't always obvious, even to LGBT people themselves.

The power of stereotypes to hold people back shows up in numerous studies of women and people of color. Social psychologists developed the concept of "stereotype threat" to explain how negative stereotypes affect the performance of members of the group that is stereotyped. When a negative stereotype comes up in a relevant context, such as by mentioning it directly or making the group identity relevant before a test, the stereotype can affect the behavior or performance of someone in that group. People perform worse because they fear they will confirm the stereotype.

Consider a couple of common (and harmful) stereotypes: Women aren't as good in math as men. African Americans aren't as smart as white people. If you tell African American students that a test is going to provide a measure of ability, they do worse than white students—and worse than African American students who are not told that it's an ability test.[56] The effect is so strong that simply asking women to answer a survey question about their sex before taking a math test appears to trigger these stereotypes in the minds of female students, leading to a poorer performance.

Given that stereotypes affect the performance of some groups, it seems likely that stereotypes also shape LGBT people's choices and job performance. So far there is only one such study, but it showed that stereotypes reduced job performance for gay men.[57] Gay and straight men were asked to interact with young children in a nursery school setting—a workplace setting that could trigger stereotypes about the dangers of gay men to children. Before they started, the men were given a survey. Half of them were asked about their sexual orientation and the other half were not.

While they played with the children, independent observers watched what happened. Afterward, they rated the men's interactions as if they were applying for a job as a childcare worker. Interestingly, the gay men were rated higher than the heterosexual men, but stereotypes took a toll on job performance. The gay men who had been asked their sexual orientation got worse ratings by the observers on childcare skills than those who had not been asked. The gay men who had to think about their sexual orientation for the survey also displayed signs of higher anxiety—likely triggered by the stereotype—that accounted for their poorer performance.

And what about those gender stereotypes? They appear to be another funnel in the workplace for LGBT people. Usually we think of gender stereotypes as limiting the job options for cisgender women, designating certain jobs as appropriate mainly for men and others as appropriate for women. These stereotypes might also limit LGBT people if employers see gay (and possibly bisexual) men as being feminine or more like women or lesbians as more like men.

Some connections are clear. A study in the US found that employers discriminated more against gay men if the job advertisement included stereotypically male characteristics—being ambitious, assertive, aggressive, or decisive.[58] It looked like those employers did not think gay men would fit those male personality stereotypes, leading employers to avoid considering them for those jobs. In a UK study, lesbians were disadvantaged where ads were looking for stereotypically feminine characteristics.[59]

However, lesbian, bisexual, and transgender (LBT) women might actually benefit in the workplace to some extent from their sexual orientation, although the research on this topic is still thin. If employers see LBT women as more masculine and less likely to have the disadvantages of current or future motherhood, then they might actually have an advantage over heterosexual women. Another possibility is that stereotypes for women are seen as less applicable to lesbians. One US study found that college students viewed lesbian mothers and nonmothers as just as competent and committed to their jobs as heterosexual men—and much more committed and competent than heterosexual mothers.[60] Another study found that LGBT women who describe themselves as having stereotypical masculine characteristics (for example, aggressive, confident, or bold) are not penalized by hypothetical employers, while non-LGBT women are rated lower for using masculine terms.[61]

Both the good and bad effects of gender stereotypes appear to funnel LGB people into jobs that are different from heterosexual people of the same sex (we don't have this kind of research for transgender people). Several studies in the US and France have looked at the jobs LGB people end up in. Lesbian and bisexual women are in occupations that have more men in them than do heterosexual women, although much segregation by sex remains for LGB women.[62] Compared to heterosexual women, study results document more lesbians who are computer scientists, surgeons, and security guards.[63] Likewise, gay and bisexual men are in occupations with more women in them than are heterosexual men, like social workers, flight attendants, and education administrators.

Are LGB people breaking free of restrictive gender stereotypes in choosing jobs? Or do they have a harder time getting jobs that come with strong gender stereotypes? It's hard to interpret what the occupational patterns are telling us, but probably some of each dynamic is at work. LGB people are not completely inoculated against gender stereotypes, though, since they are still mostly working in occupations held by people of the same sex—just less so than are heterosexual people.[64]

Stereotypes against transgender people are complicated and might be related to a transgender person's sex assigned at birth or to their gender identity—or both. A study asked Dutch students studying human resources management about their assessments of a transgender woman and an equally qualified cisgender woman who were applying for the same job. The students rated transgender women as more assertive and autonomous than cisgender women, which are traits consistent with male personality stereotypes, as well as being less likely to go on maternity leave.[65] But the students' expectation that transgender women will be more likely to go on sick leave was consistent with the negative stereotypes about transgender people as mentally or physically ill.

Funnels that nudge LGBT people into certain jobs because of stereotypes or the difficulty in staying closeted—that is, for any reason other than their skills and preparation for certain occupations—are going to mean that the best person is not being matched to the job. And that's the recipe for inefficiency and economic loss.

COUNTING THE MONETARY COSTS TO LGBT PEOPLE

Explicit barriers, implicit fences, and powerful funnels have been costly for LGBT people. On top of the psychological costs that we will return to in chapter 3, there are also financial costs to not having the same opportunities as heterosexual cisgender people. Being turned away for a job, losing a promotion, being discouraged from a high-wage occupation, or not getting the same raises are all forms of discrimination that will reduce someone's earnings and most likely their productivity too.

To get a sense of whether LGBT people earn less and, if so, how much less, good data on representative samples of LGBT people and non-LGBT people is needed. More and more government and private surveys are including sexual orientation questions along with questions about income. Good data on the wages of lesbian, gay, and bisexual people can now be found to compare with heterosexual people in Australia, Canada, France, Greece, the Netherlands, Sweden, Greece, the UK, and the US. Also, two countries so far have good data on incomes of transgender people in big data sets. These surveys allow us to compare people who have the same characteristics that affect wages, like education, experience, occupation, race, or location. We can pick up the effect of discrimination in the labor market through a difference in earnings by sexual orientation or gender identity for people who are otherwise the same in terms of other characteristics.

The first big finding in almost all of these studies is that gay and bisexual men earn less than heterosexual men who have the same qualifications. I conducted the first study like this and found that gay and bisexual men earned 11–27 percent less than heterosexual men.[66] Later studies have found similar wage gaps for the most part in every country.[67] In 2015, economist Marieka Klawitter compiled all of these studies that were completed by 2012. On average, she found that the gap for gay and bisexual men compared to heterosexual men with the same qualifications was 11 percent.[68]

Note that this gap debunks the stereotype that gay men are members of a high-earning elite who don't face discrimination.[69] Even when gay and bisexual men have high levels of education, like Jason Thorne, they might earn less than an equally qualified heterosexual man. Some sources of data show that gay men have more education than straight men, which explains why gay men's incomes appear higher in some studies. But once we hold education constant, comparing gay men with college degrees to heterosexual men with college degrees, for example, the gay men earn less.

Interestingly, the same gaps aren't evident for lesbian and bisexual women. Across the studies Klawitter gathered, lesbians earn 9 percent more than heterosexual women with the same qualifications. Some of this apparent "lesbian advantage" comes from the fact that lesbians work more hours and more weeks every year than do heterosexual women.[70] Over time, those extra hours would mean more experience and on-the-job training for lesbians, giving them extra qualifications that couldn't be measured directly but could account for their higher wages.

Economists debate whether this pattern in earnings—a gap for gay and bisexual men but an advantage for lesbian and bisexual women—reflects discrimination or just the different decisions that people in same-sex couples make. Maybe lesbians turn their freedom from a male partner's expectations that she should take primary responsibility for home and kids into more lifetime experience in the paid labor market (which can't be measured directly in most data), while heterosexual women miss out on experience and new skills when they take on more traditional female responsibilities. Also, it makes sense that lesbians might need to work more and will gain more experience to support families that won't include a male earner. These possible influences at work can be seen in the fact that this "lesbian advantage" is much lower for lesbians who were once married to men.[71] It's also important to note that women still face a large gender gap compared with men, and lesbians are no exception to that unfortunate rule—they're simply doing a bit better than the lowest paid group.

Applying the same logic to gay men is less persuasive, though. The argument is that gay men might have a lower commitment to working for pay in the labor market since their partners will be other (relatively high-earning) men. So some gay men might reduce the amount of experience and on-the-job training that they get, especially if they are in a couple. There is some evidence of that response: men in couples have bigger wage gaps (compared to heterosexual men in couples) than do single gay men (compared to heterosexual single men); men in same-sex couples work somewhat less than men married to women.[72] But as noted earlier, gay men do not have less education than we would expect, so it's not clear why they would get less on-the-job training or other experience that produces the wage gaps.

The alleged lesbian wage premium also does not mean that lesbians are exempt from employment discrimination. Remember that the real-world experiments mentioned earlier showed clear evidence of discrimination, since gay and lesbian job applicants are less likely to get job interviews than identically qualified heterosexual men and women. In his studies in Cyprus, Greece, and the UK, economist Nick Drydakis's research team asked employers about the wages that these jobs paid when an employer called to schedule an interview with an applicant. In all three studies the employers who were willing to interview a gay or lesbian applicant paid *less* than the employers who wanted to interview heterosexual applicants.

Put together, the detailed economic studies suggest that LGB people face discrimination that involves being funneled into lower-paying jobs or blocked from high-wage jobs. The studies that look at wages for broad groups of LGB people find wage gaps for gay and bisexual men that are consistent with the experiments. But researchers cannot observe all the differences between LGB women and heterosexual women, so the lesbians look like they earn more than straight women, even though they are probably facing discrimination in the labor market.

Much less data and research on income gaps are available for transgender people than for LGB people. Where data is available, though, it indicates that discrimination hurts incomes. Dutch researchers used tax records and population registries from 2003 to 2012 to identify almost three hundred transgender people in the Netherlands who could be compared before and after their transition.[73] The researchers defined transition as going through treatments such as taking sex hormones or having gender affirmation surgeries (sometimes known as "sex reassignment surgery") and changing the gender marker in official population records. Obviously, they could not identify transgender people who do not have surgical treatments, so this study captures only a subset of trans people.

Data shows that in 2003, before their transition, transgender men (those assigned as female at birth who transition to being male) earned a lot less than cisgender men and pretransition transgender women (male to female) and a bit less than cisgender women. In 2012, after their transition, trans men had roughly the same earnings (total and per hour) as they did pretransition: they worked more but still earned less than cisgender men.[74]

The economic changes were much more negative for transgender women (those transitioning from male to female). Their earnings, hourly wages, and hours of work all declined steadily over the course of their transition. Compared to cisgender men's earnings, the annual earnings for transgender women fell 18 percent after they transitioned.

The researchers argue that both groups face two changes that affect their earnings: a penalty in their incomes for transitioning, plus a gender effect. The trans men appear to get a gender benefit of being male that offsets their transition penalty, while the trans women's transition penalty is reinforced by the gender penalty of being female. A study of transgender people in the US found similar patterns—a transition penalty and a variable gender effect, although those surveyed were probably not representative of all transgender people.[75]

In the US, only one large government survey of the population has a question on gender identity to use for economic comparisons. Two studies using data on transgender people from that national health survey also find negative economic outcomes for transgender people.[76] Using the 2014–2017 surveys, economist Christopher Carpenter and his colleagues found big differences in household incomes for cisgender people and transgender people after taking into account differences in the number of adults in the household and personal characteristics like health, education, age, race, and household size. Transgender people's household income was about 17 percent less than for cisgender men. Separating out transgender women and transgender men showed similar shortfalls in household income, but transgender gender-nonconforming people had no gap compared to cisgender men.

These studies of incomes and wages give us a good measure of how the labor market treatment of LGBT people diminishes their economic well-being. The effect of being LGBT is about sex assigned at birth as much as sexual orientation and gender identity. Before their transition, transgender women get a positive earnings boost from being assigned a male sex at birth (relative to cisgender women), but after transition their earnings go down almost to the level of cisgender women. Transgender men's incomes stay at the level of cisgender women, both before and after transition. Most studies show a wage gap for gay and bisexual men, who earn less than similar heterosexuals. Lesbian and bisexual women earn less than heterosexual and gay men, but more than heterosexual women in some studies. Our best evidence suggests that is because the main likely source of the advantage for lesbians—greater experience and the higher level of skill that would result from more experience—cannot be measured.

THE COSTS TO ALL OF US

Overall, it's not a pretty picture. LGBT people are penalized with lower incomes for the barriers, funnels, and walls that push them into jobs that aren't the best fit. It's certainly not the picture of a privileged group implied by the myth of gay affluence. Having lower incomes will affect many aspects of the lives of LGBT people: access to adequate food and housing, the ability to buy other consumption goods, resources for children, the ability to save, and many other decisions that relate to income.

There's another way to view the barriers, funnels, walls, and even the pay gaps: we *all* pay for this discrimination in wasted time and effort. Think about the lost human resources. Maintaining the closet keeps LGBT people from using their whole selves at work and uses up energy they could have applied to their job. Failing to hire or promote the best qualified person who happens to be LGBT means losing some part of what they could have contributed. Harassing LGBT people in the workplace makes it harder for them to do their jobs well. Stereotypes might discourage people from pursuing the jobs that their skills and interests make them best suited for. It adds up.

But, one might ask, what if the non-LGBT person who gets hired over an LGBT person is equally qualified, as in the experiments discussed earlier? This situation may be evident when there is a lot of unemployment during a recession or in a developing country, where many well-qualified people are looking for fewer available jobs. In that case, the employer might not be worse off as a result of hiring discrimination, so there is no economic impact on the business, although harassment and other kinds of mistreatment might make LGBT workers less productive within those businesses. At a broader social level, discriminatory treatment becomes transformed into health problems and could reduce how much training and education young LGBT people decide to pursue—an unfortunate feedback effect. Gender stereotypes also get reinforced about who should do what work, and that will also hurt cisgender women, a much larger group of workers than LGBT people.

However, in many cases, a hiring supervisor who discriminates against LGBT people will end up hiring someone less qualified, and that scenario has a very different impact. For example, consider a Ugandan soccer coach who wrote about being a lesbian under the pseudonym "Pretty."[77] She is not open about the fact that she's a lesbian, but she knows that rumors circulate about her sexuality in the Ugandan soccer world. She blames those rumors as the reason that her supervisors give new opportunities to unqualified staff instead of giving them to her. In the soccer world, that kind of discrimination means that a team could be more successful with Pretty as a coach if she is more qualified.

Economists think of this such discrimination as clearly creating inefficiency—the best person for the job was not hired, so the one who was hired doesn't do as good a job or make as much of a contribution to the employer and economy. Economist Gary Becker argued that racial discrimination hurts companies for exactly that reason. When workers are less productive than they could be, employers are paying more than they need to, raising their costs and making them vulnerable to competing companies that are less discriminatory.[78]

Why don't companies see this bad effect on their bottom line and end it? Sometimes they are aware that they need to reduce discrimination, especially if they are having a hard time recruiting and retaining skilled workers. (We'll hear this from business-people in chapter 4.) However, research also shows that ending discriminatory behavior by biased supervisors or coworkers is not a simple task for organizations and businesses, and common approaches like diversity training do not work well by themselves.[79] In some cases, the bosses might be acting on their own prejudices rooted in morality or on their narrow stereotypes about appropriate behavior for men and women. Those ideas or beliefs might overshadow other motives for hiring, especially if the employer doesn't perceive the economic costs he or she is incurring. That's why clear public policies and internal rules against discriminatory behavior are so important.

RESILIENCE: THE BEST-CASE SCENARIO?

Finally, let's think about the best-case scenario, if such a thing exists where bias is concerned. That might happen when LGBT people lose a job because of discrimination or become discouraged from pursuing a particular occupation because of the fear of facing prejudice. But then they get a job or career that's just as good—in the sense that the job matches their skills and preferences—or maybe even better. Psychologists know that some people in stigmatized groups are resilient and able to create good lives in the face of oppression, and I've met some of those folks on my travels.

Several years ago, Salman Noori (a pseudonym) had a boring job in a Middle Eastern country that he desperately wanted to leave.[80] As he began to come out to himself and to others as a gay man, he started a blog to promote sexual freedom and bodily autonomy. The blog helped him to build connections and gain public exposure as a writer, and he used that visibility to begin writing successful novels. His first book beautifully explored the stories of women and gay men struggling with traditional gender roles and expectations about marriage. When that book became a best seller, he was able to move abroad for a master's degree, which in turn gave him access to a much better job when he returned home.

So how did homophobia affect Noori and his career? "I guess it all boils down to how we react to it. . . . No matter how harsh our cultural heritage is, we can always find a way to gain from it rather than focusing on being the victims," Noori said. Becoming a successful novelist and landing a more appealing day job shows the range of experiences LGBT people have.

As a kid in a small town in the UK, Bradley Secker was bullied, which gave him a boost to get away. He's now a successful photographer and lives in another country, leaving behind the challenges of his early years. However, being gay tempers his success: "The most prominent thing affecting me as a photographer, I'd say, would be being seen as the 'gay photojournalist' in the Middle East, of which there are no open others. I feel this sometimes limits which stories people think I can work on, or choose to ask me about working on them with, etc."

In many ways, those two stories have a happy ending: in spite of challenging beginnings, both have achieved economic success and have satisfying work. It's a story that others could tell, and I don't want to deny their reality. Resilience in responding to stigma or violence and perseverance in constructing a community and life might be the main weapons LGBT people have, particularly in settings where there is little acceptance or access when human rights are violated.

And yet, it might give us only part of the big picture about how homophobia and transphobia shape the lives of LGBT people. Without some parallel universe as a guide, what might have happened to any LGBT person's career in the absence of homo- and transphobia remains unknown. We can't be sure that the next homophobic boss isn't just around the corner to challenge someone's

resilience. Resilience also doesn't magically dissolve bias and hatred; resilience also requires resources, so it's not a costless strategy.

Resilience, then, is a process and way of being that can help
individuals, but the ability of LGBT people to be resilient does not
let society off the hook in making the world less homophobic and
transphobic. Homophobia and transphobia can take their toll in
other ways, adding to their social cost and, therefore, postponing
the potential benefits of inclusion. The next chapter will explore
how the experiences of stigma, discrimination, or violence can be
etched into our bodies and psyches.

CHAPTER 3

WHEN STIGMA MAKES YOU SICK

YING XIN GREW UP IN XIANGYANG, one of the smaller cities in central China. When she was young, her dream was to be the secretary-general of the United Nations. Once she got to graduate school, Ying Xin took what might turn out to be the first step in that direction, becoming an activist. She connected with other lesbians on the internet and started an LGBT organization in 2010, Wuhan Rainbow. After graduation, she got a job at the Beijing LGBT Center, and within a year she became the director of the center, which celebrated its tenth anniversary in 2018.

I asked her what her life, and the lives of other LGBT people in China, would be like if there was no stigma against being LGBT. "More people would make more contributions to society," she answered. "There would be less depression. Many LGBTs are really depressed and cannot get support. Because we do community work, we see so many people who have mental [health] issues, and they lack support."

Given her analysis, it's not surprising that the Beijing LGBT Center focuses on providing services to their community, along with events and research. One of the center's most popular services is its psychological counseling, available either in person or online. The center also educates therapists and conducts research on issues related to mental health and other challenges faced by LGBT people.

Another leader in the global fight for LGBT inclusion, Fabrice Houdart, moved from France to the United States to get an MBA. He decided to stay in the US, taking advantage of the more tolerant climate for LGBT people that he experienced, but he gave up a lot. He left his family and network, losing the safety net and social capital that would have helped launch his career in France. He's done very well for himself professionally, though, leading the introduction of LGBT issues at the World Bank and starting the discussion there about the costs of homophobia. Next he designed and implemented the United Nations campaign to encourage businesses to adopt standards for the treatment of LGBT and intersex people, all the while raising twin boys whose exploits charm Houdart's Facebook friends.

But he also sees another side of gay life on Facebook. He has received news of friends lost to liver disease, suicides, addiction, and accidents. Although he shares his friends' scars from growing up in a homophobic environment, Houdart recognizes he is privileged to have the resources to help him understand and move past those scars. The health-related costs of stigma and discrimination do not appear in the UN Standards of Conduct for Business on LGBT and intersex people, but health is at the top of Houdart's list when he talks about the cost of homophobia.

The LGBT people encountered by Ying Xin and Fabrice Houdart reflect a common experience of LGBT people in many parts of the world: homophobia and transphobia can make LGBT people sick. That conclusion, supported by hundreds of studies, should not be mistaken for another claim—that LGBT people are sick by definition. This chapter starts by outlining the global consensus among mental health professionals that being attracted to people of the same sex or having gender expressions and identities that do not conform to the gender one is born into are simply normal variations of human sexuality and gender.

But the life challenges resulting from stigma, violence, discrimination, and rejection faced by LGBT people take their toll on mental and physical health. Damaging LGBT people's health also means holding back their economic potential. Health is a form of human capital that LGBT people, like all people, bring to their economic roles, and health challenges likewise take their toll on the economy.[1] In general, poor mental and physical health for young people reduces their test scores and years of schooling as well as their future earnings and employment as adults. Adults who have poorer health or disabilities earn less, work less, and are less productive. Countries with healthier people have higher GDP per capita, so differences in health across countries provide one reason that some countries are richer than others.

The importance of health as a goal in itself and a pathway to more education and prosperity explains why good health for everyone is a sustainable development goal (SDG) for the UN, along with quality education and decent work. (The seventeen SDGs are at the heart of international development efforts.)[2] Those pathways are why health is a central link between LGBT inclusion and the economy.

BEING LGBT IS NOT AN ILLNESS

Making connections between health and homosexuality (or gender nonconformity) started long ago. Psychiatrists and early sexologists in the medical professions in Europe in the late nineteenth century were the first scientists to take the study of homosexuality and of gender-crossing people seriously. For many psychiatrists back then, homosexuality was better characterized as an illness to be cured than a sinful perversion, the earlier perspective. However, pioneering students of psychology, such as Havelock Ellis, Edward Carpenter, Magnus Hirschfeld, and even Sigmund Freud, resisted the idea that homosexuality was a disease.[3]

Later researchers like Alfred Kinsey and Evelyn Hooker used innovative methods to show how common homosexual behavior and attraction was (Kinsey) and how homosexual men could not be distinguished from straight men in common tests of psychological health (Hooker).[4] That body of research was influential in the 1973 decision by the American Psychiatric Association to remove homosexuality from its list of illnesses, the *Diagnostic and Statistical Manual of Mental Disorders* (*DSM*). The research gave activists, both outside and inside the field, the data they needed to make the case for depathologizing homosexuality.

That change in 1973 was the beginning of the depathologization era. By 2013 the final vestiges of illnesses based on sexual orientation were gone from the fifth version of the *DSM*.[5] Being transgender is no longer considered an illness either, although removing mentions of gender identity has been more complicated since diagnostic categories influence health insurance coverage for transition-related care. To balance that need with the need to reduce stigma, "gender dysphoria" remains in the *DSM-5* as a condition that captures "clinically significant distress" related to having a gender identity or expression other than the sex assigned at birth.[6]

At the global level, the job of deciding what counts as a disease is in the hands of the World Health Organization (WHO), which has reached a similar conclusion: being lesbian, gay, or bisexual or being transgender or gender nonconforming (the WHO calls this "gender incongruence") is *not* a disease or disorder. The WHO is the agency within the United Nations that coordinates efforts to fight diseases, improve health, and expand access to health services worldwide. As part of its mission, the WHO publishes the International Classification of Diseases, or ICD, which has been ratified by 194 member countries. The ICD is a catalog of globally recognized diseases and health conditions, and countries use it to guide healthcare practitioners and to standardize health statistics about diseases and death across countries. The WHO removed sexual orientation as a disorder in 1990, and gender incongruence was removed in 2018.[7]

Even with a global judgment that being LGBT is not an illness, some LGBT people are forced or pressured into efforts to change their sexual orientation or gender identity. Ying Xin reported that this is a common practice in China.[8] Homosexuality was decriminalized in China in 1997 and removed from the list of mental disorders in 2001, but some medical professions still offer and recommend so-called therapies to change individuals' sexual orientation or gender identity. The Beijing LGBT Center's 2014 survey of eight hundred LGBT people in China revealed that most had heard about conversion therapy, as it's sometimes known, especially through advertisements on the web, and almost one in ten had felt pressure from their families or other social influences to consider it. Families sometimes use threats or even force to get their LGBT children into these "treatments." In the US, almost seven hundred thousand LGBT adults have experienced these efforts at some point in their lives.[9] It's likely that tens of thousands of young LGBT people will still be subjected to efforts to change their sexual orientation or gender identity in the US.

In many cases, these so-called therapies come from religiously oriented providers, but they sound more like torture than therapy. Kidnappings, confinement, forced medication, humiliation, threats, isolation, food deprivation, electroshock treatment, and rape—these are parts of the "therapy" reported by people who've been forced into it in some countries.[10] Soraya, a lesbian in Ecuador, told the story of her partner's abduction to human rights activists:

> Some of her neighbors told me she shouted, begged for help, and she was forced into a car, worse than if she were a criminal. That is how I knew that Viviana was handcuffed as soon as she left the house. . . . They grabbed her by force. . . . All the neighbors saw how she was handcuffed and then forced into a taxi. Yajaira, the therapist, beat her![11]

Even if the moral and ethical objections to conversion therapies are ignored, they have not been shown to be effective.[12] The story of Exodus International, once a leading organization promoting sexual orientation change efforts, illustrates their failure in a particularly powerful way.[13] Michael Bussee was a cofounder of Exodus International but later exited the group to enter a relationship with another male leader of the organization. A male board member of the organization was discovered looking for sex partners at a gay bar in Washington. Alan Chambers, the last director of the organization, had gone through one of the programs as a teenager and married a woman. However, over time he realized that those conversion efforts had not eradicated his attraction to men, and the efforts didn't seem to be very effective for others either. In 2013 Chambers publicly apologized for the pain the Exodus International programs had caused LGBT people, and he shut down the organization, although the Exodus Global Alliance lives on.

Even though efforts to change LGBT people's sexual orientation or gender identity continue, the efforts to eradicate those harmful practices have also expanded globally. Three countries (Brazil, Ecuador, and Malta) ban conversion therapies, as do a growing number of provincial or state governments in Canada, Spain, and the US.[14] Numerous professional organizations around the world have condemned the treatments and discourage people from seeking them, including organizations in Australia, Brazil, Canada, Costa Rica, Hong Kong, Israel, Lebanon, Paraguay, Philippines, South Africa, Thailand, Turkey, and the United States.[15] Only Indonesia and Malaysia officially classify LGBT people as mentally ill or in need of conversion therapy.[16]

Conversion therapy is a marker of stigma for LGBT people and a symbol of ongoing resistance to the full social inclusion of LGBT people. It exists even though healthcare professionals no longer consider being homosexual or transgender an illness and even in places like the Netherlands and United States that have LGBT-inclusive public policies. Pressure to eradicate being LGBT—like discrimination, harassment, and violence against LGBT people—is part of the underlying context of stigma that LGBT people live in.

DIFFERENCES IN HEALTH BY SEXUAL ORIENTATION AND GENDER IDENTITY

The good news, then, is that the medical professions no longer believe LGBT people are sick by definition. However, public policies and social conditions in the places where they live can make them sick. The rest of this chapter shows how homophobia and transphobia faced by LGBT people make them more vulnerable to physical and mental health disorders than non-LGBT people.

Since 2000 or so, hundreds of studies have compared the health of LGBT people to that of non-LGBT people. Many of those studies come mainly from places with high-quality data on LGBT people—that is, data from random samples of individuals—mainly Europe and North America. More studies are also starting to be conducted in other parts of the world, like South America and Southeast Asia, that indicate just how common health disparities are between LGBT and cisgender heterosexual people, with studies of transgender people emerging more slowly. Many studies use data from community-based samples rather than from large-scale surveys of a random sample of the population, but together with studies of population-based probability samples, they provide important insights into the lives of LGBT people.

The vast quantity of research makes it hard to sift through the studies one by one. Fortunately, highly reputable health scholars have taken on that task and provide a clear roadmap to what the research has found. In addition to reviews of the research published in academic journals, we have a report from the prestigious Institute of Medicine in the United States, which is now known as the National Academy of Medicine and is part of the National Academies of Science, Engineering, and Medicine.[17] In 2011, the Institute of Medicine assembled a panel of eminent researchers to assess studies about LGBT health. That panel concluded that while most LGBT people do not report mental health problems, clear evidence exists that LGBT people experience higher rates of mental health problems and some physical health problems than do non-LGBT people. All of these reviews have identified several common areas where the evidence is very convincing, and most of them include data from well beyond the United States.

SUICIDE

Many studies of suicide attempts and of suicidal thinking have found that both are more common for LGBT adults than for non-LGBT adults. One review of the research from seven different countries found that LGB adults (not including transgender people) were twice as likely as heterosexual adults to have attempted suicide, and a similar finding comes from data in South Korea.[18] Young LGB people are also at a higher risk of suicide attempts and suicidal thinking, as shown in studies from Australia, Belgium, Canada, Guam, Hong Kong, New Zealand, Norway, Switzerland, Turkey, and the US.[19]

While data on transgender people is not as common as data on LGB people, the Institute of Medicine found evidence that the risk of suicide attempts and suicidal thinking is even higher for transgender people than for LGB people. A more recent study reviewed data on transgender people's suicide attempts and found very high rates in Argentina, Belgium, Brazil, Canada, Germany, Italy, Japan, the Netherlands, Norway, the UK, and the US.[20]

A couple of examples show how serious these disparities are. In the US, a survey with more than six thousand transgender participants found that 41 percent of them had attempted suicide at some point in their lives, compared with only 4.6 percent in the general population.[21] The transgender people who had experienced discrimination or violence had even higher rates of suicide attempts. A third of 482 transgender women surveyed in Argentina had attempted suicide at some point in their lives, with 3 percent making an attempt just in the past year, more than ten times the population rates cited in that study.[22]

Embedded in those suicide statistics are wrenching stories. Take Laxmi Ghalan and Meera Bajracharya, for example.[23] Laxmi and Meera fell in love in Nepal, but their families kept them apart. Meera's family locked her up so she could not run away with Laxmi. Distraught over the situation, Meera tried to kill herself with poison, and she was hospitalized and unconscious for seventeen days. Laxmi helped Meera escape from the hospital, but eventually Laxmi's father found them and beat them. The couple's narrow escape from Laxmi's father ended successfully with the two women returning to Kathmandu, where they later founded a service organization for lesbian, bisexual, and transgender women.

Although good statistics on suicide deaths of LGBT people are not available, human rights researchers tell the story of Taka, a Japanese transgender man they interviewed for a report. His family, healthcare providers, and employers all refused to accept Taka as a man. Employment discrimination against Taka took a particularly high toll on him, leading him to give in and report in job applications that he was female. Taka became depressed and considered suicide for many years—he saw no reason to live. Eventually he poured gasoline on himself and set himself on fire. Although he recovered from that attempt, six months after the last interview with the researchers he tried again and died.[24]

DEPRESSION AND ANXIETY

The Institute of Medicine concluded that research demonstrates that the percentage of LGBT people with anxiety or depression is higher than that of non-LGBT people. The review by epidemiologist Michael King and others cited earlier found that LGB people had a 1.5 times higher risk of depression and anxiety than heterosexuals.[25] Transgender people also have two to three times the odds of depression than their cisgender counterparts, according to a recent study of data from a random sample of transgender and cisgender people in the United States.[26]

SUBSTANCE USE

Many studies have also shown higher rates of smoking, alcohol, and drug use for LGBT people as compared with non-LGBT people. The

Institute of Medicine concluded that these rates are clearly higher for lesbian and bisexual women than for heterosexual women. Other reviews show, in particular, that lesbian, gay, and bisexual adults also are much more likely to smoke than heterosexual adults.[27] They document such findings in Australia, Canada, China, Mexico, South Korea, Switzerland, Taiwan, and the United States. Studies of youth in Australia, Canada, New Zealand, Thailand, and the US also show higher rates of smoking, alcohol, and drug use.[28] The odds of substance use were three times higher for lesbian, gay, and bisexual youth compared to heterosexual youth.

LIVING WITH HIV

Disparities between LGBT people and non-LGBT people also exist regarding their physical health. Even as the number of new HIV infections falls around the world, rates of new HIV infections continue to be higher for transgender women and for gay and bisexual men (also those known more generally as MSM, or men who have sex with men regardless of their sexual identity) than for the general population. UNAIDS reports that gay men and MSM made up high shares of *new* infections in every region in 2017: 57 percent of new HIV infections in North America and in western and central Europe; 41 percent in Latin America; 25 percent in Asia, the Pacific, and the Caribbean; 20 percent in eastern Europe, central Asia, and the Middle East and North Africa; and 12 percent in western and central Africa.[29]

Perhaps unsurprisingly, the Institute of Medicine and other reviews have found strong evidence that higher percentages of LGBT people have HIV (known as HIV prevalence rates) than does the general population, especially among gay men, black MSM, and transgender women. Data from 2000 to 2006 suggests that in low- and middle-income countries, the odds of MSM having HIV were nineteen times higher than the general population.[30] More recent data find that the percentage of gay men or MSM who are living with HIV ranges from 25.4 percent in the Caribbean to very low rates in countries in the Middle East and North Africa.[31]

Large numbers of transgender women are also living with HIV in many countries. One research team estimated that 28 percent of transgender women had tested positive for HIV in the US in some studies, while 12 percent self-reported in other studies that they were HIV-positive.[32] According to one study of fifteen countries, 18 percent of transgender women are living with HIV in low- or middle-income countries, and 22 percent had HIV in the high-income countries—much higher rates than for the population age fifteen to forty-nine.[33]

CANCER

The Institute of Medicine found convincing evidence that the risk of anal cancer is higher for men who have sex with men than for heterosexual men.[34] That higher risk is mainly the result of MSM's higher rates of the human papillomavirus (HPV), which is sexually transmitted and is associated with anal cancer.

One longstanding question has been whether lesbians are more likely to get breast cancer than straight women. Healthcare researchers have worried about this possibility because lesbians have higher rates of risk factors for breast cancer, such as not having had children and higher rates of substance use. However, the Institute of Medicine study concluded that the research base was not sufficient for drawing conclusions about different cancer rates for lesbian and bisexual women and for transgender people.

VIOLENCE

Violence, whether physical, sexual, or psychological, is a threat to the health of LGBT people in all countries of the world. LGBT people can be punched, kicked, spat on, or threatened. They might have objects thrown at them or weapons used on them. Perpetrators of violence could be strangers but also family members or police. It's important to point out that anti-LGBT violence leads to more than physical scars. The long-lasting effects of violence include depression, anger, anxiety, and post-traumatic stress.[35]

The Institute of Medicine pointed to evidence of high rates of violence against LGB people and even higher rates against transgender people in the United States. For example, a 2005 survey of a random sample of LGB people found that 13 percent had been hit, beaten, attacked, or sexually assaulted at some point in their lives because of their sexual orientation.[36] Almost half (49 percent) had been threatened with violence. A survey in 2013 found that 30 percent of LGBT people had been threatened or physically attacked at some point in their lives because of their sexual orientation or gender identity.[37] Violence against transgender people is pervasive and particularly harsh. In a 2015 US survey, 47 percent of transgender people reported having been sexually assaulted in their lifetimes, and 10 percent had been sexually assaulted in the last year.[38] Physical attacks were also common, with 13 percent having been attacked in the past year.

LGBT people in all parts of the world are at risk of violence. The Inter-American Commission on Human Rights (IACHR) created a Registry of Violence in 2014 to track violence based on prejudice against LGBT people in the Americas.[39] In just fifteen months, 770 acts had been registered in twenty-five different countries (including in Argentina, Brazil, Canada, Cuba, Haiti, Jamaica, and the US), 594 of which were killings of LGBT people. The IACHR argues that those more visible crimes were the tip of the iceberg, and LGBT people likely experienced attacks and rapes that were never reported. Assaults that take place in private, as are many against transgender men or bisexual people, appear greatly underreported. The murders are often horrifyingly cruel, sometimes involving torture, stonings, or decapitations. About half of the murder victims in the IACHR registry were gay men, and the other half were transgender women. Lesbian and bisexual women are vulnerable to so-called corrective rapes that perpetrators describe as a way to make them "real women," along with other less visible instances of violence by family members. Development scholar Amy Lind also notes that violence against lesbians, in particular, often happens in more intimate spaces rather than public ones.[40]

Surveys from other continents tell a similar story. One in four LGBT people in the EU experienced a physical or sexual attack or threat in the past five years and one in ten in the last year, with transgender people reporting higher rates.[41] Violent incidents were more common in some Eastern European countries and less common in others. One organization tracked 2,982 murders of transgender people over the 2008–2018 period, with 88 percent coming from the Global South and East (which typically refers to low- or middle-income countries in Africa, Asia, Latin America, and the Caribbean, often with a history of colonialism).[42]

In Asia, data from UNAIDS shows shocking levels of sexual violence: One in five transgender women in India had experienced sexual violence in the last year.[43] One in four transgender women in Bangladesh had been raped in the last year.

WHY DO DISPARITIES EXIST? MINORITY STRESS

High rates of violence against LGBT people are easy to connect to homophobia and transphobia. When a hate crime happens, the prejudice underlying that act can be very clear: anti-LGBT comments by an assailant who beats up a gay man or a family member who reacts violently to a lesbian's partner are clear signals of homophobia and transphobia.

Explaining the other health disparities is less obvious, though, especially now that being LGBT is no longer considered to be an illness in most countries. If being LGBT doesn't mean someone is sick, then what generates those differences in mental and physical health between LGBT people and heterosexual cisgender people? In a word: stigma, or society's negative view of LGBT people. Even if conversion therapy did work—and it doesn't—it would not make LGBT people "better." The problem lies with the societies LGBT people live in.

Stigma connects to poor health in several ways. First, experiences of stigma generate extra stress for LGBT people. Everybody faces stress in life, whether driving in bad traffic, dealing with unpleasant people, losing loved ones, or being laid off from a job, and those experiences can affect anyone's health. But because of stigma and prejudice LGBT people may face more stressful situations than non-LGBT people. Public health psychologist Ilan Meyer named this extra stress that LGBT people face minority stress.[44] He described four types of minority stressors: stressful events and conditions, internalized homophobia and transphobia, expectations of rejection and discrimination, and concealing or hiding one's sexual or gender identity.

Discrimination at work, bullying at school, family rejection, and pressure to change are major events that tell LGBT people that they're considered inferior because of their sexual orientation or gender identity. Along with those major stressful experiences from direct encounters with other people, the unequal treatment of LGBT people built into laws and customs also sends a message of inferiority. Even seemingly small events add stress to their lives, like a transgender person being misgendered (when someone uses the wrong pronouns), a lesbian hearing a slur from a window of a passing car, or a gay couple being disrespected at a restaurant or store.

People who have other kinds of stigmatized identities, for example, women and people of color, also face stress due to those stigmas. These intersectional identities place them at different risks for stress, and as a result, minority stress adds up, meaning that LGBT women of color would be likely to face stress from multiple sources.

It's not just that LGBT people face more stress than non-LGBT people. Just as homophobia and transphobia get baked into cultures and economies, they get baked into LGBT people as well. This second connection happens when chronic minority stress leads LGBT people to expect to be rejected. That expectation adds to their stress by making them hypervigilant, always on the lookout for looming rejection, violence, or insults. LGBT people also internalize the message they're getting and start to think of themselves negatively (known as internalized homophobia). Another common way individuals deal with the ever-present risk of homophobia or transphobia has been to hide or conceal being LGBT. All of these reactions—vigilance, internalized homophobia, and concealment—intensify the impact of stress from experiences of homophobia and transphobia.

The damage of stigma goes even deeper, potentially changing how LGBT people's brains process stigma-related stress. Psychologists have pointed out that people have a limited pool of psychological energy to make decisions and to exercise self-control.[45] Mark Hatzenbuehler, a psychologist at Columbia University, argues that coping with stigma forces LGBT people to use up those resources, which results in processes that make them more prone to depression and anxiety.[46] For example, being on the lookout for threatening situations, constantly worrying about being found out, or even trying *not* to think about stigma can lead to a repetitive focus on oneself that psychologists call rumination, which generates psychological distress.

To make matters worse, some LGBT people have less social support, a positive resource that people use to cope with stress. LGBT people who avoid social relationships to conceal their sexual orientation or gender identity status might not develop the supportive friends and family members they need for living in a homophobic or transphobic context. Being around other people who are also LGBT reduces the impact of stigma on mental health, but concealment can make finding those people difficult.[47]

That's one reason why identities have been so important to LGBT people in many places. Identities create a group out of a bunch of individuals whose sexual behavior and sexual attraction focus on people of the same sex. Labeling that behavior and attraction as a personal characteristic, like being lesbian, gay, bisexual, or transgender (or any other culturally relevant identity), makes it easier to look for and find others who have that characteristic. Sharing an identity has many benefits, like building relationships with other people to provide social support when stigma strikes. Identities also facilitate political organizing against stigma and inequality and build community-level supports for LGBT people.[48] This connection between individual LGBT people and the LGBT community may well be a source of resilience for LGBT people, the majority of whom do not report health problems related to minority stress.

INDIVIDUAL EXPERIENCES OF STIGMA EXPLAIN AT LEAST SOME DISPARITIES

In 2011 the Institute of Medicine also concluded that the evidence was strong that linked experiences of stigma and discrimination to poorer health.[49] When LGBT youth and adults experience prejudice-related events like violence, discrimination, or family rejection, their risk rises for health problems like depression and anxiety, psychological distress, suicide, substance use, and risky sexual behaviors.[50]

Mostly those associations are revealed through statistics, but individual stories show the links as well. Nana, a Japanese lesbian, gave human rights researchers a long list of negative experiences that constituted minority stress in her life: being suspended from school, pressure to see a psychiatrist, and rape to "cure" her lesbianism. After she finished junior college, being open about her attraction to women led to daily harassment and isolation in her workplace, sending her into depression. Eventually she quit her job, adding economic stress to the mental health problems she experienced as a result of the discrimination.[51]

Families' reactions to their LGBT children appear to make a big difference in the health of young LGBT people, in particular.[52] Family rejection increases the risk of attempted suicide, depression, illegal drug use, and unprotected sexual activity. Conversely, acceptance by families increases the self-esteem, and health of LGBT young people.

ANTI-LGBT LAWS AND POLICIES RESULT IN POORER HEALTH

Stigma is also perpetuated by the laws and institutions that criminalize or marginalize LGBT people, creating an additional burden on health not felt by non-LGBT people. Sometimes the health-care system itself sets up explicit barriers for LGBT people, as in the reliance on employer-provided health insurance as a form of compensation for workers in the United States. While employers provide coverage for their LGBT workers, they often exclude coverage for the transition-related care required for some transgender people, even though the costs of such care are low.[53] Also, until recently, employers would provide coverage for different-sex spouses but rarely included the same-sex partners of LGBT people, meaning that some partners had no health insurance until same-sex couples could marry.[54]

Even if LGBT people do not directly face a discriminatory experience related to the law, the mere existence of an exclusionary law can create minority stress. Legal inequality is a constant reminder of being inferior under the law. The minority stress framework shows how being considered a criminal, having no employment security, or not being worthy of the right to marry might diminish health through the internalization of these attitudes by LGBT people.

Research in several countries reveals that those connections exist. Laws that criminalize sexual behavior between two people of the same sex are potent symbols of how far LGBT people are from full inclusion in society. In India, the Supreme Court overturned a law criminalizing same-sex sexual relations (a holdover from British colonial rule) in 2018. A study conducted in India a few years before that decision showed that sexual minorities reported that the law had affected them. The effects they noted included more concealment and depression, as well as a reduction in their sense of belonging.[55] Future research will be needed to see if the decision to decriminalize leads to positive effects on health in LGBT people in India.

Nigeria went in the opposite legal direction of India, strengthening its law criminalizing homosexuality in 2014 with the "Same-Sex Marriage Prohibition Act." Actually, same-sex marriage and same-sex sexual relations were already illegal, but the new law went further by outlawing activities like participation in gay-related organizations and meetings, providing services to gay people, or being public about a same-sex relationship. Research that compared MSM who enrolled in an HIV study before the new law with those enrolling after it shows the impact of the 2014 law. The study found strong evidence of the negative psychological effects of the law.[56] After the law, more new enrollees reported fear in seeking healthcare, and more had avoided getting healthcare. The men enrolling after the new law also reported the absence of safe spaces to socialize with other MSM, which could deprive them of social support. A later study of LGBT Nigerians found more psychological distress among those living in Nigeria compared with those who moved to another country.[57]

We can also see how stigmatizing laws diminish the ability to treat, prevent, and monitor HIV. Countries that criminalize homosexuality dramatically underestimate the proportion of MSM in their HIV tracking and, not surprisingly, overestimate how well they are providing HIV services to MSM.[58] Homophobic laws and negative social attitudes about homosexuality in a country are correlated with higher levels of AIDS-related deaths for men with HIV.[59] Also, stigmatizing laws and attitudes toward LGBT people in some European countries reduce the ability to educate MSM about HIV and to treat them effectively, as well as harm the health of LGBT people more generally.[60] The study by John Pachankis and others found that stigma leads to higher odds of sexual risk behaviors, concealment of sexual orientation, and not discussing sexual behavior when getting an HIV test.

In the US, one of the best examples of the harmful impact of policies comes from the wave of votes in 2004–2005 on state constitutional amendments to ban same-sex marriage.[61] Sixteen states had public votes, while thirty-four did not, providing a natural experiment to see what would happen to the health of LGB people (only sexual orientation was asked in the survey used) when voters imposed new legal stigma. In the states with public votes, the percentage of LGB people with mood disorders (like depression), anxiety, and alcohol use disorders was higher after the votes than before. But the share of LGB people with those disorders did *not* increase in the thirty-four states that did not vote on marriage.[62] More tellingly, heterosexual people's reports of those disorders also increased in the marriage vote states, but their increases were smaller than for LGB people. These patterns suggest that these campaigns might have been bad for everyone's health but were much worse for LGB people. Spillover effects of campaigns can also increase the stress of LGBT people who see ads about ballot measures related to marriage equality, even when their own states are not taking similar votes.[63]

Approval of same-sex marriage by the general public (that is, public opinion about it and not the law itself) also appears to have an impact on LGBT health. Studies in Australia and the United States show that supportive places have smaller gaps in health for LGBT people than do unsupportive places.[64] Where support for same-sex marriage is higher, LGBT people report that their overall health is better and the gaps compared to heterosexuals are smaller. The most likely connection is that LGBT people feel more social support in those places and that helps them cope with stigma in a healthy way.

Research is beginning to show links between inclusive laws and attitudes and healthier LGBT people in the US.[65] Lesbian and gay people (although not bisexual people) have better health and access to healthcare in states that have both nondiscrimination laws and more accepting public opinion. In Massachusetts, a group of gay men—both single and partnered—had fewer healthcare visits and lower healthcare costs after gaining the right to marry. In Illinois, lesbian and bisexual women reported lower levels of stigma consciousness, depression, and negative effects of drinking after that state created civil unions for same-sex couples in 2011. In Oregon, young LGB people were less likely to attempt suicide in counties with stronger antibullying and nondiscrimination protections, and alcohol use disparities for LGBs were lower in counties with

LGBT-supportive religious communities. In the US as a whole, the earliest states to adopt marriage equality saw declines in the rate of students attempting suicide, with a larger drop in the rates for sexual minority young people, although future research will give us a fuller picture.

Another study followed disparities in psychological distress between LGB people and heterosexuals in Sweden from 2005 to 2015.[66] Over that time, public opinion about LGB people became more positive and laws equalized the right to marry, improved protection against discrimination and hate crimes, and allowed fertility treatment for lesbians. By 2015 there was no disparity for Swedish lesbians and gay men compared to heterosexual Swedes, tracking the decrease in structural stigma, although there were no changes for bisexuals.

Overall, the glass-half-empty view of these studies is a sobering one, documenting the pervasiveness of minority stress that will have harmful impacts on the health of many LGBT people. From the glass-half-full perspective, however, these findings could be seen as helpful news: voters and policymakers can take actions that should improve the health of LGBT people. Laws that limit and stigmatize LGBT people can be removed, and laws that respect their dignity and provide them with opportunities to participate fully in society can be passed. While requiring that people have more positive attitudes toward LGBT people and issues is not possible, countries can pass laws that make it easier for LGBT activists and organizations to be open and to educate the public about the lives of LGBT people. Some research suggests that inclusive laws improve attitudes toward LGBT people. (These studies will be discussed further in chapter 7.) And while the process of moving from institutionalized stigma to laws supporting greater inclusion might mean heated campaigns that create more stress for LGBT people, and perhaps even occasional backlash, it's also possible that a difficult process creates stronger and more resilient LGBT communities that will be able to push more effectively for change over the longer run.

STIGMA IN THE HEALTHCARE SYSTEM

Healthcare systems are supposed to provide services and care to prevent and treat illnesses, but for LGBT people the healthcare system is a target for improvement and greater inclusion. That's because LGBT people face barriers within the health system that keep them from getting the care they need. The healthcare system itself is a potential reason for health disparities.[67]

The HIV epidemic provides a good example of what can go wrong. Several studies of MSM from many countries show how homophobic stigma reduces healthcare access and increases risk for HIV.[68] For example, MSM from 120 countries had more suppression of the virus and better access to services in countries with lower levels of homophobic stigma. Another survey that included participants from 165 countries found that homophobia was associated with less access to condoms, HIV testing, and HIV treatment. Nigerian MSM who had experienced more stigma, including rejection, fear, harassment, and violence, were more likely to have HIV.

A closer look into healthcare systems reveals some of the problems. Outright discrimination can result in being turned away from care. One in ten South African LGBT people surveyed in 2016 had experienced discrimination in the healthcare system, for example, with similar results in Nigeria.[69] In a 2017 survey, 16 percent of LGBT people in the US reported they had faced discrimination at a doctor's office or health clinic.[70]

A gay man in Uganda gave an example of this kind of discrimination: "Reaching the counseling room I found a lady seated there and she asked for my history and I told them how I love and sleep with guys and the lady looked at me and she said, 'We don't offer services to such people [homosexuals].'"[71]

Getting access to transition-related care is an almost universal challenge for transgender people. In a 2015 survey in the US, 55 percent of transgender people had been denied insurance coverage for transition-related surgery, and 25 percent had been denied coverage for hormone therapy.[72] Community-based surveys of transgender people in eight countries between 2012 and 2014 found many respondents had been refused care: 60 percent in India, 46 percent in the Philippines, 38 percent in Serbia, 17 percent in Thailand, 68 percent in Turkey, 6 percent in Venezuela.[73] The cost of care is another major barrier, as a study in South Korea shows.[74]

Discrimination likely results from the fact that healthcare providers have prejudices against LGBT people, just as the general public does.[75] In a general South African survey, more than 40 percent of people working in healthcare reported being disgusted by gay men, lesbians, or "men [who] dress like women and women [who] dress like men."[76] In addition to reporting explicit preferences for heterosexual people, healthcare providers in the US also have been shown to have unconscious biases against lesbians and gay men.[77] Medical students who were surveyed in India, Indonesia, Serbia, and the UK displayed a wide range of attitudes toward homosexuality, from supportive to highly negative, so LGBT people cannot be sure they will be treated with respect.[78]

This prejudice apparently drives providers to shame, chastise, or proselytize their LGBT clients.[79] On top of provider prejudice, a lack of cultural competence and knowledge about the life experiences of LGBT people can result in inferior care. One transgender person in the US provided a vivid account of what that treatment feels like physically: "I was consistently misnamed and misgendered throughout my hospital stay. I passed a kidney stone during that visit. On the standard 1–10 pain scale, that's somewhere around a 9. But not having my identity respected, that hurt far more."[80]

These experiences can have devastating health consequences when LGBT people react to those experiences by avoiding care. In 2017, 18 percent of LGBT people in the US reported avoiding care to evade discrimination.[81] Almost one in four (23 percent) transgender people in the US avoided seeing a health provider because they feared being mistreated or disrespected. In Senegal, fear of being discovered as MSM reduced MSMs' use of HIV services.[82] UNAIDS reports that high percentages of gay men or MSM have had experiences of stigma that discouraged them from seeking healthcare services, including, for example, around 66 percent in Algeria, 22 percent in Côte d'Ivoire, 36 percent in Fiji, and 75 percent of gay and bisexual men and MSM in Laos.

Being deterred from getting care could mean poorer health in the future, too, although this research is still at an early stage. For example, one study in the US showed that women in same-sex relationships had more unmet healthcare needs and were less likely than women in different-sex couples to have had a recent Pap test or mammogram.[83]

Even when they do seek health services, LGBT people's relationships with their providers are not always conducive to getting good care. A survey of more than twenty-seven thousand LGB people in the UK found that they had higher levels of mistrust of their providers and reported poorer communication with doctors and nurses than did heterosexual respondents to the same survey.[84] One common consequence of that kind of mistrust is that many LGBT people are not open about their sexual orientation or gender identity to providers. In the US, for example, 31 percent of transgender respondents to a survey reported that they were not out to any of their healthcare providers about being transgender. For people with conditions like HIV, lack of disclosure can mean misdiagnosis, delayed treatment, and poorer health.[85]

PUTTING THE PIECES TOGETHER

Instead of making LGBT health better, the treatment of LGBT people in the healthcare system contributes to minority stress and makes the effects of that stress harder to treat. Add that to the other forms and effects of stress faced by LGBT people around the world—from discriminatory laws to internal coping mechanisms—and it's not surprising that their health is worse than that of heterosexual cisgender people. Poorer health means that LGBT people are clearly worse off than they should be, and it means that they can contribute less to their jobs, families, and communities than they are capable of.

We've now seen how LGBT people's inequalities in education, employment, and health are connected, creating a dangerous cycle. Experiences of harassment and discrimination in education and employment are forms of minority stress that make LGBT mental and physical health worse. Worse health makes it harder to go to school or to work, reducing education, incomes, and employment. Poorer quality jobs or unemployment provide fewer resources to improve health. While not all LGBT people are sent into a downward spiral, that threat looms large over some LGBT lives and shows how big the loss of economic resources could be for those individuals, as well as how much homophobia and transphobia reduce their contributions to the economy. The potential is there—the laws, institutions, attitudes, and stigma that get in the way of LGBT people need to be stopped.

CHAPTER 4

MAKING THE BUSINESS
CASE FOR LGBT EQUALITY

WHO GETS HURT when anti-LGBT bias rears its ugly head? The previous chapters focused on LGBT people, who face the greatest damage to their education, jobs, and health, but actually anti-LGBT bias hurts everyone. Thousands of heterosexual people in North Carolina lost out on new high-paying jobs because of discrimination against LGBT people occurring in that state. In 2016, then-governor Pat McCrory pushed a bill through the North Carolina legislature that blocked Charlotte and other cities from passing laws that would forbid discrimination based on sexual orientation or gender identity. Worse yet, House Bill 2 (HB2) actually *required* discrimination against transgender people, forbidding them from using the bathroom that matched their gender identity, earning the nickname the "Bathroom Bill."

Not surprisingly, LGBT activists from around the country responded in outrage, but notably, the most visible figures condemning HB2 in the media were business leaders—and many put their money where their mouths were:

- Deutsche Bank and Red Ventures froze planned expansions of jobs in North Carolina.[1]

- Two prominent companies called off plans to create new facilities in Charlotte: a real estate research company, CoStar Group, took its 730 new jobs to Richmond, Virginia, instead, and PayPal canceled a previously announced $3.6 million expansion in Charlotte. The PayPal departure alone left 35,000 square feet of office space empty and took 400 jobs to another state.[2]
- The National Basketball Association moved its 2017 All-Star Game from Charlotte to New Orleans, and the National Collegiate Athletic Association pulled championship games out of North Carolina in a year in which the University of North Carolina men's team won the national basketball title.

Added together, a 2017 tally of the economic impact found that the bill would cost North Carolina $3.76 billion in lost jobs and business over twelve years.[3]

The impact on the local economy from these decisions was clear: *all* citizens of the state lost out, not just LGBT people. But the reason is less obvious. Why did these businesses react so negatively to the North Carolina law? PayPal CEO Dan Schulman explained why his company took this stand:

> The new law perpetuates discrimination and it violates the values and principles that are at the core of PayPal's mission and culture.... This decision reflects PayPal's deepest values and our strong belief that every person has the right to be treated equally, and with dignity and respect.[4]

By including LGBT people in its values and making it sound like business as usual, and by acting on those values, PayPal achieved something remarkable. American companies haven't always been so welcoming to queer people, and as chapter 2 showed, workplace discrimination and harassment still happen to many LGBT people globally. Over the last three decades, though, a sea change has happened in businesses across the US, EU, and many other places as companies realized that treating LGBT people fairly is good for business. This chapter highlights how the business case for LGBT equality emerged and reshaped US workplaces for LGBT people. From there, businesses contributed to change in state capitals and Washington, and now the business case is spreading globally.

IDENTIFYING THE BUSINESS CASE FOR LGBT EQUALITY

The business case for LGBT equality argues that equal treatment is good for the bottom line. What businesses want is simple: higher profits. To improve their bottom line, businesses have two strategies. They can reduce their costs of doing business, which include paying their employees and buying the space and other things they need to create the goods or the services they sell. Or they can increase the revenue they earn from selling their goods or services. Businesses have begun to see how they could do both by treating LGBT workers more fairly.

First, companies discovered the gay consumer.[5] In the 1990s, the US marketplace began to see gay couples selling dining room tables in IKEA ads, sexy men modeling Calvin Klein underwear on big city billboards, and ads for financial planning services for affluent same-sex couples. Companies bought ad space in gay and lesbian publications, sponsored LGBT organizations' events, and marched in Pride parades.

Attention to LGBT consumers grew as gay entrepreneurs launched new marketing companies to help corporate clients better target this allegedly affluent but untapped niche market. And while later research uncovered the inconvenient fact that LGBT people are *not* an affluent elite overall (as mentioned in chapter 2), enough affluent LGBT people existed in the US and many other countries to reinforce the stereotype. Thus was born the pink dollar—and later the pink pound, pink euro, and pink yuan.

Gay consumers were also a juicy carrot that LGBT employee groups dangled in front of their employers: as much as $1 trillion in LGBT buying power in the US alone in 2018, according to one estimate.[6] The carrot got the attention of corporate officials when they were asked to provide explicit nondiscrimination protections and healthcare benefits for same-sex partners. To tap into this new market, equality had to become part of corporate values and a corporate brand, much like we see now with PayPal.

Today, images of LGBT people appear in ads for everyday products.[7] In the US, Burger King celebrated the San Francisco Pride Parade with a rainbow wrapper for a "Proud Whopper." Honey Maid featured two gay dads and their kids in an ad for graham crackers. Brazilians have seen Netflix sponsor a float at the Sao Paulo Pride Parade. In China, Alibaba held a Valentine's Day contest on its shopping site to send a few lucky same-sex couples to marry in California.

Not all businesses sell directly to consumers, though, so LGBT buying power wasn't enough to generate the equality revolution in US businesses and multinational corporations. Over the longer run, employers have increasingly focused on the other side of the equation, asking how equality can lower costs of doing business.

Successful businesses must recruit and retain talented workers to run their companies. Companies worry about losing highly valued workers, since it takes a lot of time and money to find and then train a replacement. After being hired, a new employee will also have training costs and adjustment time. Economists have found that replacing an employee typically costs about 20 percent of their annual salary.[8] High-level executives and other highly paid workers can cost even more—more than 200 percent of salary. These are costs most businesses would prefer to avoid.

In particular, companies hate to lose their valuable employees to their competitors. The real threat of employee turnover gives companies an incentive to make sure their compensation and other policies are at least keeping up with their competitors'. How can companies hang on to their LGBT employees besides by paying them more? One logical strategy is to create good workplace policies and environments that ensure fair and equal treatment.

In addition to retaining their LGBT employees, employers also need to create the conditions that allow employees to perform well.

Of course, LGBT employees bring valuable skills, knowledge, and networks to their jobs, but their work environment will shape their ability to fully use that human capital. So, employers can lower their costs of doing business if they can raise the productivity of their existing workers, since the business gains more value for the same cost of labor.

A lot of evidence suggests that productivity, recruitment, and retention are at the forefront of employers' minds when they decide to enact policies that make workplaces friendlier to LGBT people. In fact, public announcements of a business's pro-LGBT policies often call out the bottom line as the main motivation.[9] For example, a senior executive at Lockheed Martin pointed to retention and productivity as reasons for having a nondiscrimination policy and domestic partner benefits: "Ensuring a positive, respectful workplace and robust set of benefits for everyone is critical to retaining employees and helping them develop to their fullest potential."[10]

United Technologies incorporated these arguments to justify their broader diversity goals: "Maintaining a diverse workforce is a key component of our ability to meet the demands of a global business. We strive to remove all barriers—cultural or otherwise—so that we hire, develop, promote, and retain the very best talent from around the world."

The business case proved to be an extremely valuable tool for LGBT employees in the United States and helped their push for equality in their own workplaces. The pioneering companies' actions put competitive pressure on the other companies that were slower to see the value of making workplaces more welcoming to LGBT workers. The success of the business case in spreading equality is clear. By 2019, 93 percent of Fortune 500 companies had added sexual orientation to their corporate nondiscrimination policies and 85 percent included gender identity.[11] Among those big companies, 49 percent provided domestic partner benefits and 62 percent offered transgender-inclusive healthcare benefits.[12] In the US as a whole, 54 percent of workers with employer health coverage can now sign up a same-sex partner.[13]

DOES LGBT INCLUSION IMPROVE COMPANY PERFORMANCE?

A few years ago some colleagues and I wondered whether these companies' claims of improved performance are backed up by research or whether companies might point to business reasons for LGBT-related policies just to placate their shareholders or customers. We searched the databases and found that a growing body of research supports the business motivations touted by companies.

We initially located thirty-six studies, and later, more current ones, in psychology, business, and economic research that assessed the links between employers' business concerns and LGBT-supportive policies.[14] These are studies that were carefully designed and were published in peer-reviewed journals or books, the standard in academia. That focus on academic studies is important because people and companies differ from each other for many reasons, and to isolate the impact of an employee being LGBT or a company having an LGBT-supportive policy on business-related outcomes, it is essential to take those other differences into account.

The first way that researchers approached the question was through surveys of LGBT people (although mostly they included only lesbian, gay, or bisexual people). The responses of those who worked in LGBT-friendly environments were compared to those who worked in less-friendly or hostile environments. The vast majority of these studies found that LGBT workers had better outcomes when their workplaces had LGBT-positive policies and good working environments. They had greater commitment to their jobs (sixteen studies), better mental or physical health (fourteen studies), more job satisfaction (eleven studies), and were more open about being LGBT (eight studies).

These good outcomes for LGBT workers are also good for their employers. More openness generates better health for LGBT people, and better health means that workers miss less work and are more productive. These research findings can also be connected to employers' financial outcomes. Other research that is not LGBT-specific shows that greater job commitment and job satisfaction are connected to lower turnover costs and lower healthcare costs.

So when LGBT people are more committed to and satisfied with their jobs, employers are less likely to incur the costs of replacing those LGBT workers because they leave. That, in turn, means that businesses will have higher profits.

Taken as a whole, these surveys show positive effects for LGBT employees when their employers promote equality and inclusion for LGBT people. Other research shows the link between those positive employee outcomes and positive business outcomes.

An even more persuasive business case for LGBT inclusion comes from the second approach in academic research that compares employers with good LGBT policies to companies without those policies, asking who has better financial outcomes. Companies and investors judge the health of a business by using measures that capture profitability and long-term financial health. A new line of research studying US-based companies supports the business case very clearly with these traditional measures. Most of these studies use research methods designed to get beyond statistical correlations of business policies and outcomes at one point in time, so we are more confident that LGBT inclusion *causes* better business outcomes.[15]

The most popular measure of company success is stock prices, and several studies ask whether stock prices increase for companies when they adopt LGBT-positive policies.[16] Businesses care a lot about stock prices, since they influence the cost of raising capital and executive compensation. Also, higher stock prices would reflect investors' views that those companies have a stronger financial performance than before.

All the stock market studies find that LGBT-inclusive policies have a positive effect on stock performance.[17] The earliest study in 2008 found an immediate but short-lived stock price boost for companies that received a high Corporate Equality Index (CEI) rating from the Human Rights Campaign, an LGBT advocacy organization. Later studies found a persistent link when they took a longer view over time, though. The annual growth in stock prices for companies was higher when their CEI had risen in the prior year. In other words, adopting better policies in one year was rewarded with a bigger rise in stock prices the next year, compared to similar companies. Companies also had higher stock prices after they offered domestic partner benefits to employees' same-sex partners, compared with companies that did not offer partner benefits. Another study showed that this stock price effect was particularly strong for companies that also do a lot of research and development (R&D). That link makes sense, because R&D generates the need for particularly skilled workers. One company, Credit Suisse, did its own study and found that the stock prices of 270 companies with openly LGBT senior management (or other measures of LGBT equality) outperformed firms from similar industries.

More importantly for the business case, four studies went beyond stock prices to look at profitability and worker productivity. Feng Li and Venky Nagar found a boost in return on assets—a common measure of profitability—for companies once they offered partner benefits. Liwei Shan, Shihe Fu, and Lu Zheng found that average company income per employee—one possible measure of productivity—was higher in companies with higher CEI scores. Mohammed Hossain and colleague found that higher CEI scores are associated with more patents, trademarks, and copyrights for companies.[18] Shaun Pichler and his colleagues found higher productivity in more LGBT-supportive companies when they do substantial research and development and for companies that are in states without sexual orientation nondiscrimination policies. Companies that engage in R&D *and* have good LGBT policies have even higher profits in the Pichler study.

So consistent positive connections are evident between LGBT-supportiveness and business outcomes, even when researchers use slightly different measures of LGBT-supportiveness, different samples of companies, and different time periods. That consistency creates some confidence that it's not just an odd finding related to the particular companies in one single study. Another notable feature is that these studies show that the boost in financial outcomes

comes after the policy change, rather than the other possibility that companies with better financial situations are more likely to enact policies.

Maybe the best test of the impact of LGBT-inclusive policies comes when employers do not get to choose the policy. When a state adds sexual orientation and gender identity to its nondiscrimination law, all companies must comply with that policy, not just the ones that were already on board with their own voluntary polices. If positive business outcomes can be seen in that situation, it makes an even stronger business case for equality.

A 2016 study by Huasheng Gao and Wei Zhang in the journal *Management Science* used just such a "natural experiment" with state laws.[19] In particular, they wanted to know whether LGBT equality policies would increase the creativity and innovation of employees. They used a scientific measure of corporate innovation: the number of patents generated by a company. To measure the quality of those patents, they calculated the number of times a patent was cited in other patent applications. Gao and Zhang found that the number of patents and citations increased in companies headquartered in states that enacted nondiscrimination protections for LGBT people. This effect was strongest for companies that did not already have their own voluntary policies.

Companies with their own voluntary nondiscrimination policies had most likely already received the benefit of being more inclusive of LGBT people. But that last finding also suggests something important about the larger economic impact of nondiscrimination laws. Nondiscrimination laws not only speed up protection for LGBT workers, but they can also move companies into the fast lane, requiring companies to update their policies in ways that will also have business benefits. In this case, those companies appear to have become more competitive in the labor market for talented inventors when the policy said they had to treat LGBT workers fairly.

Gao and Zhang found that a changing workforce was the key factor driving this increase in corporate creativity in the LGBT-equality states. They followed individual inventors across companies and states after the laws were passed. Inventors started moving more when laws changed, both into and out of companies in the states with new laws, perhaps because more tolerant inventors were moving in and less tolerant ones were moving out. In the end, companies in the LGBT-equality states attracted the most productive inventors. They produced more patents and more highly cited patents than the inventors who left companies in the equality states.

Gao and Zhang can't tell whether those inventors were LGBT or not. Given the relatively small size of the LGBT population, most of them were probably *not* LGBT. That suggests that highly productive heterosexual cisgender inventors might also appear to prefer companies in more tolerant locations.

Of course, more research should be undertaken to understand the impact of inclusive policies. Do more inclusive policies improve the creativity and productivity of workers who do not change employers? Do the customer base and product sales expand when companies have stronger policies? Some surveys show that customers care about and consider a company's LGBT-related policies before buying. One global study showed that 71 percent of LGBT people and 82 percent of non-LGBT allies would favor companies that are LGBT supportive.[20] But no studies have yet done careful, detailed research to see whether consumer spending actually changes when employer policies change.

So far, though, the existing research tells a consistent story that strongly supports the business case: what's good for LGBT employees is good for their employers. Both the direct studies of company outcomes and the indirect studies of outcomes for LGBT employees mean positive benefits for employers with LGBT-inclusive policies. Policies that promote LGBT equality and inclusion in the workplace, whether company-level or state-level, generate positive outcomes for employees and for businesses. Those policies allow businesses to attract and retain the best employees, and they provide a platform for LGBT employees to be healthier and more loyal, and to do their best work.

A FEEDBACK LOOP IN ACTION: FROM CORPORATE POLICY TO PUBLIC POLICY

Once businesses in the United States began to understand and act internally on this business case for LGBT equality, their worldview seemed to shift. Social and legal inequality *outside* the workplace became a problem for businesses too. In the 2000s and 2010s, activist and corporate attention increasingly focused on marriage equality in the United States. The business case created a feedback loop between internal corporate policy change and external social and legal change by laying the groundwork for corporate advocacy on marriage rights for same-sex couples.

How did that happen? To start, it's important to remember that the business case for LGBT equality did not suddenly appear in a vision to corporate leaders at Apple, AT&T, or IBM, and other early converts. They could not see how they were losing out— somebody had to tell them. Gay entrepreneurs formed marketing companies to help corporations tap into the LGBT market. Stephanie Blackwood, Howard Buford, Todd Evans, Scott Seitz, Sean Strub, Bob Witeck, and other pioneers educated corporations about the gay community and what it wanted out of their employers and favorite brands. Unions like the Service Employees International and UAW often supported LGBT workers in collective bargaining over equal benefits. Now union members in the US are much more likely to have access to domestic partner health benefits than nonunion workers, 63 percent versus 38 percent.[21]

About the same time, LGBT employees started coming together to form support groups (sometimes called "employee resource groups") just as women and people of color had done.[22] Their early goals were adding sexual orientation and gender identity to their companies' nondiscrimination policies and getting benefits for same-sex partners of employees. These support groups developed the bones of the business case and presented it to anyone who would listen, from the human resources department to the CEO. When employers balked at the increased healthcare costs they feared from domestic partner benefits, these employee groups even worked with researchers (like me) to show that the number of partners signing up would be small and manageable. Then these groups enlisted new allies to educate others in the same companies and industries.

Collective action. Greater visibility. A rights strategy. Business arguments. Powerful allies. All of these tactics that helped win domestic partner benefits at the business level became familiar parts of the marriage equality campaign as well. Corporations provided a training ground for LGBT activists and a platform for non-LGBT coworkers to meet and learn about their LGBT colleagues and their same-sex partners.

And it turns out that there is a not-so-secret weapon to enhance the business case when it comes to marriage: weddings. Weddings are a special day for couples, so they invite many friends and family to celebrate. To create the magic, couples are willing to spend a lot of money. One industry source reported that the average American wedding cost $24,723 in 2018.[23] Same-sex couples' weddings have landed on the more frugal end of the spectrum, spending an average of $11,000, according to a 2016 survey.[24] Researchers Christy Mallory and Brad Sears estimated that 123,000 couples married after the US Supreme Court decision opening up marriage, generating more than $1.5 billion in spending in just one year. That's a lot of new business for hotels, caterers, restaurants, bands, photographers, jewelers, florists, and other parts of the wedding industry that have eagerly expanded into this new market.

People spend a lot of money getting married in other countries too, by the way, so this argument has widespread appeal. In 2012 I was invited to Australia to talk to policymakers, businesspeople, and the public about my research on marriage equality. My most beautiful stop was Hobart, Tasmania. The Lonely Planet travel guide lists Tasmania as a top-ten honeymoon island, and so I found an eager audience with the premier of Tasmania and her staff for research showing that the first Australian state to allow same-sex couples to marry would see a $161 million-plus economic boost as Australia's same-sex couples flocked there to get married.[25]

Next, I presented the research to Robert Mallett and Geoff Fader, two somber officials from the Tasmanian Small Business Council, who listened politely but impassively to my numbers. I finished and waited for their verdict—what would actual business people think? They admitted they hadn't thought about marriage equality as an issue for small businesses before, but the numbers convinced them they had a stake. When the premier later introduced a marriage equality bill in the Tasmanian Parliament (unsuccessfully, as it turned out), Mallett publicly praised the bill, mentioning the $100 million and the business interest: "The proposal seems sound and would help achieve what the vast majority of Tasmanian small businesses are saying. . . . We need more customers."[26]

But despite all the potential allies among CEOs, small business owners, and workplace colleagues, convincing them to speak out on a controversial public issue like marriage equality for same-sex couples took a while. Some corporations had early experiences in managing pressure against their LGBT-positive policies. In the early 1990s, the town of Williamson, Texas, withdrew proposed tax breaks for a new Apple computer plant because of Apple's domestic partner benefits. Apple pushed back, though, and it was the town that eventually backed down in the face of widespread support for Apple and its jobs.[27]

Around the same time, Disney stared down the Baptists who organized a boycott of Disneyland because of Disney's domestic partner benefits and support for LGBT employees. Disney's theme parks did not suffer from the boycott, and both episodes showed that companies would not be hurt by their support of LGBT employees.

Internal lobbying from employees increased as external pressure became less of a threat. In 2005 Microsoft announced it would not take a company stand on adding sexual orientation to Washington State's nondiscrimination law. After 1,700 employees signed a petition urging a public stand, the company changed its position and supported the bill, valuing its employees' opinions and interests in spite of lobbying by some local churches.[28]

Gaining support for marriage equality took a bit longer. Wall Street CEOs' support of a marriage equality bill in New York State in 2011 opened the door for wider corporate endorsements. By 2012, Amazon, Microsoft, Nike, and other companies had come out in support. When big marriage equality court cases got to the US Supreme Court in 2013 and 2015, hundreds of companies came together in friend-of-the-court briefs to educate the justices on the business case for marriage equality. These businesses—including Aetna, Apple, Google, Hewlett-Packard, Nike, Verizon, and Xerox—didn't like the patchwork of laws across states that affected their payroll systems. They didn't like that marriage inequality forced them to treat their LGBT workers as second-class citizens, disrupting corporate cultures of equality. So in 2013 they made the business case to the Supreme Court: laws that treat same-sex couples unequally "can impede business efforts to recruit, hire, and retain the best workers in an environment that enables them to perform at their best."[29]

Employers were the first institutions in the US to officially recognize the relationships of same-sex couples, and they helped spread official recognition to the rest of the country. In *Obergefell v. Hodges,* the 2015 US Supreme Court decision requiring marriage equality, the court pointed to the business brief as evidence of the broad social deliberations taking place in the US on the marriage issue.[30] Businesses had gone from being a site of conflict over LGBT inequality to being committed partners in the LGBT equality vanguard, in large part because they saw supporting marriage equality as not only the right thing to do but also as sensible for them as businesses.[31]

Since then, companies have used the business case to argue for equality in other countries and in other LGBT issues. In 2017, Airbnb, Amazon, Apple, IBM, Intel, Mass Mutual, and forty-seven other companies filed a friend-of-the-court brief in support of Gavin Grimm, a transgender boy who was denied the use of the boys' bathroom at his Virginia high school.[32]

Business support for marriage equality extends beyond US borders as well, as my Tasmanian small business experience showed.

In Australia, both multinational and local companies got involved to support marriage equality there, including Aussie Home Loans, the Australian Football League, Bank of Melbourne, BEST Telecom Australia, ING, Lush, Qantas Airways, Telstra Corporation, Twitter, and Vodafone.[33] Facebook, Google, Microsoft, and Twitter joined the bandwagon for marriage equality in Ireland in 2015.[34] In Taiwan, Airbnb, EY, and Google joined twelve other multinational and local companies in supporting the legislation that gave same-sex couples the right to marry in 2019, citing the value of diversity to their businesses.[35]

Given the momentum for business support, as well as the many opportunities to exercise it, companies are likely to be increasingly important players in public and policy debates over LGBT equality in the near future in other countries.

TAKING THE BUSINESS CASE ON THE ROAD

Both the evidence base and corporate statements show that the business case for LGBT equality has legs. Its potential for moving across borders suggests that it also has wings, as the marriage equality campaigns in Ireland and Australia show.

However, companies don't always take the same visible public stance on LGBT-related policies in less friendly countries. PayPal took a forceful stand to cancel plans for a new facility in North Carolina after the state legislature passed the "Bathroom Bill," but PayPal also has operations centers in Malaysia and Singapore, countries that criminalize being gay. The contrast raises important questions: Do global companies prioritize LGBT rights in one country but not another? Why wouldn't the business case apply in other countries too?

Big multinational companies say publicly that they have just one nondiscrimination policy that they apply to all employees, no matter where they are. As noted earlier, each year the Human Rights Campaign rates more than a thousand businesses on their policies toward LGBT people. In 2018, more than half (59 percent) of those rated companies had locations outside the US, and almost all of them (98 percent) reported applying their social orientation and gender identity (SOGI) nondiscrimination policies everywhere they operate.[36] Perhaps more surprisingly, two-thirds of the global business opinion leaders surveyed by the *Economist* magazine's Economist Intelligence Unit in the same year agreed that companies should stand up against government policies that discriminate against LGBT people.[37] But do they?

Not always. I've heard activists complain that they have a hard time even getting in the door to talk to corporate leaders in countries where anti-LGBT laws and attitudes are common. It took some time for businesses to come around in Taiwan, for example. In 2017, just a few years before the marriage victory in 2019, the business community was not standing up to support marriage equality, according to legislator Ching-Yi Lin.[38] And surveys show that many non-US employees of multinationals do not think their employers are doing enough to make their companies LGBT-inclusive.[39]

A study by Sylvia Ann Hewlett and Kenji Yoshino confirms that corporate actions might not line up with a company's official policies.[40] They found that multinational companies have varying strategies when operating in countries with more conservative and openly anti-LGBT climates. Some take a "when in Rome" approach, according to Hewlett and Yoshino, simply following local laws and making exceptions to their own pro-LGBT policies. Other companies act as an "embassy" in a relatively hostile climate, providing support and protective policies for LGBT employees within their walls. "Advocate" companies take the most proactive approach, going beyond the office walls to support local LGBT activists and to pressure governments to make policy changes. Hewlett and Yoshino see a company's choice as reflecting the limits imposed by a country's laws and culture, as well as companies' judgments about what is safe and sensible for the company and its own LGBT employees.

As anti-LGBT legislation pops up in many countries, companies operating in those countries increasingly believe they must act, though. The Economist Intelligence Unit surveyed global business leaders in 2018, and almost half predicted that businesses would be more prominent "agents of progress" on LGBT issues in the near future.[41] But the potential precariousness of the terrain is evident, since only a third expected that their own companies would be doing more public advocacy.

Open for Business is a coalition of large multinational companies, including American Express, AT&T, EY, Google, IBM, and Virgin, that have decided to take a collective stand against anti-LGBT laws and policies worldwide. Their well-documented argument is the business case: "Successful, enterprising businesses thrive in diverse, inclusive societies and the spread of anti-gay policies runs counter to the interests of business and economic development."[42] Open for Business acknowledges that anti-LGBT laws create risks for employees and the company, just as Hewlett and Yoshino point out. But this new coalition also recognizes that *not* taking a stand against those laws comes with risks to global brands and reputations. Merely operating in anti-LGBT countries might alienate key groups of customers and potential employees, including the global emerging middle class and millennials (those born 1980–1996).

Polling commissioned by Open for Business backs that fear up, showing that more than half of UK (53 percent) and US (51 percent) respondents would be unlikely to work for a company doing business in antigay countries.[43] Companies might also face criticism from activists and employees of hypocrisy or "pink washing," that is, using a positive image based on activities in LGBT-positive countries to hide a lack of support for LGBT rights (or other human rights) elsewhere.

Expanding the business case to accommodate the risks to reputations and brands still emphasizes the connection between LGBT equality and the bottom line. The Open for Business companies also point to the importance of tolerance and inclusion for creating stronger economies—an expansion that the next chapter takes on more fully. Presenting the business case in one collective voice raises the volume on the LGBT equality message and also protects individual companies from backlash.

In 2017 the United Nations Office of the High Commissioner for Human Rights (OHCHR) initiated a related effort to get businesses on the same page globally. OHCHR created a set of business standards of conduct related to LGBT and intersex people and has been asking companies to sign on to them.[44] The standards reflect businesses' responsibility to respect the human rights of LGBT and intersex people and calls on them to end and prevent discrimination and stigma in their workplaces, in the marketplace, and in communities. One standard calls on companies to stop human rights abuses where they do business. The UN partnered with Open for Business to outline the many "channels of influence" that companies can use to have an impact outside their own walls. These channels range from ensuring LGBT inclusion throughout their value chains, from suppliers to distributors, to working either publicly or behind the scenes on policy issues. One important principle for businesses here and in many different contexts (which we'll revisit in chapter 6) is "nothing about us without us"—the idea that anyone seeking to improve LGBT people's lives in a country must work directly with LGBT groups in these efforts.

Clearly, the business case becomes more complicated in the global setting as the variation in LGBT-related policies becomes broader, but its reach had been spreading even before the Open for Business manifesto and the UN's efforts. The big multinationals move their executives around, effectively sending the ones who are business-case advocates to more markets. Many multinationals require their suppliers to have nondiscrimination policies, and multinationals' policies put pressure on their competitors to adopt inclusive policies to attract and retain a skilled workforce.

The impact of that competitive and cultural pressure is becoming more visible beyond the usual suspects in the US and Europe. Open for Business points out that, as of 2017, twenty-nine out of the one hundred top emerging-market multinationals have added sexual orientation and gender identity to their nondiscrimination policies.[45] India's Godrej Industries and steelmaker ArcelorMittal, China's computer manufacturer Lenovo, and Brazil's aerospace company Embraer are other corporate pioneers in their countries.[46]

And yet there's room for growth in acceptance of the business case. The global business opinion leaders surveyed by the *Economist* were mostly very LGBT-supportive. However, only 29 percent thought there would be a financial return on investment, and only 18 percent saw the potential for financial benefits. The Economist Intelligence Unit noted, "Despite a firm's best intentions toward its LGBT employees, it appears that a link is missing in the chain of logic connecting LGBT [diversity and inclusion] and the bottom line."[47]

Expanding acceptance of the business case might accompany—or even drive—movement toward more LGBT-inclusive workplaces among local businesses in the Global South. Charles Goddard, editorial director of the Economist Intelligence Unit in Asia, says the gap between multinationals and local employers is evidence that there's still work to do, especially in Asia. That's one reason the *Economist* holds one of its annual Pride and Prejudice events there.

USING THE BUSINESS CASE IN THE FIELD

The gap is wide in the Philippines, for example, as I found during a speaking tour there in 2015. Addressing the Philippines Financial Industry Pride Network one morning, I spoke about the cost of LGBT exclusion. The room was filled with employees of ANZ, Thomson Reuters, Wells Fargo, and other multinationals, and they told me about their companies' partner benefits, inclusion of transgender workers, nondiscrimination policies, and LGBT employee groups. Our hosts served us a rainbow-colored cake with our coffee and tea as a symbol of supportiveness.

In the afternoon, I gave a similar talk on the cost of homophobia to human resources managers from local companies with roots in the Philippines. The business case argument was new to most of them. One panelist reported that she had to google *homophobia.* Our host, the People Management Association of the Philippines, had conducted some focus groups and found that the multinationals operating locally were way ahead of local employers. Local companies were hiring LGBT people but did not have an equal employment opportunity policy. Why not? They weren't aware of the positive outcomes they could experience, and a less-than-supportive national culture defined the terms for business policy in the absence of the business case.

Spreading the business case can work for companies in many countries. Juan Pigot is the chair of Parea Suriname, an organization for LGBT professionals in Suriname that advocates for inclusion of LGBT people. He is also the managing director of his family-owned business, so he speaks the language of local businesspeople when they discuss LGBT workplace equality. "I try to bring it from the angle of the company," he told me in an interview, adding that he tells companies that inclusion is the right thing to do. He went on: "I say also as a company you're losing money because people become less productive. Because at the workplace they cannot be themselves."[48] He warns them that they will lose valued LGBT employees to competitors who are more inclusive. Pigot and Parea have convinced many local businesses to sign on to a pledge to move toward gender-sensitive human resources policies and ending discrimination.

It's important to recognize that the business case does not go unchallenged, especially in more homophobic and transphobic countries. Irene Fedorovych, a Ukrainian activist, has had mixed success with it. She worked with managers of a sports club chain in Kyiv on diversity issues. They sometimes refused entry or memberships to LGBT clients when they "weren't sure" which locker room to assign. She summed up the club's argument: "We do not want to lose ten homophobic customers for one gay or lesbian client."[49]

She saw it work differently in another Ukrainian city, though. LGBT activists there convinced shop owners, bars, and restaurants to support safe spaces for LGBT people by putting rainbow stickers in their windows. Those activists admitted that the businesses might lose a few clients in the short term but argued they would gain more in the medium term from the LGBT people who would become regulars and bring others along with them.

When employers know about it, the power of the business case for LGBT inclusion is real. It's more than a rationalization for companies doing the right thing. A growing body of careful scientific research backs up the claim, showing that employees and businesses perform better when LGBT workers are treated equally. After they've been pushed by their employees and activists, companies have acted on the business case to improve workplace conditions for LGBT workers. Employer actions have pushed the case farther into the marketplace and now into the world of public policy debates.

The next chapter asks a related but broader question: If equality is good for LGBT employees and for their employers, is it good for national economies? Let's add it up.

CHAPTER 5

THE COST TO ECONOMIES

Adding It Up

B USINESSES ARE WORRIED about anti-LGBT discrimination because it affects their bottom line. LGBT people want to be safer, healthier, and more economically secure. Combining insights from these two perspectives reveals how they affect the larger economy, giving policymakers new motivations and new tools for fighting LGBT exclusion.

In a country's economy, the seemingly small things that happen to individual LGBT people or businesses can add up to big costs. To see how that might work, think of the economy as an orchestra. Like an economy, orchestras are complex, with many different sections, people, and instruments. The quality of the music gives us a measure of how well the orchestra is playing, just like some overall measures of an economy suggest how well it's doing.

When things are going well, you hear all sections of the orchestra playing their parts and interacting with each other to create music that is full and beautiful. If some musicians have instruments that are out of tune, or if the orchestra members haven't practiced enough, or if some musicians are tired and don't have enough energy to put into their playing, the quality of the music will be lower—perhaps dramatically and unpleasantly.

But maybe those musicians are playing off key because they have been given broken or cheap instruments to play or never received the full training they needed. Perhaps something is distracting them from giving the music their full attention, or they found the wrong music on their stand, or they are in seats where they can't see the conductor. Given these problems, some of these individual musicians have been put in a position where even their best efforts are likely to produce a poor outcome. We know that orchestras are capable of producing beautiful and inspiring music, but this one will not fulfill that expectation.

When LGBT people can't get the training they're capable of, are harassed in their workplaces, or aren't hired into jobs that fully use their skills, in essence they have been told to play the wrong music with shabby instruments while sitting in bad seats. The output of the whole economy is diminished as a result.

How much of a difference that can make for the economy is the subject of this chapter. The first way to assess the impact is to focus on individual countries, mainly on examples from Canada, India, Kenya, the Philippines, and South Africa. The basic idea is simple. The first step is to estimate how many people face discrimination or experience a health problem because of stigma related to their sexual orientation or gender identity. The next step is to figure out how to put a financial value on the problem that emerges. The final step is to add it up for the whole country. Even though the LGBT community is relatively small, typically estimated at 3–5 percent of a population, the economic losses to countries are significant—billions of dollars annually.

The second way to assess the impact is to look across borders, giving us a kind of thirty-five-thousand-foot view. If homophobia and transphobia are costly, we should see that places with more inclusion of LGBT people have stronger economies.

In some ways, this is the ultimate test of the cost of homophobia argument, and it's the most obvious weak spot according to some skeptics. "Look at Singapore," I have heard as a counterargument all over Asia. "They still criminalize homosexuality but have a thriving economy—one of the richest in the world." And what about China? The Chinese government is no friend to LGBT people, as was evident again in 2017 when the government extended a TV ban on homosexuality to online video or audio content, but China's economy continues to grow rapidly.[1]

The success of some economies that aren't LGBT-friendly appears to be a strong counterargument; however, it is not. The lesson from the first part of this book is that the costs of exclusion can be hidden, and this chapter shows they can be large, even though they are hidden. Economic success can blind us to the fact that those successful or emerging economies might perform even better if they were more inclusive.

To make the case at the level of the whole economy, an apples-to-apples comparison with a high-level view across borders is necessary. Using the orchestra analogy, orchestras with the same instrument quality but different ways of treating some musicians are compared in order to see whether that treatment matters. Many factors influence the growth and average national income of an economy, so it's important to take them into account in making comparisons of countries with differing records of LGBT inclusion. Once everything else is controlled for, we will see that there's a positive relationship—a correlation, in statistical terms—between LGBT inclusion and economic output across countries.

MEASURING A COUNTRY'S ECONOMY

First, we need a way to measure what an economy produces in order to see the impact of excluding LGBT people. The most common overall measure of a country's economy is national output, or gross domestic product (GDP), a measure developed and used by economists, policymakers, and development agencies. GDP adds up the value of goods and services produced in a country and captures whatever is bought or sold within markets. To estimate GDP, government statistical agencies collect data from businesses and workers with surveys and administrative records.[2] Since big countries will have larger economies than small ones, GDP is averaged over the country's population, or GDP per capita, to assess economic development and the average potential standard of living.

GDP per capita is not a perfect measure, however. Important unpaid work—often the work done by women, such as caring for children, household chores, and preparing food—is not counted in GDP since it isn't bought or sold in a market. GDP also doesn't account for any environmental damage that happens while producing goods and services. Another disadvantage is that GDP doesn't take into account the fact that some people make a great deal of money and others very little, so average GDP is a poor indicator of the quality of life for many people in a country. In spite of these imperfections, GDP is widely accepted by economists and policymakers as a development measure, and good data is available across countries and years to make comparisons. Some other measures take into account a broader view of well-being, such as the UN Human Development Index that includes life expectancy and educational attainment along with GDP in its measure for individual countries.

In this book, I focus on GDP per capita because it is available for many countries over many years, but the economic benefits of LGBT inclusion would apply to any other overall measure of the economy too. In the first part of the chapter, GDP per capita is shown to provide a baseline to compare the estimates of other costs. In the second part, I will examine the relationship between measures of inclusion and GDP per capita.

LGBT EXCLUSION AND LOST PRODUCTIVITY

Economists see the productivity of workers as the key to economic development and raising GDP. When they think about the concept of a person's productivity, they're trying to capture how much people can produce in some period of time, whether it's a tangible thing being produced or a service provided.

As a writer, for example, my own productivity could be measured by the number of words I write per hour. When I'm on a roll, I write faster, pounding out more words in one hour. Another way to say it is that I'm sometimes more productive than usual (assuming those extra words are of the same quality and don't get edited out later). If I were more productive, I could write this book faster than expected, and therefore more cheaply, so both my publisher and I would be happier from a business perspective. Employers want their workers to be more productive so they can produce more services or tangible goods at the same employee cost, because that would lower the company's cost per unit of whatever they're selling. Policymakers want their national economies to be more productive so that there are more goods and services for everybody. And not surprisingly, productivity is closely linked to a country's average standard of living—the economic "pie" gets bigger as workers become more productive, so at least some people (hopefully, *all* people) can get bigger slices.

As important as productivity is as an economic concept, it's difficult to measure in most employment settings. To estimate it here, I draw on economists' views of employee wages as being closely tied to productivity. If one employer is willing to pay its workers 5 percent more than another employer in the same business, then the higher paid workers must be more productive to allow their employer to be competitive. If employers are paying some employees more because of discrimination, though, the workers facing bias and earning less are not as productive as they could be.

It's not a perfect link, since wages also reflect how much bargaining power workers have to convince employers to pay them more, whether they are in unions or not. Also, sometimes employers pay workers more to make up for unpleasant working conditions or fewer benefits. That's why researchers control for as many of those other relevant factors as possible when using statistics to estimate group differences in wages.

Here's how it works with an example of the gender gap in pay: if women earn, on average, 20 percent less than men who have the same qualifications and are in similar jobs, we would estimate that the women are approximately 20 percent less productive than they would be if there were no discrimination. Maybe the more productive employers are discriminating against women in hiring, so women end up in less productive workplaces. Or women are steered into occupations that pay less because they don't fully use or value women's skills. Women might earn less if they're given fewer hours of work and get less experience and on-the-job training.

If women are exactly as productive as men but are paid 20 percent less, it's not only discriminatory but also sets up employers to lose those women to another less discriminatory employer.[3] Some economic theories of wages argue that people getting paid less in those situations will be less productive when they think they're treated unfairly. So it's not just the women themselves who are hurt by lower wages but the entire economy as well.[4]

Using wages as a proxy for productivity has some advantages, mainly because they are commonly measured by government statistical agencies as a way to track living standards. Many studies have used statistical data on wages to estimate the cost of excluding some group of workers from full participation in the labor market:

- *Cost of gender inequity in education:* In India, young women face inequality in education and access to jobs. Raising women's level of educational attainment to the next level would increase women's productivity and wages, boosting GDP by 0.5 percent. Closing the gender gap in the rate of joblessness for young women would add 4.4 percent to India's GDP.[5]
- *Cost of intimate partner violence:* Women who experience intimate partner violence (IPV) participate less in the economy because they miss days of work, have lower productivity, and other effects. In Tanzania, lower earnings from IPV costs the economy 1.2 percent. In Vietnam, lost days of work cost the economy 1.6 percent of GDP in 2011.[6]
- *Cost of Roma exclusion:* The Roma people are a marginalized ethnic group concentrated in Central and Eastern Europe. Their wage gap compared with non-Roma people costs that region €3.4 billion–9.9 billion per year in lost productivity.[7]

Calculating the impact of these wage and productivity gaps on economic output means seeing how much more labor and output a stigmatized group would contribute, measured by giving each person in the group a raise the size of the average wage gap. Then we can estimate how much more output the economy would produce with that extra labor.

Chapter 2 presented evidence that workplace discrimination against LGBT people is global. In India, many LGBT people surveyed have reported discrimination. For example, a 2013 survey of more than 300 college-educated, white-collar LGB workers found that 56 percent had experienced workplace discrimination because of their sexual orientation.[8] In the Philippines, 30 percent of 540 LGBT people surveyed in 2018 reported experiencing discrimination, bullying, or harassment at work.[9]

Unfortunately, only a handful of the world's statistical agencies ask questions on surveys that would provide evidence of wage gaps based on sexual orientation or gender identity discrimination. Those countries include Australia, France, Greece, the Netherlands, Sweden, the UK, and the US—all of which are wealthy countries with a relatively high degree of LGBT tolerance and (to some extent) legal equality for LGBT people. As described in chapter 2, Marieka Klawitter reviewed the studies using those countries' data. She found that gay and bisexual men earn 11 percent less than heterosexual men when averaged across those studies. So that 11 percent is also an approximation of the lost productivity of gay and bisexual men because of exclusion of some kind, most likely from employment discrimination.

For lesbian and bisexual women, though, the same studies show that they earn 9 percent *more* than heterosexual women on average. As chapter 2 discussed, this apparent advantage for lesbian and bisexual women likely reflects their relative freedom from the usual constraints on women's labor force participation and because they work in paid labor much more than do heterosexual women. In those countries, lesbians appear to have the ability to live on their own without marrying men, and women have enough economic opportunities to give lesbians the ability to support themselves, whether coupled or not. Lesbians and bisexual women might have more workplace experience (a form of human capital) and more freedom to pursue a high paying career than heterosexual women.

But this "lesbian advantage" over heterosexual women doesn't cancel out the productivity loss of gay and bisexual men, because men and women have very different labor market constraints. In many countries lesbians might not have the freedom and economic independence of lesbians in the US or European countries if there is more pressure to marry men and become unpaid family caregivers, or if women in general face barriers in the labor force. Forcing lesbians to marry men means losing out on their contributions to the paid labor market. The right calculation for women estimates what lesbian and bisexual women in exclusionary countries would earn in the absence of exclusion—they would earn 9 percent more than heterosexual women because of higher productivity. Finally, I'll note that this is obviously a conservative way to estimate the lost productivity from lesbians, since I don't take into account the gender wage gap for *all* women, regardless of sexual orientation.

Overall, then, LGBT men and women would earn more and be more productive in the absence of exclusion. Using studies from relatively tolerant countries, the effect of exclusion would be the average of 11 percent (men) and 9 percent (women), or 10 percent. In countries that are less accepting of LGBT people than in Europe or the US, those gaps could well be larger, although we can't know for sure without much better data. So let's use 10 percent as a conservative estimate of how much LGBT people lose—that's the hypothetical raise that we'll give each LGBT person.

The last step involves a little bit of arithmetic.[10] We need to know how many LGBT people there are, which is a hard question to answer precisely with current data.

Let's start with India. UNAIDS is the United Nations agency that coordinates the fight against HIV. In 2012 they estimated that 0.6 percent of men in India have sex with other men. That's a low rate in the range of estimates of sexual behavior that come out of academic studies, but it's a good "lower bound" for a minimum estimate of how many people are LGBT. If the percentage of LGBT people identifying as such is as high as in the United States, or about 3.8 percent by one estimate, we'll have an "upper bound" for a range of estimates. Those two figures put the number of India's employed LGBT people in the range of 2.7 million to 16.9 million people. We could end up with much higher estimates if we used measures of being LGBT that focused on sexual behavior with same-sex partners or sexual attraction to people of the same sex, or if we used measures of gender expression that count all people who don't conform to traditional norms for men and women. The 0.6–3.8 percent figures are, therefore, fairly conservative estimates of the size of the broadly defined LGBT population that could face stigma and discrimination.

The average Indian worker earned around 56,000 rupees in 2011–2012. If LGBT workers lose 10 percent from discrimination, that would be about 5,600 rupees each. Let's convert that to dollars and then multiply the lost earnings by the number of LGBT employed people in India. The result is a range of $240 million to $1.5 billion in lost income for LGBT people. Taking into account the fact that workers would use the extra effective time while working, along with other inputs, to produce goods and services, the full economic cost doubles to $500 million to $3 billion per year.[11]

A similar estimate of costs can also be calculated for the Philippines. To get the number of LGBT workers, we'll use an estimate from a well-designed survey that showed 3 percent of young Filipino men reported same-sex attraction.[12] Applying that figure to men and women of all ages in the Philippines workforce gives an estimate of about 1.1 million LGBT workers. If average earnings are raised by 10 percent for those workers, they'll earn about $255 million more per year. Taking into account the fact that workers use other inputs means that the economic loss is as high as $730 million.[13]

Open for Business researchers did a similar estimate for Kenya, estimating a loss of $42 million–$105 million in earnings. A report on South Africa used higher quality data on the labor market status of LGBT people, which allowed very direct comparisons of wages and employment between same-sex couples and different-sex couples, and among LGB-identified people, gender-nonconforming people, and heterosexual-identified people. They estimated the loss to the South African economy from wage discrimination and underemployment to be $317 million per year.[14]

Raising incomes by reducing discrimination means more money to spend in the hands of LGBT workers and more goods and services being produced in the economy. The pie gets bigger, so LGBT workers can get their fair share, and there's more for everyone else too.

THE ECONOMIC IMPACT OF POORER HEALTH

Health is a key form of human capital that has a big influence on how much people can contribute to the economy and to their families and communities.[15] Mental or physical impairments can slow people down, making them less productive. If you've ever dragged yourself to work with a cold or fever, you probably experienced the impact an illness can have on your work output and quality. Keeping people healthy also requires resources from the healthcare system. If illnesses are preventable, then the costs to treat them are avoidable, leaving more resources to treat other conditions.

We saw in chapter 3 that stigma, discrimination, and violence are bad for the health of LGBT people, leading to higher rates of many mental and physical health issues. Those health disparities become another drag on the economy that is rooted in exclusion.

To see how those higher rates of health conditions for LGBT people drag the economy down, imagine two lines of people walking into a workplace. One line has one hundred people who are heterosexual and cisgender (that is, they are not LGBT). The other line has one hundred LGBT people. If some serious health condition resulted in 5 percent of the population being unable to work, five people in each line would be lost. But what if that condition hit LGBT people harder, maybe because the stress of stigma makes

LGBT people more susceptible or because they have less access to preventive treatment? If that condition hit 10 percent of LGBT people instead of 5 percent, an extra five LGBT people would be lost because of stigma.

Of course, non-LGBT people greatly outnumber LGBT people, but those extra LGBT people who can't work still make a difference to national economies. Some studies have used detailed data on hospitalization, lost days of work, and early deaths to estimate the cost of losing people when racial and ethnic minorities have higher rates of illness than the general population in the United States.[16]

Health researcher Christopher Banks was the first to estimate the cost of health disparities for lesbian, gay, and bisexual people (he did not have data on transgender people), with a focus on Canada.[17] He found studies showing that LGB people have higher rates of suicide, murder, smoking, alcohol use, HIV/AIDS, depression, and drug use than do non-LGB people—differences that he argued were related to chronic stress related to homophobia.[18]

Calculating the cost to society and the economy involves two steps. First, he asked how many "extra" LGB deaths result from greater health problems. For example, he found studies suggesting that 40 percent of Canadian LGB people smoke compared with only 25 percent of all Canadians, presumably because of social exclusion. So, some LGB people who smoke wouldn't do so in the absence of exclusion, and some of them get sick or die each year. Banks estimated that between 2,350 and 5,500 additional LGB people die each year because of higher rates of suicide, smoking, depression, alcohol, and drug abuse among LGB people.

The second step is to estimate the financial losses from those extra deaths. Banks used a variety of economic studies to estimate the lost productivity, direct healthcare costs, and other costs. His final estimate of the total cost of health disparities was between $500 million and $2.3 billion (Canadian dollars) each year.

A similar method can be used for India, although the data isn't as extensive or precise as in Canada. We start with the difference in the rates of having a particular health condition for LGBT and non-LGBT people, such as depression, and ask how many fewer people would have the condition if LGBT people had the same lower rate as non-LGBT people. Studies of LGBT people in India have found evidence of large health disparities compared with the overall Indian population:

- Their rates of depression were six to twelve times higher than the average for all Indians, 4.5 percent of whom experience major depression.[19]
- Suicide attempts and suicidal thinking are common among LGBT people. Studies suggest that 15–45 percent of LGBT Indians have thought of suicide, compared with 2.1 percent of people in developing countries.[20]
- Indian health agencies estimate that 5.7 percent of MSM and transgender people are HIV-infected, compared with 0.3 percent of the overall population in 2011.

Studies in India show that stigma and discrimination help to create those health disparities.[21] That means that if homophobia and transphobia are reduced, the health gaps between LGBT people and the general population will narrow or disappear. So the next step is to figure out what the economic impact of the higher rates is.

Fortunately, data is available from a large project involving thousands of health scholars that periodically estimates the "global burden of disease" in most countries.[22] They measure the social and individual burden of many physical and mental illnesses in each country using the same measure: disability adjusted life years (or DALY). The DALY captures how many years of life someone with HIV, depression, or self-harm (such as suicide) loses from an early death or from poorer quality of life.

With the country-level estimates for each disease, three other pieces of information are factored in: the percentage of a country's population that is LGBT, an estimate of their greater likelihood of a condition, and the cost of a DALY. Then the LGBT share of a country's DALYs for a disease with and without the health disparity is calculated to get the extra DALYs resulting from exclusion. The last step is to multiply the extra DALYs by the economic contribution those people would have made. Here I follow the World Health Organization's Commission on Macroeconomics and Health recommendation and measure the value of a DALY by one to three times the average gross domestic product (GDP) in India.

Adding up the effects puts the health cost of homophobia in the $700 million to $23 billion range for India. A similar calculation for HIV and suicide in the Philippines, a much smaller country, is $293 million valued simply at the average GDP.

Two studies done in Kenya and South Africa mentioned earlier used a similar methodology. As with India, the data available in those countries does not allow a precise comparison of rates of HIV, depression, or suicide. Using available studies, the cost estimates show that Kenya loses $1 billion per year because of LGBT health disparities and South Africa loses $3 billion–$19.5 billion from health disparities.[23]

On one level, these estimates might be somewhat too high, since there might be overlap in these diseases—a person with HIV might be depressed and suicidal. However, it's important to remember that this estimate includes just three health conditions out of many possibilities for India, and fewer for other countries. If more information on other potential health disparities for LGBT people were available, the price tag for the health effects of LGBT exclusion would be much higher.

ADDING IT ALL UP

The most useful aspect of this approach is that these pieces can be added together to estimate how much economies might lose. Putting together the costs from lost labor productivity and the costs of three health disparities in India results in a range of $1.2 billion–$26 billion. That works out to 0.1–1.4 percent of India's GDP.

Two health disparities and the labor productivity effect, totaling $1 billion, or 0.4 percent of GDP, can be seen in data from the Philippines. That estimate falls in the range given by the India study.

The health and labor productivity estimates for the Kenya study total $1.1 billion. That report also estimates that Kenya may be losing 119,000 tourists a year who would spend $140 million. To calculate that figure, the authors extrapolated from the fact that around 50 percent of LGBT travelers surveyed in the UK and US say they wouldn't travel to countries with anti-LGBT laws (like Kenya), and 10–20 percent of non-LGBT people would also not travel there. Adding health, employment, and tourism losses suggests Kenya is losing $1.2 billion a year, or about 1.3 percent of Kenya's GDP of $75 billion in 2017.

In South Africa, the total is $3.5 billion–$20 billion a year, or 1–5.7 percent of South Africa's 2017 GDP. That estimate is higher because of a higher estimated wage gap for LGBT people (30 percent) and because the definition of being LGBT includes a broad measure of gender nonconforming people (in the absence of good measures of being transgender), leading to 15 percent of the population counting as LGBT.

While the dollar values are large, turning them into percentages of GDP might appear to generate very small effects at first glance—mostly in the neighborhood of 1 percent of GDP. However, that first glance would be misleading. If government statistical agencies and economists saw a 1 percent drop in a country's economic activity that lasted for a while, they would eventually call it a recession. So in a sense, homophobia and transphobia puts economies in a permanent recession, with economic output below what the people of a country could produce.

OTHER COSTS ARE HARDER TO MEASURE BUT ARE REAL

It's likely that the costs estimated here are just a fraction of the actual total cost of homophobia and transphobia. Other pieces could go into these calculations if the data was available, adding to the costs already estimated.

One big piece that is lacking for India, Kenya, the Philippines, and South Africa is the possibility that LGBT people face challenges getting an education. If people miss out on education, they have fewer skills and opportunities in the workforce, as well as less human capital to use at work. Unfortunately, the evidence wasn't available to make a reasonable estimate of how much education might be lost because of stigma and exclusion.

One glimpse of how large the education gaps could be comes from the 2011 census in India. For the first time, that census included a gender question with an option for "other" that transgender people could use. Some simple tallies published by India's National Statistical Office implied a potentially large education gap for that group: only 46 percent of those identified as "other" were literate, in contrast with 74 percent of the whole population. Making sure that transgender people had the same level of education and literacy as the general population would have increased the economy's amount of human capital.

Many other impacts of exclusion could also hurt the economy but aren't currently measured by government statistical agencies or academic researchers. LGBT people might have trouble finding housing, getting credit, obtaining government services, or accessing the justice system to protect their property. As a result, LGBT people won't have the resources to meet their own basic needs and might face barriers to making potentially valuable business or home investments.

Also, a focus on LGBT individuals overlooks the costs that family members might bear. Lower earnings for LGBT people would reduce the amount an extended family has to share with one another for living expenses. Again, there would be less to save or to invest in a family business. Psychologist Eric Manalastas found that young Filipino gay men (ages fifteen to twenty-four) were more likely to be working than young heterosexual men—and 60 percent of the gay men who work were contributing half or more of their earnings to their households.[24] If discrimination cuts their earnings, their families also lose out.

Another emerging concern linked to families is that LGBT people might leave their home countries to escape violence or to improve their life chances. This outflow of people creates a brain drain for the home country. One statistical study finds that link by comparing gay men in different countries: gay men are less likely to consider moving because of their sexual orientation if their countries have good legal protections for LGBT people.[25] A study by Pink Armenia, an LGBT organization, interviewed experts and LGBT people who suggested that discrimination and limits to freedom, along with economic motivations, push LGBT Armenians to leave the country. The study pointed out that all Armenians had paid the costs of education and upbringing for those individuals, but the country that receives the LGBT emigrant is likely to gain some or all the benefit of those early investments.[26] One big unanswered question is whether (and how much) LGBT migrants send remittances back to their families, which would balance out some of those losses.

Finally, tourism is a big global industry, and LGBT tourism makes up a potential market that could be lost to countries seen as overly homophobic or transphobic. Some marketing data suggest that two-thirds of LGBT travelers take into account LGBT legal rights in the places they plan to visit.[27]

And what about the costs to a country's business sector from LGBT exclusion—should they be added in too? To some extent, lower wages and other costs are borne by LGBT people themselves. However, some costs noted above will have effects on business, too, such as lower productivity or limitations resulting from lower levels of education in the workforce. The estimates above already include those effects, at least in theory where productivity is concerned. But some apparent costs to individual businesses will become benefits to other businesses. For example, if an LGBT worker moves from one company that discriminates to another that does not, then the first firm faces a loss while the other gains. So the net business effect of that turnover is probably much smaller than the cost to the first company.[28] The studies in chapter 4 are the best direct measures of the business impact, since they focus on business outcomes.

Finally, it's important to keep in mind that many LGBT people are resilient and find ways around anti-LGBT barriers to achieve some level of economic and social success. Sometimes that success is linked to other sources of privilege they might have because of their class, race, caste, or gender. We saw examples of people in chapter 2 who have turned being LGBT into successful careers. We also saw that some parts of the LGBT community might have somewhat higher levels of educational attainment in the United States. Should that resilience counterbalance the costs of stigma and exclusion? Is that the silver lining in the cloud of exclusion?

I would say no. We'll never know whether the paths not taken by LGBT people might have resulted in greater economic contributions, even when those LGBT people become very accomplished. Plus, that economic or education gain intended to compensate for stigma might come with its own costs in terms of poorer health or strained personal relationships. Being an overachieving "best little boy in the world," in the words of (eventually) openly gay financial writer Andrew Tobias, can mean shutting off important parts of oneself in a harmful way.

COMPARING COUNTRIES TO GET THE BIG PICTURE

As the first part of the chapter makes clear, trying to count all the losses and to net out the potential benefits of resilience involves too many individual components to be complete, so the cost estimates for India, Kenya, the Philippines, and South Africa, as large as they are, are likely to be too small. Fortunately, there is a second way to estimate the cost of LGBT exclusion on countries: by assessing whether countries that are more inclusive of LGBT people also have stronger economies, measured as GDP per capita. If more inclusive countries have higher output, that bonus may be the economic benefit of inclusion, as well as its flipside, the cost of exclusion for the less inclusive countries. This method has the advantage of taking all costs and benefits into account, although as we will see, it might also result in an estimate that is somewhat too high given the complexities of the relationship between economic output and LGBT inclusion.

In this section I'll be comparing GDP per capita across countries (that thirty-five-thousand-foot view) to a country-level measure of how LGBT people are treated. As chapters 1–3 show, researchers have used many different methods to measure the experiences of LGBT people. The number of LGBT people who report discrimination or violence or the level of educational attainment by LGBT people would tell us about their direct experiences in different aspects of life. However, even in 2020, there aren't any widely collected and accepted measures like that of the well-being of LGBT people that can be compared across countries. A few countries, such as Australia, Canada, the UK, and the US collect good data by sexual orientation (though rarely for gender identity), but most other countries collect little or no data that can be used to compare to other countries. The final chapter will discuss the UNDP's plan to create an LGBTI Inclusion Index (the "I" stands for intersex people) for each country, but that's at least a few years off.

The good news is that laws related to LGBT people in many countries can be measured and compared. Laws can either limit LGBT people's lives (if laws criminalize their behavior, for example) or can help open up opportunities to jobs and education (like nondiscrimination laws or laws that provide legal documents to transgender people). The value of laws in opening up societies might be best measured by the enormous effort expended by activists to get their countries to pass nondiscrimination laws or laws that decriminalize homosexuality. Whether the laws are effective is another matter, of course, but even a law protecting LGBT people that is poorly enforced can have symbolic value and offers a basis for demanding better enforcement. The cross-national evidence suggests that laws matter: a study of an online gay social network across many different countries found that gay men reported less discrimination and fewer threats and public insults if they lived in a country with legal rights for LGB people.[29]

The practical value of laws is that they can be counted. Dutch legal scholar Kees Waaldijk has created an index of eight LGBT-related laws for 132 countries that captures decriminalization, equal ages of consent for sexual activity, legal access to marriage or other forms of partnership, and nondiscrimination laws, all going back to 1966. He calls his measure the Global Index on Legal Recognition of Homosexual Orientation (GILRHO), since it focuses on sexual orientation but not gender identity.

The GILRHO can be used to assess whether there is a relationship between LGBT-positive laws and economic development. Kees Waaldijk, Yana Rodgers, Sheila Nezhad, and I started with thirty-eight countries with "emerging economies," or rapid growth, plus some other lower income countries—they're the ones development agencies are most concerned about globally and that get a lot of business attention.

Those countries can be placed on a graph to show both their GILRHO value and their GDP in 2011, as an example. Figure 1 (see page 126) measures the value of the GILRHO along the horizontal axis, showing the number of positive laws (from zero to eight) in a country. South Africa is the point the farthest to the right, demonstrating that it had all the rights for a GILRHO score of eight in 2011. Several countries on the far left of the graph have none of the protections (a score of zero) or only partially implement one of them, giving them a half a point. The vertical axis shows GDP per capita in US dollars in 2011, adjusted for differences across countries like inflation, exchange rates, and the purchasing-power strength of a country's currency.[30]

The graph puts Kenya near the lower left corner, which shows that country's GILRHO value of zero and GDP per capita of $1,318. Argentina's point shows a GILRHO value of seven and GDP per capita of $13,323. Those two examples show the higher GILRHO for Argentina goes along with a higher income compared to Kenya. The line through the points on the graph represents the positive correlation between GDP per capita and the GILRHO for

FIGURE 1: Comparing GDP per capita to Global Index on Legal Recognition of Homosexual Orientation, 2011

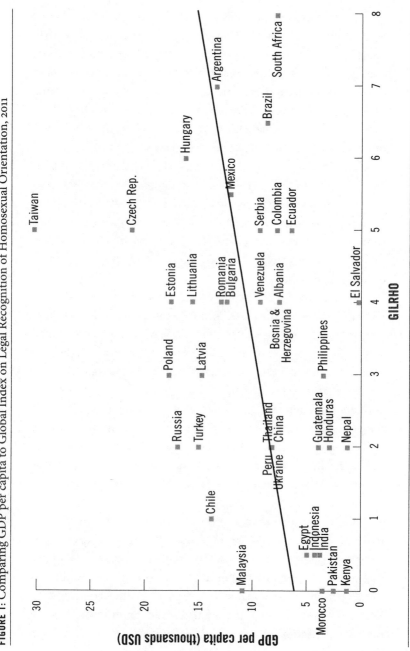

all thirty-eight countries—the more LGBT-inclusive a country is, measured as its laws, the higher GDP per capita tends to be.[31]

The same thing can be done for a more limited measure of transgender rights in 2011. Figure 2 (see page 128) shows that the relationship between transgender rights and GDP per capita is also positive: having more rights for transgender people in a country is associated with a higher GDP per capita.

However, the comparison is not yet apples to apples. To sharpen it, we used statistical tools to take into account the other characteristics of countries that affect economic growth, like the labor force, population, education levels, level of international trade, and amount of capital stock in a country. The data used for each country goes back to 1990, since most of these countries had few or none of these rights until after that year. (Unfortunately, this exercise can't be done with the transgender rights index, since it covers only one year.) That longer view is important so that the characteristics of those countries that can't otherwise be measured, like cultural, geographic, or historical differences that will not vary much over two decades, can also be controlled for. Our statistical procedure accounts for those unmeasured factors by taking out the "fixed effect" for each country, in effect looking within countries to see how their GDP rises or falls below the country's average level.

Once those other factors are taken into account, there is still a positive correlation between LGBT rights and GDP per capita. One way to describe the impact is that an additional right is associated with a $320 increase in GDP per capita, which is about 3 percent of GDP per capita for these countries averaged together. This finding does not mean that a country can increase its average output by 3 percent simply by adding another right for LGBT people—I'll address that below. But it does show that there is a strong positive relationship.

In a broader study, Kees Waaldijk, Yana Rodgers, and I expanded this analysis to 132 countries and extended it back to 1966, and we got similar findings.[32] The measure of LGBT rights

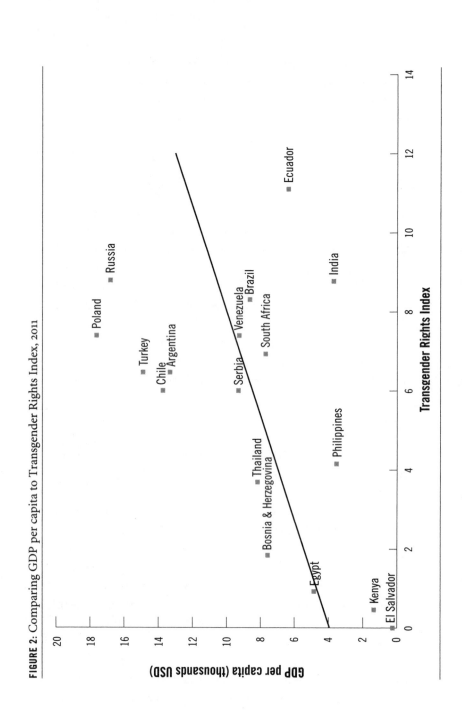

FIGURE 2: Comparing GDP per capita to Transgender Rights Index, 2011

is positively correlated with GDP per capita at a global level, with each right associated with a $2,065 increase in output per person. When we divided up countries by different regions of the world, the connection between GDP and rights is high in East Asia and Pacific countries, in Europe and Central Asia, and in the EU, but it is not statistically significant in the other parts of the world (in other words, we aren't confident that there is a correlation in those regions).

We worried that the effect across countries for LGBT people might be related to some other characteristic of those countries, such as the greater inclusion of women in the laws and economies of the 132 countries. Perhaps countries that do better with gender inclusion have stronger economies and happen to be better with respect to LGBT rights and inclusion because women are more favorably inclined to rights for LGBT people. In that case, LGBT inclusion could have nothing to do with GDP per capita on its own. To see if gender mattered, we added a measure of women's social position: women's share of seats in national legislatures. It turns out that the gender measure was not the reason for our findings, since the same positive relationship of LGBT rights and GDP per capita can still be seen, although the relationship is actually a tiny bit larger.[33] The fact that a clear impact of homosexual-related rights can be seen suggests that gender inclusion and LGBT inclusion are distinct when it comes to the economy.

Our finding that GDP and LGBT inclusion are positively correlated is so important that it's worth trying other data sources and using different measures of inclusion. In our 132-country study, we used two other sources of data on the economic variables and used somewhat different adjustments to make the data comparable across country and over time, but we found the same positive relationship between GDP per capita and LGBT rights. In a separate study, Andrew Flores, Andrew Park, and I found that countries had higher GDP per capita where there was more public acceptance of LGBT people, a different measure of inclusion, and also more supportive laws.[34] Finally, another study also found a similar correlation, as higher measures on a "homophobic climate index" (based on laws and public opinion) was associated with a lower GDP per capita in 2017.[35] So far the evidence shows that the statistical link between GDP and LGBT inclusion is strong and positive no matter the measure of inclusion or source of data.

CAUSATION OR CORRELATION? OTHER POSSIBLE CONNECTIONS

But what exactly does that positive statistical connection between LGBT rights and GDP per capita mean? Simply put, it means that countries with more rights also have higher GDP per capita than other countries with similar economic characteristics. However, one of the first things you learn in a statistics class is that correlation does not imply causation, so we can't say for sure that more LGBT rights *caused* the higher level of GDP.

The most accurate way to connect the thirty-five-thousand-foot view to the first part of this chapter and book is to say that there is now a lot of evidence from different angles that all fits the idea that more inclusion leads to increases in GDP per capita. At a personal level, LGBT people face stigma, violence, and discrimination in education, the labor force, and health that will reduce their ability to contribute to the economy. Less exclusion would mean more human capital and higher productivity. Businesses with better treatment of LGBT people have higher profits and stock prices. Countries with extensive LGBT exclusion have people who are less healthy and less productive, reducing GDP. Therefore, given the human capital perspective that underlies these links for individual people, businesses, and countries, it seems likely that at least part of that relationship seen across countries is causal.

Also, given those strong links at the person level and business level, it would be surprising and damaging to the economic case for LGBT equality if a positive connection between rights and higher GDP across countries was not evident. It's important to point out that the evidence presented throughout the book consistently supports the idea that homophobia and transphobia are harmful to economies.

The wide-angle macroeconomic view also allows us to expand our understanding of how GDP and LGBT inclusion could be connected, including a perspective the research team called "strategic modernization." Countries might adopt LGBT-supportive policies to show people in other countries that they are modern trading partners and good places to invest in and to visit. Here LGBT rights are a signal about the positive treatment of minorities and perhaps the declining role of older traditions that are less business friendly.

Richard Florida's "creative class" idea is a version of the strategic modernization argument. He argues that visibility and tolerance of LGBT people in a country send a signal to the world's creative and skilled people (not just those who are LGBT) to think about immigrating to places that welcome new ideas and a diverse population. Economic development follows LGBT rights because of the people drawn into a country, not specifically because of the work of LGBT people themselves.[36] In a study of the US, Florida and Gary Gates found that high-tech employment appeared to follow increasing visibility of same-sex couples.[37] And the 2016 study by Huasheng Gao and Wei Zhang discussed in the previous chapter found a similar link between the passage of statewide sexual orientation nondiscrimination laws and the movement of talented inventors into the state.

Even a country like Singapore, which stubbornly retains its laws making homosexuality a crime, has recognized the value of softening its image related to homosexuality for the sake of its economy. As early as 1997 and later in 2003, two different prime ministers announced that the Singapore government would hire lesbians and gay men, and others began to proclaim that Singapore had a "live and let live" attitude toward homosexuality.[38] The government also openly eased back on enforcement of the law criminalizing homosexuality. Political scientist Meredith Weiss argues that Singapore's apparent shift was a strategy to score better on Richard Florida's tolerance index, mainly because Singapore needs to be able to attract skilled foreign labor and to prevent a brain drain of its own citizens.

Singaporean LGBT activists saw an opening and began to organize an annual Pink Dot event in 2009 to increase visibility. Singapore's ambivalence continues, though. While it still allows the Pink Dot event, the government banned foreigners and multinational companies from participating in 2017. Those limitations did not deter LGBT people, however. Many local companies stepped up as sponsors, and twenty thousand people showed up for the event.[39]

And it's not just individual workers who might make decisions based on a country's policies. Individual companies considering new facilities in other countries also appear to take tolerance into account. Economist Marcus Noland looked at data on those decisions from 1997 to 2002.[40] After he accounted for the factors known to predict foreign direct investment (FDI), as those decisions are known, countries that were more accepting of homosexuality consistently had a higher level of FDI. Noland argues that tolerance is a measure of a country's political or security risk, such as for the company's local workers. More tolerant attitudes signal lower risk, giving countries an incentive to look—or better yet to *be*—more tolerant to attract foreign investors.

However, it's also possible that the link between inclusion and the economy goes in the other direction. Richer countries might be more likely to be tolerant of LGBT people and to pass laws to respect their rights if people in richer countries adopt what political scientist Ronald Inglehart calls "post-materialist values."[41] As countries get richer, his argument goes, people worry less about survival and subsistence (the post-material part) and can focus more on allowing individual rights and self-expression. The importance of traditional and religious ways of thinking fades and the importance of secular ideas and individual rights grows. The link to LGBT inclusion comes in the finding of Inglehart's and others' research that higher GDP per capita is a good predictor of more tolerant attitudes toward homosexuality. Also, with wealth comes the possibility of using resources to create organizations that focus on the rights of minorities and can lobby successfully for laws enacting respect for those rights. So in Inglehart's argument, economic output and rights are connected because higher GDP per capita causes countries to have more tolerant attitudes and to pass LGBT rights laws.

While we can't parse out how much of the link between rights and GDP per capita is because LGBT inclusion improves economic performance or because greater wealth improves attitudes, it seems reasonable to think that both are at work to some extent. Here's one way to think about it. Stigma and discrimination against LGBT people cost the Indian economy (and other emerging economies) about 1 percent of its GDP, according to the first part of this chapter. India is an emerging economy that had none of the country-level rights marked in the GILRHO at the time of the study.[42] On average, emerging economy countries (including India) that add one right have 3 percent higher GDP per capita. So the impact of inclusion on GDP is about one-third of that size (1 percent is one-third of 3 percent) or more, if we had better data on the full range of exclusions faced by LGBT people in India.[43] This simple comparison suggests that the impact of LGBT inclusion on GDP per capita is not trivial.

The good news is that both causal directions are positive from an economic development perspective, since they show that inclusion reinforces economic development and vice versa—a recipe for stable, long-term improvement for LGBT people in a growing global economy. Businesses, economic development agencies, government ministers, and legislators all have good reason to better understand these links and to act on them. Thinking about how this research can move the debate on LGBT inclusion forward is the focus of the next chapter.

CHAPTER 6

A WAY FORWARD

THE RAINBOW FLAG has become not only a visible symbol of LGBT pride but also a global commodity.[1] They're for sale in shops where I live, and I've seen them in gay bookstores and community centers in many countries. But when LGBT activists Noël Iglessias and Negede Gezahegn planned a Rainbow Photo Project social media campaign in Ethiopia in 2015, they couldn't buy a rainbow flag locally.[2] So they ventured out to a nearby neighborhood and hired a seamstress who made one for them. She didn't know that she was sewing an LGBT flag. She asked about what it meant, and Negede said with a smile, "It's a flag representing the diversity of humankind."

For the project, Noël and Negede wrapped themselves in the rainbow and Ethiopian flags, and they tweeted photos taken from the back that didn't show their faces as they looked out over Addis Ababa. They told stories about being LGBT in Ethiopia with the hashtags #stopthehate and #spreadlove.

The tweets went viral, reaching more than thirty-three-thousand people, but 99 percent of the reaction was negative. "We were prepared for the anger," recalled Noël, "but not for the exposure." The tweets and photos had reached the seamstress, who recognized her handiwork and started telling people about the two young men who had hired her to create the flag.

Revealed as the activists behind the social media campaign, Noël and Negede became targets. Their home was ransacked by police and attacked by neighbors. Death threats became common. Some of their LGBT friends living in their house were beaten. They had to pay bribes to the police to get Noël out of detention. Increasingly, Negede could imagine "being thrown in prison to rot there," with no one knowing where they were.

While the two men attended a conference in Europe, the threats kept coming. Noël and Negede realized they lacked either the local or the international support they would need to withstand government threats. They decided to seek asylum and have begun a new life in Austria, learning German and preparing for new careers. Noël and Negede have left their families, jobs, and activist networks behind but are safe and still committed to the LGBT cause in Ethiopia, maintaining their connections online.

Back home, Ethiopia also bears costs. The country lost a highly trained information technology specialist and a university student when Negede and Noël left. The hostile legal environment that criminalizes homosexuality and LGBT organizations has driven many other LGBT people away as well.[3] Negede also reports that the country loses out because the LGBT people who are still there get depressed and leave school.

This story illustrates the costs of LGBT exclusion, and their experiences also tell us about the importance of human rights protections. The Ethiopian Constitution's promise to comply with international human rights protections has proven empty with respect to LGBT rights (among others).[4] Fortunately, Noël and Negede had other human rights to exercise. They were able to claim asylum in Austria because of persecution for being gay. Otherwise, they might be in prison—or worse.

So human rights protections are still needed, and they need to mean something. Appealing to the economic costliness of exclusion isn't a stand-alone strategy that we can substitute for human rights, as the first part of this chapter discusses. It's also not about waiting for businesses and governments to discover that equality is in their self-interest; individuals must make this economic case forcefully. However, the economic case is an idea that can go places the human rights strategy cannot, putting a new kind of pressure—both carrots and sticks—on governments, businesses, education systems, and healthcare systems.

Those pursuing human rights recognition for LGBT people, including activists, businesspeople, policymakers, and development practitioners, want and need practical ideas to use in the struggle. Since human rights arguments for LGBT equality are not universally accepted and themselves cause controversy, people pushing for change need other arguments. LGBT activists, development practitioners, and human rights advocates are making the economic case for LGBT equality in their work because it opens up new discussions in new locations that have the potential to move the goal of LGBT equality and inclusion forward faster.[5]

WE CAN'T TAKE PROGRESS FOR GRANTED

Ethiopia is not the only country pushing back on LGBT rights. We need to open up new spaces for change, because the equality of queer people is still contested everywhere. It's tempting to see recent advances in legal rights in North America, Europe, Latin America, and Asia as proof that change is complete in some places and inevitable in the rest, spreading more or less on its own across borders and continents. But is it just a matter of time before the rest of the world catches up? A look at the data on legal equality and public acceptance of LGBT people suggests there are no guarantees.

Of course, a promising uptick can be seen in the adoption of equality-enhancing laws over the decades. The legal rights measure discussed in the last chapter tracked eight different laws related to criminalization of homosexuality, antidiscrimination laws, and family recognition back to the 1960s.[6] In the second half of the 1960s, the average score was 0.5—mostly because some countries never criminalized homosexuality in the first place. It wasn't until the 1990s that the average country had one positive policy. Since

1990, the average has doubled to 2.2 inclusive laws globally, but that disguises very different trends. Sub-Saharan Africa, South Asia, and the Middle East–North Africa regions have seen only a tiny increase in the average number of rights from 1966 to 2014 on the GILRHO measure, and their average scores are still less than one. In the EU and in high-income OECD countries, the score is about 5.5. For those countries, progress toward legal equality is clearly evident, but most of those places also have a long way to go.

People around the world are also still deeply divided about LGBT issues. For example, in 2013 the Pew Research Center asked people in thirty-nine countries whether society should accept homosexuality.[7] Only seventeen countries had a majority who accepted homosexuality. In Canada, the Czech Republic, Germany, and Spain, 80 percent or more agreed that society should accept homosexuality, as 60 percent did in the US. On the other end of the spectrum, less than 10 percent of those surveyed saw homosexuality as acceptable in Egypt, Ghana, Indonesia, Jordan, Kenya, Malaysia, Nigeria, Pakistan, Senegal, Tunisia, Turkey, and Uganda.

Two big projects have pulled together data to find overarching patterns in public opinion. In the first, Tom Smith, Jaesok Son, and Jibum Kim found that the most accepting countries are in northwestern Europe, followed by the English-speaking, high-income countries (including Australia, Canada, New Zealand, and the US).[8] Southern European countries fall in the middle or most accepting end in these surveys, as do Latin American countries. Former Communist countries (their term) and Asian countries tend to be in the middle or bottom tiers in the rankings. African countries and Muslim countries mostly appear in the bottom third of rankings.

In 2017, Andrew Flores and Andrew Park created the LGBTI Global Acceptance Index (GAI) for 141 countries from surveys on LGBT issues.[9] They found "polarized progress" in acceptance of LGBT people since the 1980s. Just over half of the countries (57 percent) saw increased acceptance over the three decades, while 11 percent did not change and 33 percent saw declining acceptance.

In addition, Flores and Park found an important pattern. The most accepting countries during the 2004–2008 period—such as Denmark, Iceland, the Netherlands, Norway, Spain, and Sweden—saw the biggest increases in acceptance by 2009–2013. The countries with the lowest levels of acceptance in 2004–2008—such as Azerbaijan, Bangladesh, Georgia, and Ghana—saw the biggest *decreases* in acceptance a few years later.

With polarization, the spread of acceptance of LGBT people cannot be taken for granted. These studies show that acceptance varies greatly across the globe and that acceptance can go down as well as up. Changes in national politics and leadership can rapidly reverse gains, as Donald Trump's administration revoked rights for transgender people in US schools, the healthcare system, and the military.[10] Brazilian president Jair Bolsonaro proudly admits to being homophobic, stating he would "rather his son die in a car accident than be gay."[11] When he came into office in 2019, he immediately took LGBT rights off the agenda of Brazil's human rights ministry, and later he told reporters he didn't want Brazil to be a "gay tourism paradise."[12]

WORKING ALONGSIDE HUMAN RIGHTS ARGUMENTS

One key point of this book is that the economic case for LGBT equality goes beyond describing empirical reality to have strategic value in efforts to promote public acceptance and social inclusion. Some people actively involved in the struggle for LGBT human rights are suspicious of the economic case.[13] Those activists argue that human rights belong to everyone and they are not for sale. To some, the economic approach puts a price tag on rights and only values people who make economic contributions that have a monetary value. Others object that the economic case takes too kind a view of capitalism and its goals, and they are suspicious of policies that improve business outcomes.

While I share many of the underlying values driving these concerns—the importance of human rights, the worth of unpaid labor, a concern about economic inequality—they are not diminished by an economic argument. The economic case for equality is a compatible complement to the human rights argument, not a replacement for it. Ultimately, the costs I've calculated in the previous chapter simply add up the measurable economic disadvantages that are experienced by LGBT people because of human rights violations. If there were better ways to measure and value unpaid labor or the larger costs of economic inequality, we'd likely see improvements there, too, when LGBT people are fully included.

The economic case also does not require an unquestioning acceptance of capitalism. No economic model of meeting human needs can afford to waste human potential and to harm people. More importantly, the argument supports governments in their actions to restrain unfettered capitalism, for example, by enacting policies that require treating LGBT workers (or students or patients) fairly, as the final chapter will suggest.

Other activists and even some economists have challenged me on the moral basis for a cost-based argument: "What about slavery? You could use an economic argument to justify it." Whether slavery in the US was a growth-promoting practice is a highly debatable proposition among economists and historians of the United States, but it's not a relevant one for today, in my view.[14] We now live in an era where that possibility is fully (and rightly) ruled out by clear human rights principles. Article 4 of the Universal Declaration of Human Rights sets out, "No one shall be held in slavery or servitude."

Thinking through this argument is a reminder that the economic case needs a foundation of human rights just as much as the human rights argument can be made more forceful by consideration of the cost of withholding them. Human rights specialists can see the value of the economic case, while economists can also hold deep beliefs in fairness and equality.

Philip Alston, a prominent human rights scholar and practitioner, prefers arguments rooted in dignity, but he told a reporter that he sees an instrumental value of the economic case. That perspective "forces government officials to confront it, and persuades a number of people who are otherwise . . . deeply homophobic to say, 'Well frankly, I hate gays, but I also hate losing a hundred million [dollars], so let's just ease off.'"[15]

When Kaushik Basu, the World Bank's chief economist at the time, welcomed a crowd at a World Bank LGBT event, he pointed to the economic research on LGBT people but argued that other values are more important:

> If enhancing justice and equality across human beings promotes GDP that is reason for celebration. But we must not argue that removing discrimination against minorities is good *because* it promotes GDP growth. . . . Removing discrimination and promoting greater equality and justice are good in themselves. If research reveals that removing certain kinds of discrimination . . . lowers GDP a little, I would take the line that, so be it; we will live with a little less GDP in order to achieve a more just and equitable society.[16]

The evidence in this book is strong that we don't need to make that trade-off. Even if there are some costs of eliminating discrimination and homophobia, they are likely to be small compared to the gains of inclusion.

More importantly, even though human rights advocates don't speak the same language as economists, we can agree on the larger value of full inclusion as a good in itself. Our goals are the same when it comes to LGBT rights and inclusion, even as the ideas we use to promote that end might vary.

THE ECONOMIC CASE NEEDS A VISIBLE HAND TO MAKE IT WORK

Appeals to the collective economic interest in LGBT equality need people to make that argument. Some people think that if homophobia is costly, businesses, governments, and the healthcare sector should have a sufficient incentive to end it on their own. However, as chapter 4 showed, even in the settings that are most sensitive to uncovering economic self-interest—for-profit businesses—those big organizations needed their employees to organize and push them to treat LGBT workers fairly. The problem is that many other factors also prop up prejudice and exclusion by businesses and governments, such as lack of information, the need to appease opponents of LGBT rights, the persistence of religious values, and countervailing political pressures.

An ongoing anti-LGBT political campaign in Uganda provides an example of how economic interests can clash with political interests. Uganda had a law against "unnatural offences" left over from the British colonial era.[17] But some Ugandans wanted a stronger one. In 2009, a member of Uganda's Parliament submitted a bill that would have punished homosexuality with death under certain circumstances. That bill had emerged from a growing antigay movement led by local religious leaders who were advised and aided by American pastor Scott Lively and several other American religious leaders.[18] The ensuing public discussion of the bill generated public disclosure of and threats against LGBT activists, and one of them, David Kato, was murdered.[19]

The Uganda Anti-Homosexuality Act's threat to the economy became very real, as the extreme penalty drew much global attention and disapproval. Ugandan president Yoweri Museveni opposed the 2009 bill for fear of the withdrawal of international aid for the country.[20] Four years later Parliament passed an amended version with a punishment of life imprisonment for homosexuality. That law's harshness also led to the loss of $140 million in aid by the World Bank, Denmark, the Netherlands, Norway, Sweden, the US, and other countries.[21] President Museveni signed the bill anyway in early 2014 to assert Uganda's sovereignty against cultural imperialism from abroad and, some argued, to garner votes and continued political support.[22]

Aside from the obvious appeal of political rewards, did the fear of economic repercussions stop Museveni? On one hand, no, since he signed the bill. Even when several donors followed through on their threats, Museveni professed to "not [be] moved."[23] What worried him more as an economic threat, he later claimed, was the possibility of a trade boycott generated by LGBT activists. In the end, Museveni got to make his political points without a permanent loss in funding: the Ugandan Constitutional Court annulled the Anti-Homosexuality Act because the Parliament did not have a quorum when it passed.

In the Uganda case, then, some of the actual and potential economic costs to harsh antigay laws were real and quite visible, but not enough on their own to stop a surge of politically and culturally motivated homophobia. The political logic for anti-LGBT efforts can be seen in other countries as diverse as Brazil, Russia, and parts of the US as leaders bow to the political power of religious groups, scapegoat LGBT people as a threat, or frame human rights for LGBT people as contradictory to national values or as reflecting anticolonial sentiment.[24] Because these other interests persist, the economic case requires people to use it actively.

DEPLOYING THE ECONOMIC CASE IN DEVELOPMENT INSTITUTIONS

Out of the global attention to LGBT issues has come a relatively new focus on economic development institutions by queer activists and organizations.[25] In part that's because development institutions work with low- and middle-income countries, some of which, including Indonesia, Russia, and Uganda, have passed antigay laws or policies. As noted earlier, passage of inclusive laws has been much slower in low-income regions.[26] There's also a role for putting pressure on the high-income countries that are funders and decision makers in these agencies. From the broadest perspective, creating LGBT-inclusion development agencies means pushing *all* countries to take action within the work of these agencies and their national governments.

Also, these agencies focus on reducing poverty, so they are a good place for action given that exclusion is likely to make LGBT people more vulnerable to being poor. Only a few quantitative studies documenting queer poverty exist, and the most detailed show that bisexual and transgender people are much more likely to be poor than heterosexual cisgender people in the US; lesbians and gay men are at least as likely to be poor as heterosexual people.[27]

Development agencies need ideas like the economic case to change minds and policies within the agencies and in their dealings with country-level policymakers. At least partly as the result of economic arguments, some of these agencies, like the World Bank, the UNDP, USAID, and the Swedish International Development Cooperation Agency (SIDA), have been on the leading edge of incorporating social orientation and gender identity (SOGI) issues. LGBT activists have put pressure from the outside on development agencies to end discrimination and exclusion in programs and to create new opportunities. LGBT staff and allies have pushed from within these agencies.

THE WORLD BANK

The World Bank sums up its mission succinctly: "To end extreme poverty and promote shared prosperity in a sustainable way." Its primary tools are loans and grants to developing countries, plus sharing knowledge and technical assistance. Just to confirm the obvious, it's a bank, not a human rights agency. The bank's founding document, the Articles of Agreement, is clear about the need to separate politics and economics: "The Bank and its officers shall not interfere in the political affairs of any member. . . . Only economic considerations shall be relevant to their decisions."[28] Incorporating concerns about LGBT people took some reframing of the issue to focus on the economic need for inclusion rather than politics, tying into a broader recognition of the importance of gender, racial, ethnic, and other kinds of inclusion that has become more central to the bank's work.[29]

In a nutshell, its own staff first got the bank to equalize benefits for staff with same-sex partners, then they started pushing for inclusion of LGBT issues in the bank's programs.[30] Fabrice Houdart led the LGBT employee group at the bank in that push for equal benefits but then saw the need to talk about LGBT issues in terms that the bank would recognize—namely, the economic implications of stigma and discrimination. He wrote an internal grant proposal to fund research to make the economic case.

The bank's most controversial act related to LGBT issues happened in 2014, when Uganda passed the law mentioned earlier. The bank's then-president, Jim Yong Kim, criticized Uganda's antigay law—as well as similar antigay legislation in the US and in other parts of the world—as discrimination that hurts people and economies.[31] The bank was about to make a $90 million loan to Uganda to support health clinics, but Kim decided to freeze it. He justified the reversal because the bank couldn't ensure that LGBT people would not face discrimination or imprisonment as a result of visiting the clinic.[32]

This kind of *conditionality* has been criticized by some activists who worried about backlash, coercive power dynamics, and the failure to coordinate with activists on the ground.[33] Ugandan activists urged lenders such as the bank not to withhold general aid or health-sector aid, although they agreed with a different withdrawal decision, made by the Dutch government, to strategically withdraw aid from the justice sector.[34]

Since then, the bank's SOGI core efforts have moved away from such confrontational approaches. The bank now focuses more on research and data, with studies of LGBT and intersex people in Thailand, the Balkans, Serbia, and India.[35] The bank created a SOGI task force in 2015 to coordinate the creation of knowledge and its internal dissemination. Clifton Cortez was lured away from UNDP in 2016 to become the bank's first SOGI global advisor, and he now leads the effort to promote LGBT inclusion throughout the bank's operations. He and his colleagues are using a more proactive approach to get LGBT inclusive practices into loans for countries' development efforts, including loan packages with funding to address LGBT unemployment in Argentina and the challenges that LGBT university students face in Chile.

According to Cortez, the bank's Environmental and Social Framework (ESF)—the internal policies designed to keep the World

Bank from discriminating or causing social or environmental harm in the countries where it works—has become a potentially powerful tool for inclusion.[36] Although the ESF was originally criticized for not specifically mentioning SOGI, a separate document clarifies that groups defined by SOGI may be "disadvantaged or vulnerable" to being harmed by a bank project, not realizing as many benefits from a project, or being left out of consultation processes.[37] When a project presents such risks for LGBT and intersex people, Cortez and his team can help shape the project to eliminate discrimination. (The World Bank now includes intersex people with LGBT people.)

Cortez offered an example of the creation of digital identification documents that use biometric data, like fingerprints or iris patterns. Identification is a development issue because without it, people may have a harder time accessing services, transportation, credit, jobs, or voting. And as noted in other places in this book, official documents with the correct gender are particularly hard to get for transgender people, a concern confirmed in bank consultations with LGBT and intersex groups in several countries. These groups asked the bank why a gender marker should even be included on IDs when biometric data is used. Perhaps someday the new gold standard will be to have no gender markers on IDs to avoid their being used simply to exclude transgender people.

For now, though, the bank encourages governments to assess the inclusiveness of identification systems, including for transgender people.[38] Bank reports cite examples of how *hijras*, one group of transgender people in South Asia, have been able to get digital identity documents with a transgender designation in Bangladesh, India, and Pakistan.[39] Cortez provided inputs to a project design for training people in one country to create digital identification documents. To reduce the chance that transgender people or anyone viewed as gender nonconforming would be turned away or discouraged from getting their documents, the project will identify and train LGBT and intersex nongovernmental organizations as service delivery points for producing the digital IDs. The general training would also include instructions on avoiding double discrimination, for example, discriminating against transgender people filing discrimination complaints. This kind of proactive review and engagement before a project is approved or implemented has the potential to reduce discrimination and exclusion for LGBT and intersex people in World Bank projects.

THE UNITED NATIONS

The United Nations was founded with the Universal Declaration of Human Rights at its core, so linking LGBT and intersex issues to human rights was an obvious strategy. As with the UN and the World Bank, the organizations described in the rest of this chapter and the next include intersex people, so at this point I will shift to talking about LGBTI people and organizational work. Support for LGBTI human rights at the UN officially began with a resolution by the Human Rights Council in 2011 expressing concern about violence and discrimination related to sexual orientation and gender identity.[40]

Even with that firm foundation in human rights, the United Nations is also promoting the economic case. The UN Free & Equal campaign for equal rights and fair treatment for LGBTI people includes a video, *The Price of Exclusion*. Actor Zachary Quinto narrates the video, making the key link between discrimination and the economy:

> For the individuals in question, these are personal tragedies. For the wider community, they represent an enormous waste of human potential, of talent, of creativity and productivity, that weighs heavily on society and on the economy. The cost of homophobia and transphobia is simply colossal.[41]

Other parts of the UN also draw on economic arguments. For example, UNESCO is working to create inclusive learning environments, pointing out that bullying of LGBTI students can lead to lower levels of achievement, poorer health, and reduced job prospects, which reduces their economic contributions and harms *all* students.[42] Leaders of UNAIDS, the UN agency coordinating work on the HIV epidemic, want to use the economic case to go beyond human rights and public health arguments, and they've been doing their own research.[43]

As mentioned in chapter 4, OHCHR has developed a set of standards of conduct for businesses on LGBTI issues, with more than 250 companies signing on. They point out that businesses have a responsibility to respect the human rights of LGBTI people, ending and preventing discrimination and stigma in their workplaces, in the marketplace, and in communities. In the document describing the business standards, the authors use the economic case for equality to "bolster" the human rights case.[44] They urge businesses to work with local LGBTI communities to craft the most constructive approaches.

UNDP is perhaps the most directly relevant arm of the UN for economic arguments. UNDP's first significant foray into LGBTI issues in 2012 resulted in the Being LGBTI in Asia project in partnership with USAID.[45] That program has grown to include convenings of LGBTI communities, businesses, activists, government officials, and human rights bodies to discuss how to get to full inclusion for LGBTI people. The program has also sponsored research on the extent of discrimination and other forms of exclusion in employment and education. Not surprisingly, many of the studies commissioned by the project have been cited elsewhere in this book.

With a primary goal of ending poverty, UNDP is also the home of the Sustainable Development Goals. To fully implement those goals, particularly the promise that "no one will be left behind," UNDP recognized that more data would be needed to identify inequities and to monitor progress toward inclusion of LGBTI people. In 2015, UNDP and OHCHR initiated the design of an LGBTI Inclusion Index to monitor the degree to which each country is meeting the inclusion goal. That project convened scholars, LGBTI advocates, development agencies, human rights experts, and others with knowledge about data.[46] The first phase identified five key dimensions to assess: health, education, economic well-being, political and civic participation, and personal security and violence. UNDP partnered with the World Bank in the second phase in 2017 to create a set of fifty-one indicators to use as measures of inclusion within the five dimensions.

The development of the LGBTI Inclusion Index has highlighted the lack of data on laws and policies that affect LGBTI people, and on their lived experience. As earlier chapters have noted, there is a dearth of data on LGBTI people's educational achievement, health status, and economic outcomes that can be easily compared to those outcomes for non-LGBTI people within most countries. And that also means the status of LGBTI people across countries cannot be easily compared. As the next chapter discusses, UNDP, the World Bank, and other international agencies are trying to find the resources, knowledge, and people to generate the data needed to better understand the situation of LGBTI people and how to tear down barriers and create opportunities.

USAID AND COUNTRY-LEVEL AGENCY EFFORTS

The development agencies within high-income countries are increasingly funding human rights efforts and development efforts. When Hillary Clinton was secretary of state, the US created the Global Equality Fund, which still gives grants, emergency assistance, and technical assistance to organizations working for LGBTI human rights.[47] The governments of Argentina, Australia, Canada, Chile, Croatia, Denmark, Finland, France, Germany, Iceland, Italy, Montenegro, the Netherlands, Norway, Sweden, and Uruguay contribute to the fund, along with other business and advocacy groups. Countries also provide funding through other avenues, such as the United Kingdom's Department for International Development.[48]

On the development side, the vision of USAID is "a world in which the human rights of LGBTI persons are respected and they are able to live with dignity, free from discrimination, persecution, and violence."[49] USAID wants to contribute to "inclusion, protection, and empowerment of LGBTI persons." They've institutionalized this commitment through policies and programs designed to reduce discrimination and to promote inclusion of LGBTI people.

USAID was the original partner with UNDP on Being LGBTI in Asia, but the boldest effort has been the Global Development Partnership, which debuted in 2012. Along with SIDA and other partners, USAID designed this public-private partnership and provided more than $2.8 million over the 2012–2018 period for projects that furthered LGBTI human rights and development in fourteen countries.[50] They funded a wide range of activities: capacity building in media and communications skills, conducting new research, training in democratic participation, and training in organizational leadership and management skills. The partnership also supported LGBTI entrepreneurs and businesses through networking, enrollment in an international supplier registry, and the development of LGBTI chambers of commerce. The research part of the partnership funded our study that linked GDP per capita with LGBTI rights in emerging economies that was discussed in chapter 5. USAID wanted research that would show the necessary links between development and human rights, and the economic case is cited in many USAID documents on LGBTI issues.

In addition to LGBTI-specific programs, USAID also encourages the integration of LGBTI people throughout the agency's work. The agency officially encourages all programs to analyze barriers to inclusion for LGBTI people (and other marginalized groups) and to attempt to address their needs and "bolster inclusion."[51] Integration remains a work in progress for USAID, as also appears to be true in other countries' development agencies.

LINKING TO THE LGBTI MOVEMENT ECOSYSTEM: "NOTHING ABOUT US WITHOUT US"

Development and human rights agencies are only two sectors that are working for broad social inclusion of LGBTI people. Far more important and influential to date are the various LGBTI civil

society organizations around the world, and they want to be connected with and guiding development organizations working on
their behalf.[52]

It's difficult to characterize the movement ecosystem succinctly, since it varies greatly across countries. Some groups are
large and relatively well staffed, such as the National LGBTQ
Task Force, Lambda Legal, and the Human Rights Campaign in
the US, or COC Netherlands and Stonewall UK. Most countries
have smaller organizations, however. Other organizations have also
been international leaders on transgender or intersex issues, such as
Transgender Europe or Organization Intersex International (OII)
Europe. In general, these groups have largely focused on human
rights issues through lobbying, litigation, research, or other forms
of political organizing. While they mostly work in the countries (or
regions) where they're located, some of these organizations have
extensive ties globally, such as COC Netherlands in its grants to
LGBTI groups in other countries, or with foreign policy in their
home countries.

Groups like OutRight International, the International Lesbian,
Gay, Bisexual, Trans, and Intersex Association (ILGA, an umbrella
of organizations), and ARC International are hubs for organizations working together in particular contexts, such as with the UN
or on projects like the UNDP LGBTI Inclusion Index. They also
coordinate the work of LGBTI civil society, the nongovernmental
organizations operating outside of the government and business
sectors, at large events like the Vancouver meeting of the Equal
Rights Coalition.

Whatever the size or nature of the organization, it's fair to say
that they want to work directly *with*—not be directed by—global
development organizations.[53] Economic development is an area in
which many activists would like to be engaged. They want other
entry points to create change for the LGBTI people in their countries. For example, an evaluation of a training program funded by
the Global Development Partnership uncovered some participants'
criticism of the focus on human rights: "We need to use more of a

development language on poverty reduction and economic development—not only claiming human rights using rights language."[54]

Sometimes the call for economic pressure is public. After the Ugandan antihomosexuality law was passed, a group of Ugandan activists pushed back against the World Bank's withdrawal of its health sector loan but still sought ways to use economic power to resist the law. They urged action from activists in other countries:

> Call on Multinational companies that have businesses in Uganda to go public about their concerns on the Act and their future economic engagements in Uganda. For example Heineken, KLM, British Airways, Turkish Airlines, Barclays Bank, and other companies with important interests in Uganda and that already respect and value LGBT rights in their own internal policies, should note the risk that these laws pose for the safety of their own employees, as well as the impact on their brand image of continuing to do business in Uganda.[55]

Clearly, some activists would like additional tools, and many whom I have talked with believe the economic case for LGBTI rights would catch the attention of local businesses, government agencies, and the financial sector. In fact, I've spoken with many activists who would like to see an economic study for their own countries.

OPENING DOORS AND MINDS

Open for Business, the coalition of multinational employers that is promoting the economic case in many countries and international settings, has worked in Kenya with activists to introduce the idea. The organization produced the 2019 study mentioned in chapter 5 that shows exclusion of LGBTI people cost the Kenyan economy more than $1 billion per year. That study's release generated much press coverage and social media interest. Jon Miller, who directs the coalition, saw an impact: "Overnight, the media conversation changed from a contest of morals, to a discussion about Kenya's economic strategy, its ambition for higher levels of entrepreneurialism . . . to foster the tech cluster in Nairobi."[56]

In his experience, the economic case can start discussions in countries where human rights is "a fraught space," subject to distortion by religion and politics. "Economics, on the other hand," he explained, "is a universal language which everyone understands, and economic progress is an agenda everyone can share." The economic argument appeals to businesspeople and policymakers, as well as human rights advocates. The vice chair of the Kenya National Commission on Human Rights, an agency established by the government, pledged to use the study's findings to advocate for LGBTI inclusion with the government.[57]

At the country level and at the global level, powerful global institutions have been mobilized to begin work toward LGBTI equality and inclusion. The economic case has helped to bring some on board, and the work of businesses, UNDP, the World Bank, and USAID alongside the LGBTI community is helping to strengthen everyone's resolve and effectiveness in expanding those efforts. But there is still a need for clear strategies that will increase all of this work and make it more effective.

CHAPTER 7

STRATEGIES FOR REALIZING THE GAINS FROM LGBT (AND LGBTI) EQUALITY

CREATING A WORLD that treats LGBT people with dignity and allows them the full range of opportunities and resources means creating a world where all will receive the economic benefits of LGBT equality and inclusion. LGBT organizations, along with some policymakers, multinational businesses, development agencies, human rights institutions, and other stakeholders mentioned in the last chapter, are working to get us there. In addition to providing a goal, the economic case for LGBT equality will help mobilize and motivate those groups to act in support of that goal. This book makes that case for LGBT people, but in the new global arena, the discussions and debates on LGBT issues increasingly include intersex people and their concerns. Although there is no research base to draw on for thinking about the gains from intersex people's inclusion, the same general principles applied in earlier chapters are likely to be relevant. Accordingly, in this chapter I will shift from talking about LGBT people to the more inclusive LGBTI acronym to note the collaboration of LGBT and intersex movements and organizations.

Beyond generating motivation and organizational effort, economic arguments can support three interconnected strategies to change LGBTI lives. First, more resources are needed for LGBTI organizations to mobilize, educate, and innovate in their own countries. Some of the work that institutions need to do, such as training or data collection, will require resources as well. Second, countries need to change laws and policies to create opportunities and eliminate barriers that hold back LGBTI people. While that's not a novel strategy, using economic reasoning gives a new boost to those efforts. Third, more information is needed about the lives of LGBTI people in every country. To track whether LGBTI people's lives and our economies are improving, better data and more research are required.

MORE RESOURCES TO FEED THE ECOSYSTEM

Social change requires a lot of time and money. Getting large crowds of people to volunteer their time for demonstrations or lobbying efforts often means having well-staffed, financially stable organizations to plan and coordinate that work. Working through smaller institutions for change isn't free either. In the US, the LGBTI movement requires hundreds of millions of dollars every year. Globally, the need is much, much larger, but resources fall short.

In the US, the Movement Advancement Project reported on the financial health of forty large and influential LGBT organizations in 2017 (the data does not include any intersex groups).[1] Those organizations came from the advocacy, legal, research, and public education realm—a large chunk of the movement iceberg—and reported a combined revenue of $270 million. About 17 percent of that money came from foundations, along with 5 percent from corporations and 3 percent from government sources. Individuals provided 48 percent, in the form of contributions, events, and bequests. These organizations spent $250 million, employing 964 people full time, and another 127 part time.

In 2015–2016, the most recent year of data available, funding at the global level for LGBTI organizations totaled almost twice that of the forty US organizations: $524 million from 511 foundations and from 15 government and international agencies.[2] There is a decided skew in funding toward the US and Canada, which received 55 percent of that half billion, and Western Europe received 7 percent ($38 million). The rest of the world, with 89 percent of the global population, received only 38 percent of LGBTI foundation and government funding.[3]

The sources of funding are also skewed. Almost two-thirds of government and multilateral agency funding came from just two countries, the governments of Sweden ($29 million) and the Netherlands ($38 million), compared with $10 million from the US State Department's Global Equality Fund (2015 only) and $5.8 million from the World Bank. The total for all government and multilateral agency funding was $103 million, which looks very small next to the $274 *billion* in total international development assistance in the same years. In other words, for every one hundred dollars spent on development assistance only four cents goes to LGBTI issues.[4] Foundations contributed a bit more heavily to LGBTI issues, but it was still only seventeen cents out of every one hundred dollars in foundation giving.

Corporate giving has so far been a minor part of the resources available—about 4 percent of donations to LGBTI groups outside the United States. USAID's Global Development Partnership was designed to be a public-private partnership, but the private side has not been much of a source of funding. The Global Equality Fund listed only two corporate financial contributors in 2015: Hilton Worldwide and Deloitte LLP.

Governments, international agencies, foundations, and businesses could and should do much more to contribute financial support for change efforts. Overall, the need is large and the current funding level inadequate. To give one example, the Global Equality Fund's technical assistance call for proposals generated requests for $20 million in funding, ten times the $2 million that the GEF had available.

The economic case can draw together potential funders, particularly businesses and development agencies, two groups that already are using the business or economic case separately in their own policies and programs. Activists and LGBTI organizations want to use the economic case with those two groups, and they want to be in the room where these discussions happen. I've been on panels and in meetings in those places where activists, businesspeople, and development professionals are present and talking with each other about their mutual interests in diversity, equality, and change. More of those meetings need to take place, though, and they need to produce more in the way of resolve and resources for LGBTI inclusion.

PRACTICAL AND SYMBOLIC LEGAL GOALS

The best reason to think about expanding resources is that every country needs to be more inclusive, and within each country there are many possible goals. To reduce the cost of homophobia and transphobia, some very clear steps can be taken, some of which a subset of countries have pursued. The economic case for equality provides an important rationale for fulfilling those goals.

The UNDP LGBTI Inclusion Index provides a helpful starting framework. As noted earlier, UNDP wanted to be able to measure and compare countries' progress (or regress) in making LGBTI people fully equal and included (including intersex people). UNDP convened researchers, LGBTI activists, human rights specialists, lawyers, statistical experts, and businesspeople from all over the world to help design this measure. After choosing the core dimensions of health, education, economic well-being, personal security and violence, and political and civic participation in 2015, this group of specialists spent another six months in 2017 developing 51 "indicators" that would measure whether countries are fully including LGBTI people in each of the five dimensions. These indicators are obviously not the only possible markers of inclusion, but they are measures that informed people—most of whom were LGBTI—agreed on as a way to capture a country's level of inclusion (for example, how inclusive Hungary is) that is comparable to other countries (whether Hungary is more or less inclusive than Taiwan).

A large portion of the indicators captured opportunities open to LGBTI people, such as nondiscrimination laws related to employment, health, and education. The indicators of legal rights suggest a good checklist of laws that put LGBTI people on an equal footing with other citizens:

- EDUCATION:
  - Laws against bullying and harassment of LGBTI students in the educational system
  - Laws prohibiting discrimination against LGBTI students in educational settings

- POLITICAL AND CIVIC PARTICIPATION:
  - Decriminalization of private, consensual same-sex activity by adults
  - No laws criminalizing people because of their gender expression
  - Laws recognizing the right of people to choose their gender and allow them to do so in official records and documents
  - No laws restricting LGBTI people's freedom of expression, civic participation, or association
  - LGBTI people are allowed to form organizations with the same legal standing that other NGOs have

- ECONOMIC WELL-BEING:
  - Laws prohibiting discrimination against LGBTI people in public and private sector workplaces
  - Pension systems for civil servants that provide the same benefits to same-sex partners and different-sex spouses

- **HEALTH, PERSONAL SAFETY, AND VIOLENCE:**
  - Laws prohibiting discrimination against LGBTI people in the healthcare system
  - Laws forbidding conversion therapies that purport to change LGBTI people to being heterosexual or cisgender
  - Laws forbidding nonconsensual "normalizing" medical interventions for children born with variations in sex characteristics
  - Laws punishing hate crimes include sexual orientation and gender identity
  - LGBTI people can be granted asylum because of actual or feared persecution based on their sexual orientation or gender identity

Overall, this list reflects many of the goals in the sights of LGBTI human rights organizations.[5] In particular, laws that ban discrimination have value both as a symbol and as a practical means to promote equal and fair treatment in government programs, businesses, schools, and healthcare settings. Very little is known at this stage about how well such laws are enforced and the extent to which they reduce discrimination (see below). Existing studies in the United States have found that employment nondiscrimination laws improved some labor market outcomes for lesbian, gay, and bisexual people (no one has yet studied the effect of nondiscrimination policies on transgender people).[6]

In addition to (or instead of) the practical value, policies can have symbolic value. A policy that bans discrimination against LGBTI people by employers, for instance, makes a statement that LGBTI people should be considered equally worthy, since treating non-LGBTI people more favorably than LGBTI people is not acceptable. A policy that allows transgender people to choose their own gender designation on official documents and records also conveys the idea that transgender people's dignity requires official recognition and the right to make that decision for themselves.

Symbols matter, as chapter 3 presented evidence of the health damage that anti-LGBTI laws can cause and showed how to undo that damage by changing laws.

Changing laws can also change minds. The general public might internalize those inclusive ideas, increasing their acceptance of LGBTI people. It seems obvious that elected officials are more likely to make such a statement when the public supports those actions. But it turns out that inclusive laws themselves also push public attitudes into a more inclusive direction, generating a positive feedback loop for these efforts.

Jumps in public acceptance of LGBTI people can be seen after countries enact positive laws, thanks to researchers who have tracked changes in public opinion before and after legal changes. One study looked at the impact of a country's legalization of homosexuality on whether people thought their city or area was a good or a bad place for gay and lesbian people to live. The percentage saying their country was a bad place dropped where a country legalized homosexuality between 2006 and 2016.[7] Often decriminalization of homosexuality is the first legal step toward equality for LGBTI people, and these findings suggest that it might pave the way for other changes through greater acceptance.

Similar findings come from several studies on the hot button issue of marriage equality in Europe and the US. People who lived in countries or states that enacted marriage equality (or other legal recognition for same-sex couples) became more accepting of lesbians and gay men than people in the states or countries without legal recognition.[8] Also, same-sex marriage *bans* led to less acceptance over time—so negative laws also appear to have a symbolic effect that reduces acceptance.

To change these laws, legislatures and courts will be important sites of decision-making in the future, as they have been in the past. The economic case can play a role in both settings.

For legislative decision-making, the economic case might play a direct role in persuading elected officials to enact laws that are inclusive. It's hard to know when the economic case is persuasive, but it is something that legislators want to hear about, as I've learned from being asked to brief or testify before policymakers in many states in the US and several other countries.

Economic arguments have also motivated public advocacy by businesses in support of good laws and against bad ones, as examples in chapter 5 showed. The economic case has proven useful for convincing businesses to adopt nondiscrimination policies and to advocate for nondiscrimination laws, and in the US it played a role in tapping into hidden sources of business support for marriage equality. The US Chamber of Commerce studied forty-eight large companies and found that 88 percent publicly support policies promoting LGBTI equality, and 59 percent publicly oppose policies of inequality.[9]

Businesses have also supported litigation related to rights for LGBTI people in court, as in their friend-of-the-court briefs in marriage equality cases. The economic case has shown up in important court decisions on LGBTI rights too. In the marriage equality case that changed California law, the trial court judge noted the negative economic impact inequality had on same-sex couples, the state of California, and the city and county of San Francisco.[10]

The Supreme Court of India made an economic case in 2018 when it ruled that the law criminalizing homosexuality, Section 377, was unconstitutional. As part of that process, the court heard the petition of LGBTI people who were current and former students of the prestigious Indian Institutes of Technology. Those scientists, teachers, entrepreneurs, and others testified on how the stigma emanating from Section 377 had affected them. In addition to personal pain, they pointed to harms to the Indian economy, including brain drain from India and people avoiding highly productive jobs that were unwelcoming. In its opinion in *Navtej Singh Johar v. Union of India*, the court cited their examples of lost job and educational opportunities and the depression and suicide attempts caused by stigma.

MORE KNOWLEDGE AND DATA

The third type of strategy that can help to reduce the costs of homophobia and transphobia is the development of more knowledge. The economic case for equality outlined in this book has taken advantage of existing knowledge about the lives of LGBTI people and their ability to participate fully in the economy. It's a rich and growing body of knowledge, even though only 6 percent of global LGBTI funding outside the US goes to research.[11] However, the research using the most rigorously obtained data comes from only a few high-income countries, such as Canada, the Netherlands, the UK, and the US. Other countries have useful data that allows for comparisons within the population of LGBTI people but is not as useful for comparisons with non-LGBTI people. In 2017, my colleague Phil Crehan and I studied the research needs related to LGBTI issues, and we found that everyone discussed so far in this book—activists, development agencies, human rights agencies, foundations, governments, businesses, and scholars—all agreed that more data and knowledge are needed.[12]

As noted earlier in the book, data and solid academic research have helped to counter stereotypes and morality-based arguments in many countries. LGBTI people are not mentally ill, incredibly affluent, bad parents, or pedophiles. In the US and elsewhere, data on LGBTI people has played an important role in raising awareness about health needs, for documenting the need for nondiscrimination laws, and for justifying marriage equality. Decision makers, including voters, policymakers, and government officials, need to understand the extent, location, and reasons for social, health, and economic problems everywhere before they will have clear ideas about how to address them. Also, much less is known about transgender people and intersex people than about lesbian, gay, and bisexual people, so research on those groups is particularly important.

The biggest problem is that to get the best measures of health, education, poverty, violence, political participation, discrimination, income, and other outcomes, more data is needed from random samples of the population. That kind of data will be necessary for the LGBTI Inclusion Index measures and for many other kinds of research. For the activists, policymakers, development officials, human rights practitioners, and scholars who worked to create the LGBTI Inclusion Index, the issue of data collection was so important that they made a country's collection of data itself an indicator of inclusion.

A second target for expanding data and knowledge is to see how the challenges faced by LGBTI people affect societies in other ways. In addition to reducing the strength of economies, stigma and discrimination create challenges for public health systems through minority stress and its health effects. Restrictive gender roles and bullying can affect people of all gender identities and sexual orientations, not just LGBTI people. Education systems may also be disrupted by homophobic and transphobic bullying in ways that affect every student's learning environment. This kind of research makes it clear that everyone has a stake in LGBTI equality.

The third main target should be research that provides effective tools for increasing acceptance and reducing stigma and discrimination. We need to know what works. The Institute of Medicine (IOM) in the US made this recommendation back in 2011 when it noted how little is known about effective interventions.[13] For example, the IOM found no intervention research on LGBTI youth suicide or homelessness. A 2017 study of interventions (mainly in the US) found that most had attempted to reduce stigma expressed through prejudice and policies, while a smaller set focused on increasing coping resources for lesbian, gay, and bisexual people.[14] While not all had been studied using control groups, several appeared to be effective. For example, training of medical students on LGBTI issues increased their knowledge and their willingness to treat transgender people.

Work in the education sector is another area of experimentation. Schools in some places are revising curricula to be more inclusive. Others are training teachers and school staff in preventing violence and promoting inclusion, as well as working through their own attitudes. Trainings and diversity efforts in employment are another area needing more research. Programs designed to help LGBTI people find jobs or to start businesses, including job fairs, job search skills workshops, and lending circles, are also relatively new and unstudied.[15] Businesses want more workplace data and research on best practices that will help them design effective strategies for LGBTI inclusion.[16]

Many more LGBTI organizations in different countries have likely created their own interventions to address the needs they see, and drawing on their experience with these programs would also move knowledge forward greatly. Studying a wide range of on-the-ground efforts to create change would also allow us to see how well those efforts work across different cultures or across the different groups under the LGBTI umbrella.

To get this research underway, the existing research infrastructure will need to expand. Networks and partnerships that include scholars, LGBTI organizations, international agencies, foundations, government agencies, businesses, and development banks are needed.[17] Also, as with the recommendations discussed earlier for development agencies and businesses, researchers should be working with LGBTI groups to design and carry out those research projects. In many cases, community advisory boards, collaborative projects, and direct engagement with the community at many stages of the research project can result in stronger research that will have more of a public impact.

A new generation of social scientists and health scientists will be needed to take up this responsibility of conducting meaningful research on LGBTI issues in many places around the world. Exciting projects are emerging in my own field of economics that use newly available data to learn more about discrimination in the workplace for LGBTI people and about LGBTI families in particular. Much more attention to research is needed in the field of economic development—where it is almost completely absent—to provide guidance on making LGBTI inclusion part of economic development strategies.

CONCLUSIONS

When I interviewed Ying Xin, the director of the Beijing LGBT Center, I asked her what her own life would be like in China without stigma for being LGBTI. "Of course, I think I wouldn't do this job, firstly. I wouldn't have to!" she quickly answered, adding with a laugh, "So maybe [I would be] the curator of the women's film festival." Or maybe she would be a gender studies professor, another career goal she had considered during her university days. Building a global LGBT movement to fight homophobia and transphobia has soaked up the talent and time of many brilliant and committed people like Ying, leading them away from other life courses.

Ying has put her intellectual inclinations to work, though. Through a leadership training program, she got to visit the Los Angeles LGBT Center. She recalled, "It helped me to imagine what we can achieve in China." She also met with professors in the US and realized that even without being an academic, she could use her practical experience to advance knowledge. I've seen this side of Ying in action. In every conversation I've had with her, she wants to hear about the latest research and talk about how she can use it.

Most importantly, she also saw that she could *organize* research through the Beijing LGBT Center. For example, her center partnered with UNDP (the funder) and Peking University on the first national survey on LGBTI issues in China, reaching eighteen thousand LGBTI people and twelve thousand non-LGBTI people.[18] Their report found that few LGBTI people are fully out in their families, jobs, schools, or healthcare settings, but even so, they have experienced violence and discrimination in those settings. That research has informed the center's programs and is helping them to make a case for antidiscrimination laws, education about gender diversity, and training of healthcare professionals. A month before I spoke with her, she had organized a workshop for NGOs on how to do their own research, including how to work with academics, so the organizations can "use data to advance their work," as Ying put it.

LGBTI activists and allies are putting these powerful strategies—combining knowledge, data, resources, and ideas—to work in many other countries too. With good strategies to move toward worthy goals, the economic harm of homophobia and transphobia can begin to be reversed and human rights for LGBTI people realized.

Working from this economic perspective on LGBTI equality also reminds us that the world's economies are linked in ways that most of us can't fully imagine. Economic motives drive many of our individual and collective important decisions, so we have a clear stake in the health of all economies. Who will we hire to provide a needed good or service? Where will we spend our tourist dollars or open a new branch of our business? Would I accept a transfer to that country? Where will I find a job that accepts me as an LGBTI employee? How can we attract more investment and more jobs to our city or country? How will we afford the resources to improve our healthcare and education systems?

Because of those economic linkages, people who want to promote LGBTI inclusion must think globally. The exchange of news and knowledge across borders has given us the metaphor of living in a global village. The latest news about the first same-sex couples marrying in Taiwan or a court decision in Kenya upholding the criminalization of homosexuality will easily find us, whether we want it to or not. That news will go to allies and opponents of LGBTI issues. So, expanding rights for LGBTI people in my country might be seen as something to celebrate in yours—or something to guard against. We are in a moment of great flux that sometimes enhances rights for our LGBTI friends, family members, coworkers, and, in my case, ourselves, and sometimes withholds rights. Only if we are aware of those struggles can we promote LGBTI inclusion in our own countries in a way that will help, or at least not hurt, people in other places.

LGBTI people have many social change "technologies" or tools to use in their work for social justice, and most of those tools already incorporate a global awareness. Some strategies are as old as diplomacy, human rights, and social movement building.[19] Some are newer, such as the power of social media, the Sustainable Development Goals, consumer marketing, and celebrity culture. For example, as I completed this book, Hong Kong's LGBTI community successfully used a social media campaign to convince the airport and railway authorities to allow a billboard ad showing two men holding hands—all within twenty-four hours of the first news report about the authorities' ban on the Cathay Pacific Airways ad.[20]

Each of these technologies comes with its own theory of how change happens. A quiet word from a diplomat in one country to a diplomat in another country transmits support or threats to convince leaders to set a more equal course. A human rights complaint in a national or regional human rights body leads to a decision that requires one or more countries to enact laws that recognize LGBTI people's right to parenthood. Consumer marketing and celebrity endorsements raise awareness of LGBTI lives and, perhaps, acceptance.

In this book I have argued that what is needed is a twenty-first century idea from economics that will enhance all of those existing strategies in addition to standing alone: the economic case for LGBTI equality. The evidence is strong that individual LGBTI people are hurt by homophobia and transphobia. We see it in how they are treated in schools and health clinics. We see the harm from higher rates of mental and physical illness. We can see it in how LGBTI people are treated at work. What we haven't seen is just how much it sets economies back, so this book puts some of the key pieces together and adds them up.

Adding up the world's economic output shows that the "world GDP" was expected to be about $88 trillion in US dollars in 2019.[21] To get a sense of the global cost of homophobia and transphobia, apply the 1 percent loss to GDP in India (and similar losses in other countries) to the whole world. That would equal $880 billion, about the size of the economies of Turkey and the Netherlands—the seventeenth- and eighteenth-largest economies in the world.[22]

Huge numbers that show the potential gains from inclusion open eyes, and even their country-specific versions catch the attention of businesses, development practitioners, and policymakers, three groups of potentially powerful allies. Let's get those people into a room to have a conversation; eventually we want them to get on the bus, supporting and contributing to change. The economic case can help with both.

The economic case would broaden the potential supporters of efforts to make health, education, employment, social services, criminal justice, family law, immigration law, and many other areas of life and policy more inclusive of LGBTI people. The economic case could also strengthen a commitment to human rights, showing how much individuals lose from discrimination, violence, and stigma, and how much we all lose once we add it up.

The often-cited proposition that the flapping of a butterfly's wings in China can cause a hurricane on the other side of the globe captures the impact that small changes can make in creating larger, more meaningful changes in complex systems. The economic case for LGBTI equality can start those butterfly wings moving. Small business owners in Tasmania lobby for marriage equality. Human resources professionals in Manila learn about the economic benefits of nondiscrimination policies for their employees. Scientists and teachers in India convince Supreme Court justices that their economic contributions are diminished by stigma and discrimination. Medical students learn to treat LGBTI patients with dignity. Development agencies tout the economic benefits of LGBTI inclusion. A school's teachers and students work together to stop bullying. Legislatures enact rights; courts recognize them. Small and large pockets of change emerge and merge, creating more space for LGBTI individuals to find supportive places to work, learn, and heal, and for our economies to grow.

ACKNOWLEDGMENTS

ON A STICKY DECEMBER DAY in Manila in 2016, I sat on a platform at the Asian Development Bank with other speakers from the local business and political world for a panel on LGBT inclusion and economic development. While watching the audience fill the auditorium, I got a sudden brain flash telling me that I needed to write up the talk I was about to give on the cost of homophobia and transphobia.

However, it took a little more convincing before I would commit to another book project. That came a few months later at a gathering of the Salzburg Global LGBT+ Forum. A week in a gorgeous setting with many thoughtful, committed people from all over the globe created just the right atmosphere of idealism and sense of purpose. In our big, gushing final session, I pledged to write this book, and many others pledged to help me. I am incredibly grateful to the fellows who shared their stories with me and allowed me to tell them in this book. I hope that I did them justice. Without those stories, this book would be just a bunch of numbers. Thank you to Pema Dorji, Irene Fedorovych, Negede Gezahegn, Noël Iglessias, Salman Noori (a pseudonym), Juan Pigot, Bradley Secker, and Ying Xin. I also thank Klaus Mueller and the Salzburg Global Seminar staff for including me in this life-changing fellowship.

I will be forever grateful to Fabrice Houdart and Claire Lucas, who each lured me in with the irresistible temptation of working on an interesting question that matters. In partnering with the World Bank, USAID, UNDP, and their advocacy partners, I found a new community of people who strive every day to make the world a better place, but still had time to share their knowledge with me. Thank you in particular to Suki Beavers, Aengus Carroll, J. B. Collier (who gets extra credit for housing and feeding me in Washington), Clif Cortez, Anthony Cotton, Phil Crehan, Felicity Daly, Mandeep Dhaliwal, Justus Eisfeld, Micah Grzywnowicz, Boyan Konstantinov, Randy Sell, Edmund Settle, and Jessica Stern.

Many other people worked with me on some of the research presented in the book. For their friendship and collaboration, I thank Michael Ash, Laura Durso, Devika Dutt, Andrew Flores, Amira Hasenbush, Jody Herman, Angel Kastanis, Winston Luhur, Christy Mallory, Brody Miller, Avanti Mukherjee, Sheila Nezhad, Andrew Park, Yana Rodgers, Alyssa Schneebaum, Brad Sears, Randy Sell, Jennifer Smith, Suen Yiu Tung, Kees Waaldijk, and Bianca Wilson. I am also grateful to a group of people from Salzburg and beyond who created opportunities for me to try these ideas out in other places: Jonas Bagas, Rodney Croome, Laurindo Garcia, Bess Hepworth, Hyun Kim, Anne Lim, Minhee Ryu, Suen Yiu Tung, and Wei Wei. I also benefited from two speaking trips, organized by the US State Department, which sent me to Peru and to the Philippines, where I met and learned from many people. The book has also been influenced by the conversations and collaborations I've had with other UMass Amherst colleagues and Williams Institute colleagues over the years.

I send out special thanks to those who read and commented on drafts of chapters: Taylor Brown, Kerith Conron, Clif Cortez, Margo Beth Fleming, Andrew Flores, Jody Herman, Winston Luhur, Ilan Meyer, Adam Romero, Madin Sadat, and Elizabeth Silver. All of your encouragement and suggestions helped me keep going.

Kiran Asher (the queen of write-on-site) and Toni Lester contributed to this book with their friendship and their creation of spaces to write in the company of others, making a lonely task much more collegial. The first chapter of this book was developed during a research and education residency at the Gardarev Center (www.gardarev.org) held in New Hampshire in 2018. Thanks to the Gardarev Center for its generous support of my work.

It has been thrilling to work with the Beacon Press team. Michael Bronski and I talked for years before finding the right project for this series. Gayatri Patnaik was an excellent editor, providing many good ideas and other gentle and insightful feedback. I am also grateful to Maya Fernandez and others at Beacon.

As always, special thanks go to my friends and family for putting up with this process yet again. My wife, Elizabeth Silver, read every chapter at least once and listened thoughtfully to ideas and problems on many long walks. Without her support and love, books would not be worth writing.

A NOTE FROM THE SERIES EDITOR

DISCUSSIONS OF ECONOMICS, the market, and capitalism have never happened easily throughout the history of the LGBT movement. Harry Hay, an inactive Communist Party member, founded the Mattachine Society, the first gay rights group in the United States, in 1950. For a Communist he was relatively uninterested in discussing the intricacies of how economics might interact with LGBT oppression. The members of the Gay Liberation Front—the first queer group that emerged after the Stonewall Riots in 1969—were mostly radical socialists in their political orientation and dismissive of how even a progressive economic analysis that worked within capitalism might benefit anyone. Later, various incarnations of the gay rights movement were interested in how LGBT people might prosper uncritically using the tools of capitalism. None of these groups were particularly interested in examining how the inclusion of LGBT people within capitalism might be achieved by working with businesses within the framework of capitalism.

Lee Badgett's *The Economic Case for LGBT Equality: Why Fair and Equal Treatment Benefits Us All* is an incisive, critically astute, and radical analysis of how working to make economic institutions—businesses, education, and health sectors—act in a responsible, equitable, and humane way toward LGBT people effectively ensures wider LGBT equality. The bottom line is that homophobia and transphobia, manifested in a wide range of ways, has a negative effect on the economy and on business.

Badgett's argument is an elegant combination of economic critiques, personal stories, analysis of business models, surveys of LGBT health and life outcomes, and the interplay of how political, social, and religious homophobia shape legal decisions and social policy. Most important, Badgett's analysis is global. In the seventy years since Harry Hay founded Mattachine and the fifty years since Stonewall occurred, the LGBT movement has become a global movement.

We must always look at how LGBT politics play out in specific communities and nations. *The Economic Case for LGBT Equality*, however, calls for a new formulation of how to *think* about activism that is not just about fairness for LGBT people in business, schools, and health settings, particularly at the local level and in industries, but the implications of that on an international level: How can the World Bank use its power to promote equality under the law in countries with draconian anti-LGBT laws? How can development programs and economic policies work in tandem with traditional human rights arguments—the efficacy of which vary from culture to culture—to make the lives of LGBT people safer? How do we make more concrete connections, between economic realities and the ideals of human dignity and integrity, that benefit everyone?

The Economic Case for LGBT Equality is revelatory in its argument in large part because it is a completely new way to look at how to make the world a better place for LGBT people. In the twenty-first century we are now dealing with interconnected, global issues of LGBT health, poverty, safety, social and political disenfranchisement, and physical harm. The LGBT movement needs all the powerful instruments it can garner to bring its vision and message of equality and justice to the world. That is a message that communist Harry Hay and the founders of the Gay Liberation Front would have endorsed.

—Michael Bronski
Series Editor, Queer Action/Queer Ideas

NOTES

INTRODUCTION

1. *Madam Secretary* is a popular television show in the US about a brilliant, idealistic, and charismatic woman who serves as secretary of state, solving a new diplomatic problem each week with political skill, geopolitical knowledge, and a sense of humor.

2. For transgender suicide attempts, see Ann P. Haas, Philip L. Rodgers, and Jody L. Herman, *Suicide Attempts among Transgender and Gender Non-Conforming Adults: Findings of the National Transgender Discrimination Survey* (Los Angeles: Williams Institute, UCLA School of Law, 2014), https://williamsinstitute.law.ucla.edu/wp-content/uploads/AFSP-Williams-Suicide-Report-Final.pdf, and chap. 3. For employment discrimination, see Pew Research Center, *A Survey of LGBT Americans: Attitudes, Experiences and Values in Changing Times* (Washington, DC: 2013), and chap. 2.

3. Gallup, "Gay and Lesbian Rights," accessed September 25, 2018, https://news.gallup.com/poll/1651/gay-lesbian-rights.aspx; Anna Brown, "Republicans, Democrats Have Starkly Different Views on Transgender Issues," Pew Research Center, November 8, 2017, http://www.pewresearch.org/fact-tank/2017/11/08/transgender-issues-divide-republicans-and-democrats.

4. Justin McCarthy, "Two in Three Americans Support Same-Sex Marriage," Gallup, May 23, 2018, https://news.gallup.com/poll/234866/two-three-americans-support-sex-marriage.aspx.

5. Equal Rights Coalition, "Joint Communiqué of the Equal Rights Coalition Global Conference 2018," accessed December 17, 2018, https://www.international.gc.ca.

6. On homosexuality, see Lucas Ramón Mendos, *State-Sponsored Homophobia* (Geneva: ILGA World, 2019), https://ilga.org/state-sponsored-homophobia-report. In that report, seventy countries still criminalized homosexuality, but India's law was struck down in 2018. For transgender people, see Transgender Europe, "Criminalisation and Prosecution of Trans People," accessed May 28, 2019, https://transrespect.org/en/map/criminalization-and-prosecution-of-trans-people.

7. M. V. Lee Badgett, *The Economic Cost of Stigma and the Exclusion of LGBT People: A Case Study of India* (Washington, DC, 2014), http://www .worldbank.org/content/dam/Worldbank/document/SAR/economic-costs -homophobia-lgbt-exlusion-india.pdf; M. V. Lee Badgett, "The New Case for LGBT Rights: Economics," *Time*, November 25, 2014, http://time.com /3606543/new-case-for-lgbt-rights.

8. The 2001 recession in the US involved a drop in GDP of about 1 percent. Kimberly Amadeo, "2001 Recession, Its Causes, Impact, and What Ended It," *Balance*, January 23, 2019, https://www.thebalance.com/2001 -recession-causes-lengths-stats-4147962.doi.

9. Frank Newport, "In U.S., Estimate of LGBT Population Rises to 4.5%," Gallup, May 22, 2018, https://news.gallup.com/poll/234863/estimate -lgbt-population-rises.aspx; Gary J. Gates, *How Many People Are Lesbian, Gay, Bisexual, and Transgender?* (Los Angeles: Williams Institute, UCLA School of Law, 2011).

10. See Ilan H. Meyer et al., "'We'd Be Free': Narratives of Life without Homophobia, Racism, or Sexism," *Sexuality Research and Social Policy* 8 (2011): 204–14, https://doi.org/10.1007/s13178–011–0063–0. The quotations are from that study.

11. United Nations, Universal Declaration of Human Rights, Article 22, https://www.un.org/en/universal-declaration-human-rights. Emphasis mine.

12. See Joseph E. Stiglitz, *The Price of Inequality: How Today's Divided Society Endangers Our Future* (New York: W. W. Norton, 2013); Thomas Piketty, *Capital in the Twenty-First Century* (Cambridge, MA: Belknap Press of Harvard University Press, 2014); Heather Boushey, *Unbound: How Inequality Constricts Our Economy and What We Can Do about It* (Cambridge, MA: Harvard University Press, 2019). Trends in inequality by country are calculated by Piketty's chapter 9.

13. For research on gender, see Stephan Klasen and Francesca Lamanna, "The Impact of Gender Inequality in Education and Employment on Economic Growth: New Evidence for a Panel of Countries," *Feminist Economics* 15, no. 3 (2009): 91–132, https://doi.org/10.1080/13545700902893106; Jonathan Woetzel et al., *The Power of Parity: How Advancing Women's Equality Can Add $12 Trillion to Global Growth*, (New York: McKinsey Global Institute, 2015); Era Dabla-Norris and Kalpana Kochhar, "Closing the Gender Gap," *Finance and Development*, March 2019, https://doi.org/10.1044/leader.in.17122012.2. On the Roma, see Europe and Central Asia Region Human Development Sector Unit, *Roma Inclusion: An Economic Opportunity for Bulgaria, Czech Republic, Romania and Serbia* (Washington, DC: World Bank, 2010). On people with disabilities, see Lena Morgon Banks and Sarah Polack, *The Economic Costs of Exclusion and Gains of Inclusion of People with Disabilities: Evidence from Low and Middle Income Countries* (London: International Centre for Evidence in Disabilty, 2015), http://disabilitycentre.lshtm.ac.uk/files/2014/07/Costs-of

-Exclusion-and-Gains-of-Inclusion-Report.pdf. On immigrants to the US, see National Academies of Sciences, Engineering, & Medicine, *The Economic and Fiscal Consequences of Immigration* (Washington, DC: National Academies Press, 2017), https://doi.org/10.17226/23550.

14. Later chapters include examples.

CHAPTER 1: STIGMA AND SCHOOLS

1. This story appears in Louise Hallman and Klaus Mueller, eds., *Building a Global Community: Salzburg Global LGBT Forum; The First Five Years, 2013–2017* (Salzburg Global Seminar, 2017), 66, https://www.salzburgglobal.org/fileadmin/user_upload/Documents/2010–2019/2017/Session_578/Salzburg Global_LGBT_Forum_Building_a_Global_Community__lo-res_.pdf, and is used with Pema Dorji's permission.

2. For examples, see Alan B. Krueger and Mikael Lindahl, "Education for Growth: Why and for Whom?," *Journal of Economic Literature* 39, no. 4 (2001): 1101–36, https://doi.org/10.1257/jel.39.4.1101; Robert J. Barro, "Human Capital and Growth," *American Economic Review* 91, no. 2 (2001): 12–17; Eric A. Hanushek and Ludger Woessmann, *The Knowledge Capital of Nations: Education and the Economics of Growth* (Cambridge, MA: MIT Press, 2015); Daron Acemoglu and Joshua Angrist, *How Large Are Human-Capital Externalities? Evidence from Compulsory Schooling Laws, NBER Macroeconomics Annual* 15 (2000), https://doi.org/10.2307/3585383. In addition, some evidence exists in the United States that all workers benefit when the average level of education increases, known as the social value of education or "externalities of education," although these effects are small compared to the private value of education for an individual's wages.

3. United Nations, *The Millennium Development Goals Report* (New York: United Nations, 2015), https://www.un.org/millenniumgoals/2015/_MDG_Report/pdf/MDG%202015%20rev%20(July%201).pdf.

4. OECD, *PISA 2015 Results*, vol. 3, *Students' Well-Being* (Paris: OECD, 2017), 136, http://dx.doi.org/10.1787/9789264273856-en. PISA is the Program for International Student Assessment.

5. Joseph G. Kosciw et al., *The 2015 National School Climate Survey* (New York: GLSEN, 2016), 22, www.glsen.org. More specifically, 70 percent reported verbal harassment because of their sexual orientation in the prior year, and 55 percent were verbally harassed because of their gender expression.

6. Kosciw et al., 23. Additional studies of US data are reviewed in Stephen T. Russell et al., "Safe Schools Policy for LGBTQ Students," *Social Policy Report* 24, no. 4 (2010).

7. UNESCO, *Out in the Open: Education Sector Responses to Violence Based on Sexual Orientation and Gender Identity/Expression* (Paris: UNESCO, 2016). Except for the United States, all of the surveys related to bullying and violence reported in this section are summarized in the UNESCO report.

8. UNESCO, 36–37.

9. UNESCO, 28. For a review of US-based evidence, see Russell et al., "Safe Schools Policy for LGBTQ Students."

10. See Kosciw et al., *2015 National School Climate Survey*, 44–45, for US statistics in this paragraph and the next.

11. Christopher S. Carpenter, Samuel T. Eppink, and Gilbert Gonzales, "Transgender Status, Gender Identity, and Socioeconomic Outcomes in the United States," *Industrial and Labor Relations Review*, forthcoming.

12. Marie-Anne Valfort, "LGBTI in OECD Countries: A Review," in *OECD Social, Employment and Migration Working Papers* (Paris: OECD, 2017), https://doi.org/10.1787/d5d49711-en.

13. M. V. Lee Badgett, "Left Out? Lesbian, Gay, and Bisexual Poverty in the U.S.," *Population Research and Policy Review* 37, no. 5 (2018): 682–83, https://doi.org/10.1007/s11113-018-9457-5.

14. Koji Ueno, Teresa A. Roach, and Abráham E. Peña-Talamantes, "The Dynamic Association between Same-Sex Contact and Educational Attainment," *Advances in Life Course Research* 18, no. 2 (2013): 127–40, https://doi.org/10.1016/j.alcr.2012.09.002; Jennifer Pearson and Lindsey Wilkinson, "Same-Sex Sexuality and Educational Attainment: The Pathway to College," *Journal of Homosexuality* 64, no. 4 (2017): 538–76, https://doi.org/10.1080/00918369.2016.1194114; Stefanie Mollborn and Bethany Everett, "Understanding the Educational Attainment of Sexual Minority Women and Men," *Research in Social Stratification and Mobility* 41 (2015): 40–55, https://doi.org/10.1016/j.rssm.2015.04.004.

15. Donald C. Barrett, Lance M. Pollack, and Mary L. Tilden, "Teenage Sexual Orientation, Adult Openness, and Status Attainment in Gay Males," *Sociological Perspectives* 45, no. 2 (2002): 163–82, https://doi.org/10.1525/sop.2002.45.2.163.

16. Nick Drydakis, "Bullying at School and Labour Market Outcomes," *International Journal of Manpower* 35, no. 8 (2014): 1185–1211, https://doi.org/10.1108/IJM-08-2012-0122.

17. Kosciw et al., *2015 National School Climate Survey*, 28–29.

18. Human Rights Watch, *Forbidden: Institutionalizing Discrimination against Gays and Lesbians in Burundi* (New York: Human Rights Watch, July 2009), 13.

19. Stephen T. Russell, Hinda Seif, and Nhan L. Truong, "School Outcomes of Sexual Minority Youth in the United States: Evidence from a National Study," *Journal of Adolescence* 24, no. 1 (2001): 111–27, https://doi.org/10.1006/jado.2000.0365.

20. Kenya Human Rights Commission, *The Outlawed amongst Us: A Study of the LGBTI Community's Search for Equality and Non-Discrimination in Kenya* (Nairobi: Kenya Human Rights Commission, 2011), 32–33.

21. Organización Trans Reinas de la Noche, Red Latinoamericana y del Caribe de Personas Trans, International Gay and Lesbian Human Rights

Committee, Heartland Alliance for Human Needs & Human Rights and George Washington University Law School International Human Rights Clinic, *Human Rights Violations of Lesbian, Gay, Bisexual, and Transgender (LGBT) People in Guatemala: A Shadow Report* (New York: OutRight Action International, 2012), 12.

22. Arina Alam, "The Struggles of a Rural Muslim Transgender Woman," *Gaylaxy*, January 5, 2018, http://www.gaylaxymag.com/articles/queer-voices/struggles-rural-muslim-transgender-woman/#gs.YyrSMHQ.

23. World Bank Group, *Discrimination against Sexual Minorities in Education and Housing: Evidence from Two Field Experiments in Serbia* (Washington, DC: World Bank Group, 2018), 10.

24. Kosciw et al., *2015 National School Climate Survey*, 36.

25. KAB, "Art Has Become My Safe Haven," *Bombastic: Our Voices, Our Stories, Our Lives,* 2016, 7–8, https://www.kuchutimes.com/wp-content/uploads/2017/05/BOMBASTIC_3_final.pdf.

26. Kosciw et al., *2015 National School Climate Survey*, 117.

27. Daniel Chesir-Teran and Diane Hughes, "Heterosexism in High School and Victimization among Lesbian, Gay, Bisexual, and Questioning Students," *Journal of Youth and Adolescence* 38, no. 7 (2009): 963–75, https://doi.org/10.1007/s10964-008-9364-x.

CHAPTER 2: EMPLOYMENT

1. Jason Thorne is a pseudonym. These details are based on personal communication.

2. Gary Becker, *The Economics of Discrimination*, 2nd ed. (Chicago: University of Chicago Press, 1971).

3. Brad Sears, Christy Mallory, and Nan D. Hunter, "The Legacy of State Laws, Policies, and Practices, 1945–Present," in *Documenting Discrimination on the Basis of Sexual Orientation and Gender Identity in State Employment* (Los Angeles: Williams Institute, UCLA School of Law, 2009), 1–71, https://williamsinstitute.law.ucla.edu/wp-content/uploads/5_History.pdf.

4. Before homosexuality was decriminalized in India in 2018, LGBT public employees were vulnerable to losing their positions if arrested. *Pokkuluri v. Union of India*, Supreme Court of India, "Note on Arguments on Behalf of the Petitioner by Dr. Menaka Guruswamy," 2018, https://scobserver-production.s3.amazonaws.com/uploads/case_document/document_upload/334/Note_on_Arguments_by_Dr._Menaka_Guruswamy.pdf.

5. David K. Johnson, *The Lavender Scare: The Cold War Persecution of Gays and Lesbians in the Federal Government* (Chicago: University of Chicago Press, 2009).

6. See Sears, Mallory, and Hunter, "The Legacy of State Laws, Policies, and Practices, 1945–Present."

7. Sears, Mallory, and Hunter, "The Legacy of State Laws, Policies, and Practices."

8. Because he studied Nathaniel Hawthorne of *The Scarlet Letter* fame, Arvin was later dubbed "The Scarlet Professor" by biographer Barry Werth in a book of the same name.

9. Sears, Mallory, and Hunter, "The Legacy of State Laws, Policies, and Practices."

10. K. K. Rebecca Lai, Troy Griggs, Max Fisher, and Audrey Carlsen, "Is America's Military Big Enough?," *New York Times*, March 22, 2017, https://www.nytimes.com/interactive/2017/03/22/us/is-americas-military-big-enough.html

11. G. J. Gates, *Lesbian, Gay, and Bisexual Men and Women in the US Military: Updated Estimates* (Los Angeles, CA: Williams Institute, UCLA School of Law, 2010), https://williamsinstitute.law.ucla.edu/wp-content/uploads/Gates-GLBmilitaryUpdate-May-20101.pdf.

12. Kate Dyer, ed., *Gays in Uniform: The Pentagon's Secret Reports* (Boston: Alyson Publications, 1990).

13. Joshua Polchar et al., *LGBT Military Personnel: A Strategic Vision for Inclusion,* (The Hague Centre for Strategic Studies, 2014), https://hcss.nl/sites/default/files/files/reports/HCSS_LGBT_webversie.pdf.

14. Tom O'Connor, "Trump's Transgender Military Ban Leaves Only 18 Countries with Full LGBT Rights in Armed Forces," *Newsweek*, 2017, http://www.newsweek.com/trump-transgender-military-ban-leaves-few-countries-lgbt-rights-642342. As of this writing, the Trump administration has reinstated the ban and is defending it in court against lawsuits.

15. Aaron Belkin and Frank J. Barrett, *Discharging Transgender Troops Would Cost $960 Million,* Blueprints for Sound Public Policy, Palm Center, 2017, https://www.palmcenter.org/wp-content/uploads/2017/08/cost-of-firing-trans-troops-3.pdf.

16. Aaron Belkin, "Caring for Our Transgender Troops—The Negligible Cost of Transition-Related Care," *New England Journal of Medicine* 373, no. 12 (2015): 1089–92, https://doi.org/10.1056/NEJMp1415160; Belkin and Barrett, *Discharging Transgender Troops Would Cost $960 Million*; Agnes Schaefer Gereben et al., *Assessing the Implications of Allowing Transgender Personnel to Serve Openly* (Santa Monica, CA: RAND Corporation, 2016), https://doi.org/10.1038/sj.clpt.6100308. The US Department of Defense found low numbers of service members seeking transition-related care, similar to the estimates of the other reports: "Department of Defense Report and Recommendations on Military Service by Transgender Persons," US Department of Defense, 2018, https://media.defense.gov/2018/Mar/23/2001894037/-1/-1/0/MILITARY-SERVICE-BY-TRANSGENDER-INDIVIDUALS.PDF.

17. "Read Trudeau's Full Apology to Members of the LGBTQ Community," CTV News, 2017, https://www.ctvnews.ca/politics/read-trudeau-s-full-apology-to-members-of-the-lgbtq-community-1.3697975. Also see the video of the speech on YouTube, accessed May 29, 2019, https://www.youtube.com/watch?v=xi23IL3b6cs.

18. Pew Research Center, *A Survey of LGBT Americans*; *Discrimination in America: Experiences and Views of LGBTQ Americans*, NPR, Robert Wood Johnson Foundation, and Harvard T. H. Chan School of Public Health, November 2017, https://www.npr.org/documents/2017/nov/npr-discrimination -lgbtq-final.pdf.

19. S. E. James et al., *The Report of the 2015 U.S. Transgender Survey* (Washington, DC: 2016), 148.

20. *Discrimination in America*, 11.

21. *Evans v. Georgia Regional Hospital*, U.S. Dist. Ct., S. Dist. GA, Complaint No. CV415-103, 2015; Lambda Legal Defense, "Waiting on the Supremes," *Impact*, 2017. Her lawsuit argued that she had been subjected to sex discrimination because of her sexual orientation, but the courts dismissed her case, ruling that sex discrimination did not cover sexual orientation discrimination.

22. *EU LGBT Survey: Main Results*, European Union Agency for Fundamental Rights, 2014, https://doi.org/10.2811/37969; *Life on the Margins: Survey Results of the Experiences of LGBTI People in Southeastern Europe*, World Bank Group, September 2018, http://documents.worldbank.org/curated/en /123651538514203449/pdf/130420-REPLACEMENT-PUBLIC-FINAL-WEB -Life-on-the-Margins-Survey-Results-of-the-Experiences-of-LGBTI-People -in-Southeastern-Europe.pdf.

23. Luong The Huy and Pham Quynh Phuong, *"Is It Because I Am LGBT?" Discrimination Based on Sexual Orientation and Gender Identity in Viet Nam* (Hanoi: Institute for Studies of Society, Economy, and Environment, 2015), https://doi.org/10.1057/9781137275196.0007.

24. UN Development Programme, *Being LGBTI in China: A National Survey on Social Attitudes Towards Sexual Orientation, Gender Identity and Gender Expression* (Beijing: UNDP, 2016), 40, http://www.cn.undp.org /content/china/en/home/library/democratic_governance/being-lgbt-in -china.html.

25. World Bank, *Economic Inclusion of LGBTI Groups in Thailand* (Washington, DC: World Bank, 2018), http://documents.worldbank.org /curated/en/269041521819512465/pdf/124554-WP-PUBLIC-LGBTI-Report2018 -full-report-English-23March.pdf.

26. Instituto Nacional de Estadistica Y Censos, "Estudio de Caso Sobre Condiciones de Vida, Inclusión Social y Cumplimiento de Derechos Humanos de La Población LGBTI Del Ecuador," *INEC*, 2013, www.ecuador encifras.gob.ec.

27. A comprehensive review of fourteen of these studies is found in Valfort, "LGBTI in OECD Countries." Others have also been published: Emma Mishel, "Discrimination against Queer Women in the U.S. Workforce," *Socius: Sociological Research for a Dynamic World* 2 (2016), https://doi.org /10.1177/2378023115621316; Make the Road New York, *Transgender Need Not Apply: A Report on Gender Identity Job Discrimination* (Brooklyn, NY: 2010).

One study separately tested four Asian countries so is counted as four studies. Sam Winter et al., *Denied Work: An Audit of Employment Discrimination on the Basis of Gender Identity in South-East Asia*, (Bangkok: Asia Pacific Transgender Network and UNDP, 2018), http://www.asia-pacific.undp.org/content/dam/rbap/docs/Research&Publications/hiv_aids/RBAP-HHD-2018-Denied-Work-An-Audit-of-Employment-Discrimination.pdf.

28. András Tilcsik, "Pride and Prejudice: Employment Discrimination against Openly Gay Men in the United States," *American Journal of Sociology* 117, no. 2 (2011): 586–626, https://doi.org/10.1086/661653.

29. Make the Road New York, *Transgender Need Not Apply*.

30. Winter et al., *Denied Work*.

31. Christine L. Williams, Patti A. Giuffre, and Kirsten Dellinger, "The Gay-Friendly Closet," *Sexuality Research and Social Policy* 6, no. 1 (2009): 29–45, https://doi.org/10.1525/srsp.2009.6.1.29; Christine Williams and Patti Giuffre, "From Organizational Sexuality to Queer Organizations: Research on Homosexuality and the Workplace," *Sociology Compass* 5, no. 7 (2011): 551–63, https://doi.org/10.1111/j.1751–9020.2011.00392.x; Kristen Schilt and Laurel Westbrook, "Doing Gender, Doing Heteronormativity: 'Gender Normals,' Transgender People, and the Social Maintenance of Heterosexuality," *Gender & Society* 23, no. 4 (2009): 440–64, http://gas.sagepub.com/content/23/4/440.

32. Kenji Yoshino, *Covering: The Hidden Assault on Our Civil Rights* (New York: Random House Trade Paperbacks, 2007).

33. Deena Fidas and Liz Cooper, *The Cost of the Closet and the Rewards of Inclusion* (Washington, DC: Human Rights Campaign, 2014), http://hrc-assets.s3-website-us-east-1.amazonaws.com//files/assets/resources/Cost_of_the_Closet_May2014.pdf.

34. See James D. Woods, *The Corporate Closet: The Professional Lives of Gay Men in America* (New York: Free Press, 1994); Catherine Connell, *School's Out: Gay and Lesbian Teachers in the Classroom* (Los Angeles: University of California Press, 2014); David J. Lick and Kerri L. Johnson, "Perceptual Underpinnings of Antigay Prejudice: Negative Evaluations of Sexual Minority Women Arise on the Basis of Gendered Facial Features," *Personality and Social Psychology Bulletin* 40, no. 9 (2014): 1178–92, https://doi.org/10.1177/0146167214538288.

35. Overall, 52 percent of lesbian and gay actors who responded to a survey said that others could at least sometimes tell that they're lesbian or gay. The figure was 20 percent for bisexual actors. M. V. Lee Badgett and Jody L. Herman, *Sexual Orientation & Gender Identity Diversity in Entertainment of SAG-AFTRA Members* (Los Angeles: SAG-AFTRA and Williams Institute, UCLA School of Law, 2013), 33.

36. In total, 45 percent of transgender respondents to one survey said, "People can tell I'm trans even if I don't tell them" either sometimes, most of the time, or always. James et al., *Report of the 2015 U.S. Transgender Survey*.

37. John Browne, *The Glass Closet: Why Coming Out Is Good Business* (New York: Random House, 2014), 2.

38. Browne, *The Glass Closet*, 70.

39. Woods, *The Corporate Closet*; James M. Croteau, Mary Z. Anderson, and Bonnie L. Vanderwal, "Models of Workplace Sexual Identity Disclosure and Management," *Group & Organization Management* 33, no. 5 (2008): 532–65, https://doi.org/10.1177/1059601108321828.

40. Benjamin A. Everly, Margaret J. Shih, and Geoffrey C. Ho, "Don't Ask, Don't Tell? Does Disclosure of Gay Identity Affect Partner Performance?," *Journal of Experimental Social Psychology* 48, no. 1 (2012): 407–10, https://doi.org/10.1016/j.jesp.2011.08.005.

41. Erik Plug and Dinand Webbink, "Sexual Orientation, Prejudice, and Segregation," *Journal of Labor Economics* 32, no. 1 (2014): 123–59; M. V. Lee Badgett and Mary C. King, "Occupational Strategies of Lesbians and Gay Men," in *Homo Economics: Capitalism, Community, and Lesbian and Gay Life*, eds. Amy Gluckman and Betsy Reed (New York: Routledge Press, 1997).

42. András Tilcsik, Michel Anteby, and Carly R. Knight, "Concealable Stigma and Occupational Segregation: Toward a Theory of Gay and Lesbian Occupations," *Administrative Science Quarterly* 60, no. 3 (2015): 446–81, https://doi.org/10.1177/0001839215576401. Another possible reason for this pattern, though, is that LGBT people are less likely to be hired into jobs that require more contact with other workers: Angeline Cuifang Lim, Raymond Nam Cam Trau, and Maw Der Foo, "Task Interdependence and the Discrimination of Gay Men and Lesbians in the Workplace," *Human Resource Management* 57, no. 6 (2018): 1385–97, https://doi.org/10.1002/hrm.21912.

43. Michael E. Martell, "Identity Management: Worker Independence and Discrimination Against Gay Men," *Contemporary Economic Policy* 36, no. 1 (2018): 136–48, https://doi.org/10.1111/coep.12233.

44. Tilcsik, Anteby, and Knight, "Concealable Stigma and Occupational Segregation."

45. Andrew Reynolds, *The Children of Harvey Milk: How LGBTQ Politicians Changed the World* (New York: Oxford University Press, 2019).

46. Gallup, "Gay and Lesbian Rights."

47. Pew Research Center, "Section 2: Knowing Gays and Lesbians, Religious Conflicts, Beliefs about Homosexuality," *Support for Same-Sex Marriage at Record High, but Key Segments Remain Opposed*, June 8, 2015, http://www.people-press.org/2015/06/08/section-2-knowing-gays-and-lesbians-religious-conflicts-beliefs-about-homosexuality.

48. Anna Brown, "Republicans, Democrats Have Starkly Different Views on Transgender Issues," Pew Research Center, November 8, 2017, http://www.pewresearch.org/fact-tank/2017/11/08/transgender-issues-divide-republicans-and-democrats.

49. These estimates come from Pew Research Center, *A Survey of LGBT Americans: Attitudes, Experiences and Values in Changing Times*, which

reported on a random sample of almost 1,197 LGBT people in the US, and Fidas and Cooper, *The Cost of the Closet and the Rewards of Inclusion.*

50. UN Development Programme, *Being LGBTI in China.* The second survey from China is Aibai, "Online Survey Report on the Work Environment for China's LGBT Community," n.d.

51. Aibai, "Online Survey Report on the Work Environment for China's LGBT Community."

52. Huy and Phuong, *"Is It Because I Am LGBT?,"* 37.

53. Sylvia Ann Hewlett et al., *The Power of "Out" 2.0: LGBT in the Workplace* (New York: Center for Talent Innovation, 2013), 14–16, 27.

54. Ian Johnson and Darren Cooper, *LGBT Diversity: Show Me the Business Case* (Utrecht, Netherlands: Out Now, 2015), 19, https://www.outnow consulting.com/media/13505/Report-SMTBC-Feb15-V17sm.pdf.

55. Michael Bronski, Ann Pellegrini, and Michael Amico, *"You Can Tell Just by Looking": And 20 Other Myths About LGBT Life and People* (Boston: Beacon Press, 2013).

56. Claude M. Steele, Steven J. Spencer, and Joshua Aronson, "Contending with Group Image: The Psychology of Stereotype and Social Identity Threat," *Advances in Experimental Social Psychology* 34 (2002): 379–440.

57. Jennifer K. Bosson, Ethan L. Haymovitz, and Elizabeth C. Pinel, "When Saying and Doing Diverge: The Effects of Stereotype Threat on Self-Reported versus Non-Verbal Anxiety," *Journal of Experimental Social Psychology* 40, no. 2 (2004): 247–55, https://doi.org/10.1016/S0022–1031(03)00099–4.

58. Tilcsik, "Pride and Prejudice: Employment Discrimination against Openly Gay Men in the United States"; Nick Drydakis, "Sexual Orientation Discrimination in the United Kingdom's Labour Market: A Field Experiment," *Human Relations* 68, no. 11 (2015): 1769–96, https://doi.org/10.1177 /0018726715569855.

59. Drydakis, "Sexual Orientation Discrimination in the United Kingdom's Labour Market."

60. Letitia Anne Peplau and Adam Fingerhut, "The Paradox of the Lesbian Worker," *Journal of Social Issues* 60, no. 4 (2004): 719–35, https://doi .org/10.1111/j.0022–4537.2004.00382.x.

61. Marina Mileo Gorsuch, "Gender, Sexual Orientation, and Behavioral Norms in the Labor Market," *ILR Review* (2019): 1–28, https://doi.org/10.1177 /0019793919832273.

62. Tilcsik, Anteby, and Knight, "Concealable Stigma and Occupational Segregation"; Koji Ueno, Teresa Roach, and Abráham E. Peña-Talamantes, "Sexual Orientation and Gender Typicality of the Occupation in Young Adulthood," *Social Forces* 92, no. 1 (2013): 81–108, https://doi.org/10.1093 /sf/sot067; Wilfried Rault and Elizabeth Hargrett, "Sectors of Activity and Occupations of Gays and Lesbians in a Union: A Smaller Gender Divide," *Population* (English ed.) 72, no. 3 (2017): 385–418, https://doi.org/10.3917 /pope.1703.0385; Coral Del Río and Olga Alonso-Villar, "Occupational

Segregation by Sexual Orientation in the U.S.: Exploring Its Economic Effects on Same-Sex Couples," *Review of Economics of the Household* 17 (2019): 439–67, https://doi.org/10.1007/s11150-018-9421-5; A. K. Baumle, D. Compton, and D. L. Poston Jr., *Same-Sex Partners: The Social Demography of Sexual Orientation* (Albany: State University of New York Press, 2009).

63. Del Río and Alonso-Villar, "Occupational Segregation by Sexual Orientation in the U.S."

64. Del Río and Alonso-Villar, "Occupational Segregation by Sexual Orientation in the U.S.," 453.

65. Hannah Van Borm and Stijn Baert, "What Drives Hiring Discrimination against Transgenders?," *International Journal of Manpower* 39, no. 4 (2018): 581–99, https://doi.org/10.1108/IJM-09-2017-0233.

66. M. V. Lee Badgett, "The Wage Effects of Sexual Orientation Discrimination," *Industrial and Labor Relations Review* 48, no. 4 (1995): 726–39.

67. See Valfort, "LGBTI in OECD Countries." The only study that finds higher wages for gay than straight men in the US was not able to control for living in an urban area, which is important since urban areas have higher wages and more gay men. As a result, the higher gay earnings might just be picking up the fact that gay men earn more on average because they are more likely than heterosexual men to be living in cities. Christopher S. Carpenter and Samuel T. Eppink, "Does It Get Better? Recent Estimates of Sexual Orientation and Earnings in the United States," *Southern Economic Journal* 84, no. 2 (2017): 426–44, https://doi.org/10.1002/soej.12233.

68. Marieka Klawitter, "Meta-Analysis of the Effects of Sexual Orientation on Earnings," *Industrial Relations: A Journal of Economy and Society* 54, no. 1 (2015): 4–32, https://doi.org/10.1111/irel.12075.

69. M. V. Lee Badgett, *Money, Myths, and Change: The Economic Lives of Lesbians and Gay Men* (Chicago: University of Chicago Press, 2001); Vanessa E. Hettinger and Joseph A. Vandello, "Balance Without Equality: Just World Beliefs, the Gay Affluence Myth, and Support for Gay Rights," *Social Justice Research* 27, no. 4 (2014): 444–63, https://doi.org/10.1007/s11211-014-0226-2.

70. Heather Antecol and Michael D. Steinberger, "Labor Supply Differences between Married Heterosexual Women and Partnered Lesbians: A Semi-Parametric Decomposition Approach," *Economic Inquiry* 51, no. 1 (2013): 783–805, https://doi.org/10.1111/j.1465-7295.2010.00363.x.

71. Nasser Daneshvary, C. Jeffrey Waddoups, and Bradley S. Wimmer, "Previous Marriage and the Lesbian Wage Premium," *Industrial Relations* 48, no. 3 (July 2009): 432–53, https://doi.org/10.1111/j.1468-232X.2009.00567.x.

72. Carpenter and Eppink, "Does It Get Better? Recent Estimates of Sexual Orientation and Earnings in the United States"; Cevat G. Aksoy, Christopher S. Carpenter, and Jeff Frank, "Sexual Orientation and Earnings: New Evidence from the United Kingdom," *Industrial and Labor Relations Review* 71, no. 1 (2018): 242–72, https://doi.org/10.1016/j.annals.2006.06.001.

73. Lydia Geijtenbeek and Erik Plug, "Is There a Penalty for Registered Women? Is There a Premium for Registered Men? Evidence from a Sample of Transsexual Workers," *European Economic Review* 109 (2018): 334–47, https://doi.org/10.1016/j.euroecorev.2017.12.006.

74. Transgender men earn a small amount more than they did before transitioning, but the increase was not statistically significant.

75. Kristen Schilt and Matthew Wiswall, "Before and After: Gender Transitions, Human Capital, and Workplace Experiences," *B. E. Journal of Economic Analysis & Policy* 8, no. 1 (2008), http://www.bepress.com/bejeap /vol8/iss1/art39.

76. Carpenter, Eppink, and Gonzales, *Transgender Status, Gender Identity, and Socioeconomic Outcomes in the United States*; Janelle M. Downing and Julia M. Przedworski, "Health of Transgender Adults in the U.S., 2014–2016," *American Journal of Preventive Medicine* 55, no. 3 (2018): 336–44, https://doi.org/10.1016/j.amepre.2018.04.045. Figures in this paragraph come from table 3 in Carpenter et al.

77. "My Success Will Speak for Me—Pretty," *Bombastic: Our Voices, Our Stories, Our Lives*, 2016, 64. https://www.kuchutimes.com/wp-content/uploads /2017/05/BOMBASTIC_3_final.pdf.

78. Becker, *The Economics of Discrimination.*

79. Alexandra Kalev, Frank Dobbin, and Erin Kelly, "Best Practices or Best Guesses? Assessing the Efficacy of Corporate Affirmative Action and Diversity Policies," *American Sociological Review* 71, no. 4 (August 2006): 589–617, https://doi.org/10.1177/000312240607100404.

80. These two stories are based on personal communications and are used with permission.

CHAPTER 3: WHEN STIGMA MAKES YOU SICK

1. For a review of the literature on the impact of health on economic outcomes for children and adults, see Daniel Prinz et al., "Health and Economic Activity over the Lifecycle: Literature Review," NBER Working Paper Series, 2018, http://www.nber.org/papers/w24865. For a study of the impact of health on GDP per capita, see David N. Weil, "Accounting for the Effect of Health on Economic Growth," *Quarterly Journal of Economics* 122, no. 3 (2007): 1265–306, http://www.nber.org/papers/w11455. It's important to note that richer people and richer countries might have better health because of more healthcare resources, for example. The studies referenced in this note have used a variety of methods to account for this difference so that the effect of health on economic outcomes is more accurately measured.

2. United Nations, Sustainable Development Goals, https://sustainable development.un.org/sdgs, accessed May 31, 2019.

3. Ronald Bayer, *Homosexuality and American Psychiatry: The Politics of Diagnosis* (New York: Basic Books, 1981), reviews this history in his account

of the APA removal of homosexuality as an illness from its *Diagnostic and Statistical Manual*, which is discussed later in chapter 3.

4. Alfred C. Kinsey, Wardell B. Pomeroy, and Clyde E. Martin, *Sexual Behavior in the Human Male* (Philadelphia: W. B. Saunders, 1948); Alfred C. Kinsey et al., *Sexual Behavior in the Human Female* (Philadelphia: W. B. Saunders, 1953); Evelyn Hooker, "The Adjustment of the Male Overt Homosexual," *Journal of Projective Techniques* 21, no. 1 (1957): 18–31.

5. See Jack Drescher, "Queer Diagnoses Revisited: The Past and Future of Homosexuality and Gender Diagnoses in DSM and ICD," *International Review of Psychiatry* 27, no. 5 (2015): 386–95, https://doi.org/10.3109/09540261.2015.1053847, for discussion of *DSM*-5 categories.

6. Drescher, "Queer Diagnoses Revisited"; Kenneth J. Zucker, "Management of Gender Dysphoria," in *Management of Gender Dysphoria: A Multidisciplinary Approach*, ed. C. Trombetta (Springer-Verlag Italia, 2015), 33–37, https://doi.org/10.1007/978–88–470–5696–1.

7. Susan D. Cochran et al., "Proposed Declassification of Disease Categories Related to Sexual Orientation in the International Statistical Classification of Diseases and Related Health Problems (ICD-11)," *Bulletin of the World Health Organization* 92, no. 9 (2014): 672–79, https://doi.org/10.2471/BLT.14.135541; Ben Pickman and Brandon Griggs, "The World Health Organization Will Stop Classifying Transgender People as Mentally Ill," CNN.com, 2018, https://www.cnn.com/2018/06/20/health/transgender-people-no-longer-considered-mentally-ill-trnd/index.html.

8. Jonathan Tcheng, *"Have You Considered Your Parents' Happiness?" Conversion Therapy Against LGBT People in China* (Human Rights Watch, 2017), https://www.hrw.org/sites/default/files/report_pdf/china1117_web_0.pdf.

9. Christy Mallory, Taylor N. T. Brown, and Kerith J. Conron, *Conversion Therapy and LGBT Youth* (Los Angeles: Williams Institute, UCLA School of Law, 2018), https://williamsinstitute.law.ucla.edu/wp-content/uploads/Conversion-Therapy-LGBT-Youth-Jan-2018.pdf.

10. Inter-American Commission on Human Rights and Organization of American States, *Violence against Lesbian, Gay, Bisexual, Trans and Intersex Persons in the Americas* (2015), www.oas.org/en/iachr/reports/pdfs/violencelgbtipersons.pdf; Timothy W. Jones et al., *Preventing Harm, Promoting Justice: Responding to LGBT Conversion Therapy in Australia* (Melbourne: GLHV@ARCSHS and Human Rights Law Centre, 2018).

11. Natalia Marcos and Tatiana Cordero, *The Situation of Lesbian and Trans Women in Ecuador: Shadow Report; International Covenant on Civil and Political Rights* (Taller de Comunicación Mujer, September 2009).

12. Barry S. Anton, "Proceedings of the American Psychological Association for the Legislative Year 2009: Minutes of the Annual Meeting of the Council of Representatives and Minutes of the Meetings of the Board of

Directors," *American Psychologist* 65, no. 5 (2010): 385–475, https://doi.org /10.1037/a0019553.

13. Jonathan Merritt, "The Downfall of the Ex-Gay Movement," *Atlantic*, October 2015, https://www.theatlantic.com/politics/archive/2015/10/the-man -who-dismantled-the-ex-gay-ministry/408970.

14. Mendos, *State-Sponsored Homophobia*, 269–73.

15. Inter-American Commission on Human Rights and Organization of American States, *Violence against Lesbian, Gay, Bisexual, Trans and Intersex Persons in the Americas*; Mendos, *State-Sponsored Homophobia*; Lebanese Psychiatric Society, "Statement from the Lebanese Psychiatric Society," 2013; Psychological Society of South Africa, "Sexual and Gender Diversity Position Statement," (2013), http://www.psyssa.com/documents/PsySSA_sexual _gender_position_statement.pdf; letter from Graeme Reid and Brad Adams, Human Rights Watch, to Nila Moeloek, Minister of Health of Indonesia, April 11, 2016, https://www.hrw.org/sites/default/files/supporting_resources /hrw_letter_to_indonesia_moh_on_lgbt_final.pdf.

16. Mendos, *State-Sponsored Homophobia*.

17. Institute of Medicine, *The Health of Lesbian, Gay, Bisexual, and Trans-gender People: Building a Foundation for Better Understanding*, (Washington, DC: National Academies Press, 2011), https://doi.org/10.17226/13128; Michael King et al., "A Systematic Review of Mental Disorder, Suicide, and Deliberate Self Harm in Lesbian, Gay and Bisexual People," *BMC Psychiatry* 8 (2008): 1–17, https://doi.org/10.1186/1471–244X-8–70; Karel Blondeel et al., "Evidence and Knowledge Gaps on the Disease Burden in Sexual and Gender Minorities: A Review of Systematic Reviews," *International Journal for Equity in Health* 15, no. 1 (2016): 1–9, https://doi.org/10.1186/s12939–016–0304–1; Martin Plöderl and Pierre Tremblay, "Mental Health of Sexual Minorities: A Systematic Review," *International Review of Psychiatry* 27, no. 5 (2015): 367–85, https:// doi.org/http://dx.doi.org/10.3109/09540261.2015.1083949.

18. King et al., "A Systematic Review of Mental Disorder, Suicide, and Deliberate Self Harm in Lesbian, Gay and Bisexual People." The samples for the studies they use came from Australia, Austria, the Netherlands, Norway, Taiwan, the UK, and the US. A study of LGB people in Korea also found a much higher suicide attempt rate compared with the general population. Horim Yi et al., "Health Disparities between Lesbian, Gay, and Bisexual Adults and the General Population in South Korea: Rainbow Connection Project I," *Epidemiology and Health* 39 (2017): e2017046, https://doi.org /10.4178/epih.e2017046.

19. Elizabeth M. Saewyc, "Research on Adolescent Sexual Orientation: Development, Health Disparities, Stigma, and Resilience," *Journal of Research on Adolescence* 21, no. 1 (2011): 256–72, https://doi.org/10.1111/j.1532–7795.2010 .00727.x; Tumaini R. Coker, S. Bryn Austin, and Mark A. Schuster, "The Health and Health Care of Lesbian, Gay, and Bisexual Adolescents," *Annual*

Review of Public Health 31, no. 1 (2010): 457–77, https://doi.org/10.1146 /annurev.publhealth.012809.103636.

20. Jay McNeil, Sonja J. Ellis, and Fiona J. R. Eccles, "Suicide in Trans Populations: A Systematic Review of Prevalence and Correlates," *Psychology of Sexual Orientation and Gender Diversity* 4, no. 3 (2017): 341–53, https:// doi.org/10.1037/sgd0000235. See also the review by Jeffrey H. Herbst et al., "Estimating HIV Prevalence and Risk Behaviors of Transgender Persons in the United States: A Systematic Review," *AIDS and Behavior* 12, no. 1 (2008): 1–17, https://doi.org/10.1007/s10461-007-9299-3.

21. Haas, Rodgers, and Herman, "Suicide Attempts among Transgender and Gender Non-Conforming Adults."

22. Brandon D. L. Marshall et al., "Prevalence and Correlates of Lifetime Suicide Attempts among Transgender Persons in Argentina," *Journal of Homosexuality* 63, no. 7 (2016): 955–67, https://doi.org/10.1080/00918369 .2015.1117898.

23. Kyle Knight, *Bridges to Justice: Case Study of LGBTI Rights in Nepal* (New York: Astraea Lesbian Foundation for Justice, 2015), http://www .astraeafoundation.org/uploads/files/Astraea Nepal Case Study.pdf.

24. International Gay and Lesbian Human Rights Commission, *Violence: Through the Lens of Lesbians, Bisexual Women and Trans People in Asia* (New York, 2014).

25. King et al., "A Systematic Review of Mental Disorder, Suicide, and Deliberate Self Harm in Lesbian, Gay and Bisexual People."

26. Downing and Przedworski, "Health of Transgender Adults in the U.S., 2014–2016."

27. J. G. L. Lee, G. K. Griffin, and C. L. Melvin, "Tobacco Use among Sexual Minorities in the USA, 1987 to May 2007: A Systematic Review," *Tobacco Control* 18, no. 4 (2009): 275–82, https://doi.org/10.1136/tc.2008.028241; John Blosnich, Joseph G. L. Lee, and Kimberly Horn, "A Systematic Review of the Aetiology of Tobacco Disparities for Sexual Minorities," *Tobacco Control* 22, no. 2 (2013): 66–73, https://doi.org/10.1136/tobaccocontrol-2011-050181.A.

28. Michael P. Marshal et al., "Sexual Orientation and Adolescent Substance Use: A Meta-Analysis and Methodological Review," *Addiction* 103, no. 4 (2008): 546–56, https://doi.org/10.1111/j.1360-0443.2008.02149.x; Saewyc, "Research on Adolescent Sexual Orientation: Development, Health Disparities, Stigma, and Resilience"; Coker, Austin, and Schuster, "The Health and Health Care of Lesbian, Gay, and Bisexual Adolescents." A higher rate for lesbian and bisexual women (but not men) was found in South Korea. Yi et al., "Health Disparities."

29. UN Programme on HIV/AIDS (UNAIDS), "UNAIDS Data 2018," 8, https://doi.org/978-92-9173-945-5.

30. Stefan D. Baral et al., "Elevated Risk for HIV Infection among Men Who Have Sex with Men in Low- and Middle-Income Countries 2000–2006: A

Systematic Review," *PLoS Medicine* 4, no. 12 (2007): 1901–11, https://doi.org /10.1371/journal.pmed.0040339.

31. Chris Beyrer et al., "Global Epidemiology of HIV Infection in Men Who Have Sex with Men," *Lancet* 380, no. 9839 (July 28, 2012): 367–77, https://doi.org/10.1016/S0140–6736(12)60821–6.

32. Herbst et al., "Estimating HIV Prevalence and Risk Behaviors of Transgender Persons in the United States."

33. Stefan D. Baral et al., "Worldwide Burden of HIV in Transgender Women: A Systematic Review and Meta-Analysis," *Lancet Infectious Diseases* 13, no. 3 (2013): 214–22, https://doi.org/10.1016/S1473–3099(12)70315–8.

34. Institute of Medicine, *Health of Lesbian, Gay, Bisexual, and Transgender People*; Blondeel et al., "Evidence and Knowledge Gaps on the Disease Burden in Sexual and Gender Minorities"; Ulrike Boehmer, Timothy P. Cooley, and Melissa A. Clark, "Cancer and Men Who Have Sex with Men: A Systematic Review," *Lancet Oncology* 13, no. 12 (2012): e545–53, https:// doi.org/10.1016/S1470–2045(12)70347–9.

35. Institute of Medicine, *Health of Lesbian, Gay, Bisexual, and Transgender People*, 213.

36. Gregory M. Herek, "Hate Crimes and Adults in the United States," *Journal of Interpersonal Violence* 24, no. 1 (2009): 61.

37. Pew Research Center, *A Survey of LGBT Americans: Attitudes, Experiences and Values in Changing Times*. Also, a 2012 review of hundreds of studies found similar levels of violence. Sabra L. Katz-Wise and Janet S. Hyde, "Victimization Experiences of Lesbian, Gay, and Bisexual Individuals: A Meta-Analysis," *Journal of Sex Research* 49, no. 2–3 (2012): 142–67, https:// doi.org/10.1080/00224499.2011.637247.

38. James et al., *Report of the 2015 U.S. Transgender Survey*. A review of many studies finds similarly high rates of violence against transgender people in the US. Rebecca L. Stotzer, "Violence against Transgender People: A Review of United States Data," *Aggression and Violent Behavior* 14, no. 3 (2009): 170–79, https://doi.org/10.1016/j.avb.2009.01.006.

39. Inter-American Commission on Human Rights and Organization of American States, *Violence against Lesbian, Gay, Bisexual, Trans and Intersex Persons in the Americas*.

40. Amy Lind, "No Governing Intimacy, Struggling for Sexual Rights: Challenging Heteronormativity in the Global Development Industry," *Development* 52, no. 1 (2009): 34–42.

41. *EU LGBT Survey*.

42. Lukas Berredo et al., *Global Trans Perspectives on Health and Well-being: TvT Community Report* (Trans Respect Versus Transphobia (TvT) Worldwide, 2018), https://transrespect.org/wp-content/uploads/2018/12/TvT -PS-Vol20–2018_EN.pdf.

43. UN Programme on HIV/AIDS (UNAIDS), "UNAIDS Data 2018."

44. The discussion of minority stress here relies on Ilan H. Meyer, "Minority Stress and Mental Health in Gay Men," *Journal of Health and Social Behavior* 36, no. 1 (1995): 38–56; Ilan H. Meyer, "Prejudice, Social Stress, and Mental Health in Lesbian, Gay, and Bisexual Populations: Conceptual Issues and Research Evidence," *Psychology Bulletin* 129, no. 5 (2003): 674–97. The theory has also been applied to transgender people using the same arguments described here. Walter O. Bockting et al., "Stigma, Mental Health, and Resilience in an Online Sample of the US Transgender Population," *American Journal of Public Health* 103, no. 5 (2013): 943–51, https://doi.org/10.2105/AJPH .2013.301241; Walter Bockting et al., "Adult Development and Quality of Life of Transgender and Gender Nonconforming People," *Current Opinion in Endocrinology, Diabetes, and Obesity* 23, no. 2 (2016): 188–97.

45. Daniel Kahneman, *Thinking, Fast and Slow* (New York: Farrar, Straus and Giroux, 2011).

46. Mark L. Hatzenbuehler, "How Does Sexual Minority Stigma 'Get Under the Skin'? A Psychological Mediation Framework," *Psychological Bulletin* 135, no. 5 (2009): 707–30, https://doi.org/10.1037/a0016441; Mark L. Hatzenbuehler, Susan Nolen-Hoeksema, and John Dovidio, "How Does Stigma 'Get Under the Skin'?," *Psychological Science* 20, no. 10 (2009): 1282–89, https:// doi.org/10.1111/j.1467-9280.2009.02441.x.

47. Deborrah E. S. Frable, Linda Platt, and Steve Hoey, "Concealable Stigmas and Positive Self-Perceptions: Feeling Better around Similar Others," *Journal of Personality and Social Psychology* 74, no. 4 (1998): 909–22, https://doi.org/10.1037/0022-3514.74.4.909.

48. Meyer, "Prejudice, Social Stress, and Mental Health in Lesbian, Gay, and Bisexual Populations"; Ilan H. Meyer and David M. Frost, "Minority Stress and the Health of Sexual Minorities," in *Handbook of Psychology and Sexual Orientation*, ed. Charlotte J. Patterson and Anthony R. D'Augelli (Oxford, UK: Oxford University Press, 2013), 252–66.

49. Institute of Medicine, *Health of Lesbian, Gay, Bisexual, and Transgender People*, p. 171 for youth; p. 233 for early/middle age adults; p. 282 for older adults.

50. In addition to the Institute of Medicine report, see also Saewyc, "Research on Adolescent Sexual Orientation," and Coker, Austin, and Schuster, "The Health and Health Care of Lesbian, Gay, and Bisexual Adolescents." While relatively little research has found these patterns for transgender people in the US, Jaclyn M. White Hughto, Sari L. Reisner, and John E. Pachankis argue that stigma is also linked to transgender health outcomes in "Transgender Stigma and Health: A Critical Review of Stigma Determinants, Mechanisms, and Interventions," *Social Science and Medicine* 147 (2015): 222–31, https:// doi.org/10.1016/j.socscimed.2015.11.010.

51. International Gay and Lesbian Human Rights Commission, *Violence: Through the Lens of Lesbians, Bisexual Women and Trans People in Asia*.

52. Caitlin Ryan et al., "Family Acceptance in Adolescence and the Health of LGBT Young Adults," *Journal of Child and Adolescent Psychiatric Nursing: Official Publication of the Association of Child and Adolescent Psychiatric Nurses* 23, no. 4 (2010): 205–13, https://doi.org/10.1111/j.1744-6171.2010.00246.x; C. Ryan et al., "Family Rejection as a Predictor of Negative Health Outcomes in White and Latino Lesbian, Gay, and Bisexual Young Adults," *Pediatrics* 123 (2009): 346–52, https://doi.org/10.1542/peds.2007-3524.

53. Jody L. Herman, *Costs and Benefits of Providing Health Care Coverage in Employee Health Benefits Plans* (Los Angeles: Williams Institute, 2013); William V. Padula, Shiona Heru, and Jonathan D. Campbell, "Societal Implications of Health Insurance Coverage for Medically Necessary Services in the U.S. Transgender Population: A Cost-Effectiveness Analysis," *Journal of General Internal Medicine* 31, no. 4 (2016): 394–401, https://doi.org/10.1007/s11606-015-3529-6.

54. Michael A. Ash and M. V. Lee Badgett, "Separate and Unequal: The Effect of Unequal Access to Employment-Based Health Insurance on Same-Sex and Unmarried Different-Sex Couples," *Contemporary Economic Policy* 24, no. 4 (2006): 582–99, https://doi.org/10.1093/cep/byl010; Thomas C. Buchmueller and Christopher S. Carpenter, "Disparities in Health Insurance Coverage, Access, and Outcomes for Individuals in Same-Sex versus Different-Sex Relationships, 2000–2007," *American Journal of Public Health* 100, no. 3 (2010): 489–95, https://doi.org/10.2105/AJPH.2009.160804; Thomas C. Buchmueller and Christopher S. Carpenter, "The Effect of Requiring Private Employers to Extend Health Benefit Eligibility to Same-Sex Partners of Employees: Evidence from California," *Journal of Policy Analysis and Management* 31, no. 2 (2012): 388–403, https://doi.org/10.1002/pam; Gilbert Gonzales and Lynn A. Blewett, "National and State-Specific Health Insurance Disparities for Adults in Same-Sex Relationships," *American Journal of Public Health* 104, no. 2 (February 2014): e95–104, https://doi.org/10.2105/AJPH.2013.301577.

55. Sharanya Rao and Chandra D. Mason, "Psychology of Sexual Orientation and Gender Diversity Minority Stress and Well-Being Under Anti-Sodomy Legislation in India," *Psychology of Sexual Orientation and Gender Diversity* 5, no. 4 (2018): 432–44, https://doi.org/10.1037/sgd0000291.

56. Sheree R. Schwartz et al., "The Immediate Effect of the Same-Sex Marriage Prohibition Act on Stigma, Discrimination, and Engagement on HIV Prevention and Treatment Services in Men Who Have Sex with Men in Nigeria: Analysis of Prospective Data from the TRUST Cohort," *Lancet HIV* 2, no. 7 (2015): e299–306, https://doi.org/10.1016/S2352-3018(15)00078-8.

57. Bisi Alimi et al., *Not Dancing to Their Music: The Effects of Homophobia, Biphobia, and Transphobia on the Lives of LGBTQ People in Nigeria* (Bisi Alimi Foundation, 2017).

58. Sara L. M. Davis et al., "Punitive Laws, Key Population Size Estimates, and Global AIDS Response Progress Reports: An Ecological Study of

154 Countries," *Journal of the International AIDS Society* 20, no. 1 (2017): 1–8, https://doi.org/10.7448/IAS.20.1.21386.

59. Erik Lamontagne et al., "A Socioecological Measurement of Homophobia for All Countries and Its Public Health Impact," *European Journal of Public Health* 28, no. 5 (2018): 967–72, https://doi.org/10.1093/eurpub/cky023.

60. John E. Pachankis et al., "Hidden from Health: Structural Stigma, Sexual Orientation Concealment, and HIV across 38 Countries in the European MSM Internet Survey," *AIDS* 29, no. 10 (2015): 1239–46, https://doi.org/10.1097/qad.0000000000000724. For more general effects of acceptance on self-rated health of same-sex couples in Europe, see Arjan Van Der Star and Richard Bränström, "Acceptance of Sexual Minorities, Discrimination, Social Capital and Health and Well-Being: A Cross-European Study among Members of Same-Sex and Opposite-Sex Couples," *BMC Public Health* 15, no. 1 (2015): 1–11, https://doi.org/10.1186/s12889–015–2148–9.

61. Mark L. Hatzenbuehler et al., "The Impact of Institutional Discrimination on Psychiatric Disorders in Lesbian, Gay, and Bisexual Populations: A Prospective Study," *American Journal of Public Health* 100, no. 3 (2010): 452–59, https://doi.org/10.2105/AJPH.2009.168815. Other studies have also found that LGB people's psychological health suffered in states with marriage votes, although those studies only looked at differences after the vote and did not have heterosexual people to compare to. Sharon Scales Rostosky et al., "Marriage Amendments and Psychological Distress in Lesbian, Gay, and Bisexual (LGB) Adults," *Journal of Counseling Psychology* 56, no. 1 (2009): 56–66, https://doi.org/10.1037/a0013609. An insightful early qualitative study of this topic is Glenda M. Russell, *Voted Out: The Psychological Consequences of Anti-Gay Politics* (New York: New York University Press, 2000).

62. Only one outcome increased in the states without marriage votes— the percent of people with a drug use disorder. That marker also rose for heterosexual people in those states over the same period.

63. Andrew R. Flores, Mark L. Hatzenbuehler, and Gary J. Gates, "Identifying Psychological Responses of Stigmatized Groups to Referendums," *Proceedings of the National Academy of Sciences* 115, no. 15 (2018): 3816–21, https://doi.org/10.1073/pnas.1712897115.

64. Francisco Perales and Abram Todd, "Structural Stigma and the Health and Wellbeing of Australian LGB Populations: Exploiting Geographic Variation in the Results of the 2017 Same-Sex Marriage Plebiscite," *Social Science and Medicine* 208 (January 2018): 190–99, https://doi.org/10.1016/j.socscimed.2018.05.015; Mark L. Hatzenbuehler, Andrew R. Flores, and Gary J. Gates, "Social Attitudes Regarding Same-Sex Marriage and LGBT Health Disparities: Results from a National Probability Sample," *Journal of Social Issues* 73, no. 3 (2017): 508–28, https://doi.org/10.1111/josi.12229.

65. The studies referred to in this paragraph are Alexa Solazzo, Tony N. Brown, and Bridget K. Gorman, "State-Level Climate, Anti-Discrimination

Law, and Sexual Minority Health Status: An Ecological Study," *Social Science and Medicine* 196 (2018): 158–65, https://doi.org/10.1016/j.socscimed.2017 .11.033; Mark L. Hatzenbuehler et al., "Effect of Same-Sex Marriage Laws on Health Care Use and Expenditures in Sexual Minority Men: A Quasi-Natural Experiment," *American Journal of Public Health* 102, no. 2 (2012): 285–91, https://doi.org/10.2105/AJPH.2011.300382; Mark L. Hatzenbuehler, "The Social Environment and Suicide Attempts in Lesbian, Gay, and Bisexual Youth," *Pediatrics* 127, no. 5 (2011): 896–903, https://doi.org/10.1542 /peds.2010-3020; Mark L. Hatzenbuehler and Katherine M. Keyes, "Inclusive Anti-Bullying Policies and Reduced Risk of Suicide Attempts in Lesbian and Gay Youth," *Journal of Adolescent Health* 53, no. 1 SUPPL (2013): S21–26, https://doi.org/10.1016/j.jadohealth.2012.08.010; Mark L. Hatzenbuehler, John E. Pachankis, and Joshua Wolff, "Religious Climate and Health Risk Behaviors in Sexual Minority Youths: A Population-Based Study," *American Journal of Public Health* 102, no. 4 (2012): 657–63, https://doi.org/10.2105 /AJPH.2011.300517; Bethany G. Everett, Mark L. Hatzenbuehler, and Tonda L. Hughes, "The Impact of Civil Union Legislation on Minority Stress, Depression, and Hazardous Drinking in a Diverse Sample of Sexual-Minority Women: A Quasi-Natural Experiment," *Social Science and Medicine* 169 (2016): 180–90, https://doi.org/10.1016/j.socscimed.2016.09.036; Julia Raifman et al., "Difference-in-Differences Analysis of the Association between State Same-Sex Marriage Policies and Adolescent Suicide Attempts," *JAMA Pediatrics* 171, no. 4 (2017): 350–56, https://doi.org/10.1001/jamapediatrics.2016.4529.

66. Mark L. Hatzenbuehler, Richard Bränström, and John E. Pachankis, "Societal-Level Explanations for Reductions in Sexual Orientation Mental Health Disparities: Results from a Ten-Year, Population-Based Study in Sweden," *Stigma and Health* 3, no. 1 (2018): 16–26, https://doi.org/10.1037 /sah0000066.j.

67. Institute of Medicine, *The Health of Lesbian, Gay, Bisexual, and Transgender People: Building a Foundation for Better Understanding*. Reviews evidence from the United States demonstrating the points identified later in this chapter.

68. Studies discussed here are Sonya Arreola et al., *Access to HIV Prevention and Treatment for Men Who Have Sex with Men: Findings from the 2012 Global Men's Health and Rights Study* (Oakland, CA: Global Forum on MSM & HIV [MSMGF], 2012); George Ayala and Glenn Milo Santos, "Will the Global HIV Response Fail Gay and Bisexual Men and Other Men Who Have Sex with Men," *Journal of the International AIDS Society* 19, no. 1 (2016): 1–5, https://doi.org/10.7448/IAS.19.1.21098; Cristina Rodriguez-Hart et al., "Sexual Stigma Patterns Among Nigerian Men Who Have Sex with Men and Their Link to HIV and Sexually Transmitted Infection Prevalence," *AIDS and Behavior* 22, no. 5 (2017): 1662–70, https://doi.org/10.1007/s10461-017-1982-4; Carrie E. Lyons et al., "Potential Impact of Integrated Stigma Mitigation Interventions in Improving HIV/AIDS Service Delivery and Uptake for Key

Populations in Senegal," *Journal of Acquired Immune Deficiency Syndromes* 74 (2017): S52–S59, https://doi.org/10.1097/QAI.0000000000001209.

69. OUT LGBT Well-Being, *Hate Crimes Against Lesbian, Gay, Bisexual and Transgender (LGBT) People in South Africa, 2016* (Pretoria, South Africa: OUT LGBT Well-Being, 2016). Retrieved from http://www.out.org.za/index .php/library/reports?download=30:hate-crimes-against-lgbt-people-in-south -africa-2016; Alimi et al., "Not Dancing to Their Music."

70. NPR, Robert Wood Johnson Foundation, and Harvard School of Public Health, *Discrimination in America: Experiences and Views of LGBTQ Americans.*

71. Austin Bryan, *"Even If They Spit at You, Don't Be Surprised": Health Care Discrimination Against Uganda's Sexual and Gender Minorities* (2017), 22.

72. James et al., *Report of the 2015 U.S. Transgender Survey.*

73. Charlese Saballe, Carsten Balzer, and Carla Lagata, *Transrespect versus Transphobia: The Social Experiences of Trans People in the Philippines* (Berlin, 2015), https://transrespect.org/wp-content/uploads/2015/08/TvT-PS-Vol11 -2015.pdf.

74. Hyemin Lee et al., "Experiences of and Barriers to Transition-Related Healthcare among Korean Transgender Adults: Focus on Gender Identity Disorder Diagnosis, Hormone Therapy, and Sex Reassignment Surgery," *Epidemiology and Health* 40 (2018): e2018005, https://doi.org/10.4178/epih .e2018005.

75. Mollie E. Aleshire et al., "Primary Care Providers' Attitudes Related to LGBTQ People: A Narrative Literature Review," *Health Promotion Practice* 20, no. 2 (2019): 173–87, https://doi.org/10.1177/1524839918778835.

76. S. N. Nyeck and Debra Shepherd, *The Economic Cost of LGBT Stigma and Discrimination in South Africa* (Los Angeles: Williams Institute, UCLA School of Law, forthcoming).

77. Janice A. Sabin, Rachel G. Riskind, and Brian A. Nosek, "Health Care Providers' Implicit and Explicit Attitudes toward Lesbian Women and Gay Men," *American Journal of Public Health* 105, no. 9 (2015): 1831–41, https:// doi.org/10.2105/AJPH.2015.302631.

78. G. Banwari et al., "Medical Students' and Interns' Knowledge about and Attitude towards Homosexuality," *Journal of Postgraduate Medicine* 61, no. 2 (2015): 95, https://doi.org/10.4103/0022–3859.153103; Bojana Dunjić-Kostić et al., "Knowledge: A Possible Tool in Shaping Medical Professionals' Attitudes towards Homosexuality," *Psychiatria Danubina* 24, no. 2 (2012): 143–51; Ade Nea, Rudi Wisaksana, and Enny Rohmawaty, "Knowledge, Attitude, and Behavior Regarding Homosexuality among New Students in Universitas Padjadjaran," *Althea Medical Journal* 5, no. 4 (2018): 179–86; Vishnu Parameshwaran et al., "Is the Lack of Specific Lesbian, Gay, Bisexual, Transgender and Queer/Questioning (LGBTQ) Health Care Education in Medical School a Cause for Concern? Evidence from a Survey of Knowledge and Practice Among UK Medical Students," *Journal*

of Homosexuality 64, no. 3 (2017): 367–81, https://doi.org/10.1080/00918369 .2016.1190218.

79. Arreola et al., *Access to HIV Prevention and Treatment for Men Who Have Sex with Men*; Venkatesan Chakrapani, Priya Babu, and Timothy Ebenezer, "Hijras in Sex Work Face Discrimination in the Indian Health- Care System," *Research for Sex Work* 7 (2004): 12–14.

80. James et al., *Report of the 2015 U.S. Transgender Survey*, 96.

81. For US statistics, see NPR, Robert Wood Johnson Foundation, and Harvard School of Public Health, *Discrimination in America: Experiences and Views of LGBTQ Americans*; James et al., *Report of the 2015 U.S. Transgender Survey*.

82. For Senegal, see Lyons et al., "Potential Impact of Integrated Stigma Mitigation Interventions in Improving HIV/AIDS Service Delivery and Uptake for Key Populations in Senegal." For other countries, see UN Pro- gramme on HIV/AIDS (UNAIDS), "UNAIDS Data 2018."

83. Buchmueller and Carpenter, "Disparities in Health Insurance Cover- age, Access, and Outcomes for Individuals in Same-Sex versus Different-Sex Relationships, 2000–2007." The Institute of Medicine report discusses other studies of inadequate care.

84. Marc N. Elliott et al., "Sexual Minorities in England Have Poorer Health and Worse Health Care Experiences: A National Survey," *Journal of General Internal Medicine* 30, no. 1 (2015): 9–16, https://doi.org/10.1007 /s11606–014–2905-y.

85. Arreola et al., *Access to HIV Prevention and Treatment for Men Who Have Sex with Men.*

CHAPTER 4: MAKING THE BUSINESS CASE FOR LGBT EQUALITY

1. Colleen Jenkins, "North Carolina Governor Tweaks Transgender Law After Backlash," Reuters, April 12, 2016, http://www.reuters.com/article/us -north-carolina-lgbt-governor-idUSKCN0X92ER; Ken Elkins, "Red Ven- tures Reconsiders Job Growth at Charlotte Office After HB2," *Charlotte Business Journal*, April 5, 2016, http://www.bizjournals.com/charlotte/blog /outside_the_loop/2016/04/red-ventures-reconsiders-staff-up-at-charlotte .html.

2. For PayPal, see Ken Elkins and Ashley Fahey, "PayPal Inc. Opening Global Operations Center in Charlotte, Creating 400 Jobs and Investing $3.6M," *Charlotte Business Journal*, March 18, 2016, http://www.bizjournals .com/charlotte/news/2016/03/18/sourcespaypal-to-announce-300-jobs-in -new.html; Rick Rothacker, "Losing PayPal May Have Cost Charlotte More Jobs Than Announced," *Charlotte Observer*, April 22, 2016, http://www .charlotteobserver.com/news/business/article73426437.html; Rick Rothacker, "Charlotte Loses 730-Job Operations Center over House Bill 2," *Charlotte Observer*, October 25, 2016, http://www.charlotteobserver.com/news/business /article110349597.html.

3. Associated Press, "How AP Tallied the Cost of North Carolina's 'Bathroom Bill,'" APNews.com, March 27, 2017, https://apnews.com/ec6e9845827 f47e89f40f33bb7024f61/How-AP-tallied-the-cost-of-North-Carolina's-%22 bathroom-bill%22.

4. Dan Schulman, "PayPal Withdraws Plan for Charlotte Expansion," April 5, 2016, https://www.paypal.com/stories/us/paypal-withdraws-plan -for-charlotte-expansion.

5. See Badgett, *Money, Myths, and Change* for an account of this history.

6. LGBT Capital, "Estimated LGBT Purchasing Power: LGBT-GDP 2018," http://www.lgbt-capital.com/docs/Estimated_LGBT-GDP_(table) _-_2018.pdf.

7. Brendan Snyder, "LGBT Advertising: How Brands Are Taking a Stance on Issues," *Think with Google*, March 2015, https://www.thinkwith google.com/articles/lgbt-advertising-brands-taking-stance-on-issues.html.

8. Heather Boushey and Sarah Jane Glynn, *There Are Significant Business Costs to Replacing Employees* (Washington, DC: Center for American Progress, 2012), https://www.americanprogress.org/issues/economy/reports/2012 /11/16/44464/there-are-significant-business-costs-to-replacing-employees.

9. For these and other examples, see Badgett, *Money, Myths, and Change*; Brad Sears and Christy Mallory, introduction and key findings, "Economic Motives for Adopting LGBT-Related Workplace Policies," Williams Institute, UCLA School of Law, October 2011, https://williamsinstitute.law.ucla.edu/wp -content/uploads/Mallory-Sears-Corp-Statements-Oct2011.pdf.

10. Lockheed Martin and United Technologies quote are from Sears and Mallory, "Economic Motives for Adopting LGBT-Related Workplace Policies."

11. Human Rights Campaign, "LGBTQ Equality at the Fortune 500," http://www.hrc.org/resources/lgbt-equality-at-the-fortune-500, accessed May 31, 2019.

12. Human Rights Campaign, *Corporate Equality Index 2019* (Washington, DC: Human Rights Campaign Foundation, 2019), 6, https://assets2.hrc .org/files/assets/resources/CEI-2019-FullReport.pdf.

13. US Bureau of Labor Statistics, *National Compensation Survey: Employee Benefits in the United States, March 2016*, Bulletin 2785 (Washington, DC: US Departments of Labor and Statistics, September 2016), https://www .bls.gov/ncs/ebs/benefits/2016/ebbl0059.pdf.

14. For the thirty-six studies, see M. V. Lee Badgett et al., *The Business Impact of LGBT-Supportive Workplace Policies* (Los Angeles: Williams Institute, UCLA School of Law, 2013). For later studies, see citations below.

15. The goal is to distinguish the question of whether the LGBT inclusion measures are actual causes of better business performance from the possibility that better-performing companies are more likely to adopt inclusion policies. These authors use various statistical strategies for focusing on the inclusion-causes-performance angle, including longitudinal data, differences in differences, propensity score matching, and lagged variables.

16. Companies received higher ratings from the Human Rights Campaign for having sexual orientation and gender identity nondiscrimination policies, domestic partner benefits, support for an LGBT employee resource group, and other pro-LGBT policies and practices.

17. This paragraph discusses these studies, in order: Derek Johnston and Mary A. Malina, "Managing Sexual Orientation Diversity," *Group & Organization Management* 33, no. 5 (2008): 602–25, https://doi.org/10.1177/1059601108321833; Peng Wang and Joshua L. Schwarz, "Stock Price Reactions to GLBT Nondiscrimination Policies," *Human Resource Management* 49, no. 2 (2010): 195–216, https://doi.org/10.1002/hrm; Liwei Shan, Shihe Fu, and Lu Zheng, "Corporate Sexual Equality and Firm Performance," *Strategic Management Journal* 38, no. 9 (2017): 1812–26, https://doi.org/10.1002/smj; Feng Li and Venky Nagar, "Diversity and Performance," *Management Science* 59, no. 3 (2013): 529–44, https://doi.org/10.1287/mnsc.1060.0678; Shaun Pichler et al., "Do LGBT-Supportive Corporate Policies Enhance Firm Performance?," *Human Resource Management* 57, no. 1 (2018): 263–78, https://doi.org/10.1002/hrm.21831; Credit Suisse, "LGBT: The Value of Diversity," 2016, https://www.slideshare.net/creditsuisse/lgbt-the-value-of-diversity.

18. Mohammed Hossain et al., "Do LGBT Workplace Diversity Policies Create Value for Firms?," *Journal of Business Ethics*, 2019, https://do.org/10.1007/s10551–019–04158–z.

19. Huasheng Gao and Wei Zhang, "Employment Non-Discrimination Acts and Corporate Innovation," *Management Science* 63, no. 9 (2016): 2982–99, https://doi.org/10.2139/ssrn.2473250.

20. Sylvia Ann Hewlett and Kenji Yoshino, *Out in the World: Securing LGBT Rights in the Global Marketplace* (New York: Center for Talent Innovation, 2016).

21. US Bureau of Labor Statistics, "Unmarried Domestic Partner Benefits: Access, Civilian Workers, March 2018," https://www.bls.gov/ncs/ebs/benefits/2018/ownership/civilian/table44a.pdf.

22. Badgett, *Money, Myths, and Change*; Nicole Raeburn, *Changing Corporate America from Inside Out: Lesbian and Gay Workplace Rights* (Minneapolis: University of Minnesota Press, 2004); Carlos Ball, *The Queering of Corporate America: How Big Business Went from LGBTQ Adversary to Ally* (Boston: Beacon Press, 2019).

23. "2018 Average Wedding Cost," CostofWedding.com, https://www.costofwedding.com/index.cfm/action/search.weddingcost, accessed May 31, 2019.

24. Christy Mallory and Brad Sears, *Estimating the Economic Impact of Marriage for Same-Sex Couples after Obergefell* (Los Angeles: Williams Institute, UCLA School of Law, 2016), http://williamsinstitute.law.ucla.edu/wp-content/uploads/Estimating-the-Economic-Impact-of-Marriage-for-Same-Sex-Couples-after-Obergefell.pdf.

25. M. V. Lee Badgett and Jennifer Smith, "The Economic Impact of Extending Marriage to Same-Sex Couples in Australia," Williams Institute,

UCLA School of Law, 2012, https://williamsinstitute.law.ucla.edu/wp-content/uploads/Badgett-Smith-Econ-Impact-Marriage-Feb-2012.pdf.

26. "Advocates Hail Tasmanian Government's Commitment to State Marriage Equality," TasmanianTimes.com, August 5, 2012, https://tasmaniantimes.com/2012/08/advocates-hail-tasmanian-governments-commitment-to-state-marriage-equality.

27. The Apple and Disney stories are in Badgett, *Money, Myths, and Change.*

28. Sarah Kershaw, "In a Reverse, Microsoft Says It Supports Gay Rights Bill," *New York Times*, May 7, 2005, http://www.nytimes.com/2005/05/07/us/in-a-reverse-microsoft-says-it-supports-gay-rights-bill.

29. "Brief of American Companies as Amici Curiae in Support of Respondents," 2013, https://www.scribd.com/document/127847969/Perry-Amicus-Brief-of-American-Companies. In 2015, a larger set of businesses filed a similar brief: "Brief of 379 Employers and Organizations Representing Employers in Obergefell v. Hodges," 2015, https://www.supremecourt.gov/ObergefellHodges/AmicusBriefs/14–556_379_Employers_and_Organizations_Representing_Employers.pdf.

30. Obergefell v. Hodges, 135 S. Ct. 2584 (2015), at 2605.

31. A similar argument comes from Ball, *Queering of Corporate America.*

32. Elliott Kozuch, "Major Companies Join Amicus Brief Supporting Trans Student in SCOTUS Case," Human Rights Watch, blog, March 2, 2017, http://www.hrc.org/blog/breaking-major-companies-join-amicus-brief-supporting-trans-student-gavin-g.

33. Australian Marriage Equality, "Join 851 Corporations That Support Marriage Equality," http://www.australianmarriageequality.org/open-letter-of-support, accessed May 31, 2019.

34. Shane Darcy, "Business Said Yes! To Marriage Equality—But Will the Circle Be Widened?" *Business & Human Rights in Ireland*, blog, May 28, 2015, https://businesshumanrightsireland.wordpress.com/2015/05/28/business-said-yes-to-marriage-equality-but-will-the-circle-be-widened.

35. Hugo Greenhalgh, "Multinationals See Benefits in Taiwan Same-Sex Marriage," Reuters, April 24, 2019, https://www.reuters.com/article/us-taiwan-lgbt-economy/multinationals-see-benefits-in-taiwan-same-sex-marriage-idUSKCN1S029C; Open for Business, *Businesses Support the Freedom to Marry in Taiwan as an Economic Growth Imperative* (2018), https://open-for-business.org/s/Taiwan-the-economic-and-business-case-for-marriage-equality-and-LGBT-inclusion.pdf.

36. Human Rights Campaign, *Corporate Equality Index 2018* (Washington, DC: Human Rights Campaign, 2018), 4, https://assets2.hrc.org/files/assets/resources/CEI-2018-FullReport.pdf.

37. Economist Intelligence Unit, *Pride and Prejudice: Agents of Change* (London: Economist Intelligence Unit, 2017), 12, https://prideandprejudice.economist.com/wp-content/uploads/2017/03/Pride-Prejudice-report-final.pdf.

38. Ching-Yi Lin, presentation at 2017 Economist conference in Hong Kong.

39. Kate Vernon and Amanda Yik, *Hong Kong LGBT Climate Study 2011–12* (Hong Kong, 2012).

40. Hewlett and Yoshino, *Out in the World.*

41. Economist Intelligence Unit, *Pride and Prejudice: The Future of Advocacy* (London: Economist Intelligence Unit, 2018), https://prideandprejudice .economist.com/key-findings-economists-lgbt-research.

42. Jon Miller and Lucy Parker, *Open for Business: The Economic and Business Case for Global LGB&T Inclusion* (Open for Business, 2015), 1.

43. Miller and Parker, *Open for Business.*

44. UN Office of the High Commissioner for Human Rights, "Tackling Discrimination Against Lesbian, Gay, Bi, Trans, & Intersex People: Standards of Conduct for Business" (New York: OHCHR, 2017).

45. Miller and Parker, *Open for Business,* 10.

46. Suman Layak, "How the Godrej Group Is Creating an Inclusive Culture to Accept Its LGBT Colleagues," *Economic Times,* December 27, 2015, http://economictimes.indiatimes.com/news/politics-and-nation/how-the -godrej-group-is-creating-an-inclusive-culture-to-accept-its-lgbt-colleagues /articleshow/50335649.cms; Miller and Parker, *Open for Business.*

47. Economist Intelligence Unit, *Pride and Prejudice: Agents of Change* (2017), https://prideandprejudice.economist.com/wp-content/uploads/2017 /03/Pride-Prejudice-report-final.pdf.

48. Juan Pigot, telephone interview with author, July 26, 2017.

49. Irene Fedorovych, email message to author, July 24, 2017.

CHAPTER 5: THE COST TO ECONOMIES

1. Manya Koetse, "New Rules for Online Videos in China: 'No Displays of Homosexuality,'" What's on Weibo: Reporting Social Trends in China (website), 2017, https://www.whatsonweibo.com/new-rules-online-videos -china-no-displays-homosexuality.

2. For a good overview of GDP measurement in the US, see J. Steven Landefeld, Eugene P. Seskin, and Barbara M. Fraumeni, "Taking the Pulse of the Economy: Measuring GDP," *Journal of Economic Perspectives* 22, no. 2 (2008): 193–216, https://doi.org/10.1257/jep.22.2.193.

3. Gary Becker's theory suggests that if there are enough nondiscriminatory employers in the economy, the wage gap should go away as women (or employees from other stigmatized groups) are hired at higher wages.

4. And of course when people are paid less, they have less cash to spend on what other people have to sell in the economy. That macroeconomic effect is not the same as seeing the wage gap as reflecting lower productivity than possible, though.

5. Jad Chaaban and Wendy Cunningham, "Measuring the Economic Gain of Investing in Girls: The Girl Effect Dividend," policy research working paper, World Bank, 2011, http://elibrary.worldbank.org/doi/pdf/10.1596 /1813-9450-5753.

6. Nata Duvvury et al., *Intimate Partner Violence: Economic Costs and Implications for Growth and Development*, Women's Voice, Agency, & Participation Research Series 2013 (Washington, DC: World Bank, 2013).

7. Europe and Central Asia Region Human Development Sector Unit, *Roma Inclusion.*

8. Hewlett et al., *The Power of "Out" 2.0: LGBT in the Workplace*, 16.

9. UN Development Programme (UNDP) and International Labor Organization, *LGBTI People and Employment: Discrimination Based on Sexual Orientation, Gender Identity and Expression, and Sex Characteristics in China, the Philippines, and Thailand* (Bangkok: UNDP, ILO, 2018).

10. This section mixes in data and methods to estimate the cost developed in my World Bank study of India with some calculations that do not appear there in this form. Sources for these figures are in Badgett, *The Economic Cost of Stigma and the Exclusion of LGBT People.*

11. Here I use the wage share of GDP as a measure of how much the capital and other factors of production contribute to output when workers use them. If output equals capital multiplied by labor, then increasing the labor input by $240 million increases output by $240 million divided by the wage share. So if, for example, workers get 50 percent of income (one estimate is 48.6 percent for Indian workers; see Robert C. Feenstra, Robert Inklaar, and Marcel P. Timmer, "The Next Generation of the Penn World Table" [National Bureau of Economic Research working paper, July 2013]), then divide $240 million by 0.5 to get $480 million. Other mathematical forms of the relationship of labor and capital to output would produce different estimates.

12. About 12 percent of young women in the same survey had some kind of same-sex attraction, so 3 percent is a conservative estimate for women. Eric Julian Manalastas, "(Local) Sexual Orientation and Suicide Risk in the Philippines: Evidence from a Nationally Representative Sample of Young Filipino Men," *Philippine Journal of Psychology* 46, no. 1 (2013): 1–13; Eric Julian Manalastas, "Suicide Ideation and Suicide Attempt among Young Lesbian and Bisexual Filipina Women: Evidence for Disparities in the Philippines," *Asian Women* 32, no. 3 (2016): 101–20.

13. The wage share was 34.9 percent in the Philippines in 2014, Philippine Statistics Authority, Open STAT database, "Wage Share in GDP(%)," openstat.psa.gov.ph, accessed September 5, 2019.

14. For Kenya, see Open for Business, *The Economic Case for LGBT+ Inclusion in Kenya* (2019). For South Africa, see S. N. Nyeck et al., "Economic Cost of LGBT Stigma and Discrimination in South Africa."

15. Health means something different from having a disability. People with disabilities can have either good or poor health, and they can still participate in the economy—and many do.

16. Carrie Hanlon and Larry Hinkle, *Assessing the Costs of Racial and Ethnic Health Disparities: State Experience* (Rockville, MD: Healthcare Cost

and Utilization Project, 2011), http://www.hcup-us.ahrq.gov/reports/race
/CostsofDisparitiesIB.pdf; Thomas A. LaVeist, Darrell J. Gaskin, and Patrick
Richard, *The Economic Burden of Health Inequalities in the United States*
(Washington, DC: Joint Center for Political and Economic Studies, 2009).

17. Christopher Banks, "The Cost of Homophobia: Literature Review of
the Economic Impact of Homophobia in Canada" (review, Gay and Lesbian
Health Services of Saskatoon, 2001). In a later study, Banks calculated the
estimated additional deaths of LGB people: Christopher Banks, "The Cost of
Homophobia: Literature Review on the Human Impact fo Homophobia on
Canada," Community-University Institute for Social Research, University of
Saskatchewan, 2003.

18. The studies Banks used were limited to those on sexual orientation
health disparities, so here I drop the T from LGBT for accuracy.

19. Steven A. Safren et al., "Depressive Symptoms and Human Immu-
nodeficiency Virus Risk Behavior among Men Who Have Sex with Men in
Chennai, India," *Psychology, Health & Medicine*. 14, no. 6 (2009): 705–15,
https://doi.org/10.1080/13548500903334754.Depressive; Murugesan Sivasu-
bramanian et al., "Suicidality, Clinical Depression, and Anxiety Disorders
Are Highly Prevelant in Men Who Have Sex with Men in Mumbai, India:
Findings from a Community-Recruited Sample," *Psychology, Health &
Medicine* 16, no. 4 (2011): 450–62, https://doi.org/10.1080/13548506.2011
.554645.Suicidality; Venkatesan Chakrapani et al., "Structural Violence
against Kothi-Identified Men Who Have Sex with Men in Chennai, India: A
Qualitative Investigation," *AIDS Education and Prevention* 19, no. 4 (August
2007): 346–64, https://doi.org/10.1521/aeap.2007.19.4.346; CREA, *Count Me In!
Research Report, Violence against Disabled, Lesbian, and Sex-Working Women
in Bangladesh, India, and Nepal* (Delhi: CREA, 2012), http://web.creaworld
.org/files/cmir.pdf.

20. This rate combines India with other developing countries but is
the only comparison rate available. CREA, *Count Me In!*; Family Planning
Association of India, *The People Living with HIV Stigma Index: A Report from
India* (Mumbai: Family Planning Association of India, n.d.); Chakrapani et
al., "Structural Violence against Kothi-Identified Men Who Have Sex with
Men in Chennai, India: A Qualitative Investigation"; Bina Fernandez and
N. B. Gomathy, *The Nature of Violence Faced by Lesbian Women in India*
(Mumbai: Research Centre on Violence Against Women, Tata Institute of
Social Sciences, 2003).

21. Note that the studies referenced here are based on non-random
samples. In case those studies overestimate the rates of health disparities, I conservatively cut in half the difference in rates of suicide attempts
and depression between LGBT people and non-LGBT people. For HIV, I
assume that the prevalence would be the same for LGBT people as for the
general population. George Ayala et al., *Social Discrimination Against Men
Who Have Sex with Men (MSM): Implications for HIV Policy and Programs*

(Oakland, CA: Global Forum on MSM & HIV [MSMGF], 2010); Arreola et al., *Access to HIV Prevention and Treatment for Men Who Have Sex with Men*; Steven A. Safren et al., "A Survey of MSM HIV Prevention Outreach Workers in Chennai, India," *AIDS Education and Prevention* 18, no. 4 (August 2006): 323–32, https://doi.org/10.1521/aeap.2006.18.4.323; Chakrapani et al., "Structural Violence against Kothi-Identified Men Who Have Sex with Men in Chennai, India"; P. A. Newman et al., "Determinants of Sexual Risk Behavior Among Men Who Have Sex with Men Accessing Public Sex Environments in Chennai, India," *Journal of LGBT Health Research* 4, no. 2–3 (May 29, 2008): 81–87, https://doi.org/10.1080/15574090902913669; Beena Thomas et al., "Unseen and Unheard: Predictors of Sexual Risk Behavior and HIV Infection among Men Who Have Sex with Men in Chennai, India," *AIDS Education and Prevention* 21, no. 4 (2009): 372–83, https://doi.org/10.1521/aeap.2009.21.4.372.UNSEEN; Beena Thomas et al., "The Influence of Stigma on HIV Risk Behavior among Men Who Have Sex with Men in Chennai, India," *AIDS Care* 24, no. 11 (2012): 1401–6, https://doi.org/10.1080/09540121.2012.672717.

22. See more details at the Institute for Health Metrics and Evaluation website, http://www.healthdata.org/gbd. These estimates in the model for India use the 2010 Global Burden of Disease study.

23. The South Africa study also estimates a loss of $10 million–$65 million because of disproportionate rates of sexual assault against LGBT people.

24. Eric Manalastas, "Work, Wage Autonomy, and Contributions to Household Expenditures among Young Filipino Gay Men," presentation slides, 2009.

25. Niclas Berggren, Christian Bjørnskov, and Therese Nilsson, "What Aspects of Society Matter for the Quality of Life of a Minority? Global Evidence from the New Gay Happiness Index," *Social Indicators Research* 132, no. 3 (2017): 1163–92, DOI: 10.1007/s11205-016-1340-3.

26. Pink Armenia, *The Impact of LGBT Emigration on Economic Indicators of Armenia* (Yerevan, Armenia: Public Information and Need of Knowledge and Socioscope, 2015), http://www.pinkarmenia.org/publication/lgbtemigrationen.pdf.

27. Claire Thurlow, *The Economic Cost of Homophobia* (London: Peter Tatchell Foundation, 2018), https://www.petertatchellfoundation.org/wp-content/uploads/2018/06/report-a4-lo-res-1.pdf.

28. One study tried to add up the impact of employee turnover on businesses in ten countries. The study includes Australia, Brazil, Canada, France, Germany, India, Italy, Mexico, the UK, and the US. While their general argument about the cost of turnover makes sense at the business level, their measures and approach of adding up business losses make their overall estimate too high. Johnson and Cooper, *LGBT Diversity*.

29. Berggren, Bjørnskov, and Nilsson, "What Aspects of Society Matter for the Quality of Life of a Minority?"

30. We made adjustments so we can make comparisons across countries and years. More information on the data and study of emerging economics can be found in M. V. Lee Badgett et al., "The Relationship between LGBT Inclusion and Economic Development: An Analysis of Emerging Economies," Williams Institute, UCLA School of Law and USAID, 2014, http://williamsinstitute.law.ucla.edu/wp-content/uploads/lgbt-inclusion-and-development-november-2014.pdf.

31. The line drawn in is the one that best fits these simple data, calculated by a regression of the GILRHO on GDP per capita.

32. M. V. Lee Badgett, Kees Waaldijk, and Yana van der Meulen Rodgers, "The Relationship between LGBT Inclusion and Economic Development: Macro-Level Evidence," *World Development* 120 (2019): 1–14, https://doi.org/10.1016/j.worlddev.2019.03.011.

33. We only had data on the gender variable for 1997–2011. In the estimates for just those years, the LGBT inclusion effect increased slightly from $510 to $514 with the addition of the gender variable. In the study of thirty-eight emerging economies, the impact of one additional right fell from $320 to $289 when the gender variable was added.

34. M. V. Lee Badgett, Andrew Flores, and Andrew Park, *Links Between Economic Development and New Measures of LGBT Inclusion* (Los Angeles: Williams Institute, UCLA School of Law, 2018), https://williamsinstitute.law.ucla.edu/wp-content/uploads/GDP-and-LGBT-Inclusion-April-2018.pdf.

35. Lamontagne et al., "A Socioecological Measurement of Homophobia for All Countries and Its Public Health Impact."

36. Richard Florida, "The Global Map of Homophobia," CityLab, *Atlantic*, February 7, 2014, http://www.theatlanticcities.com/politics/2014/02/global-map-homophobia/8309/; Richard Florida and Irene Tinagli, "Europe in the Creative Age," February 2004, http://www.creativeclass.com/rfcgdb/articles/Europe_in_the_Creative_Age_2004.pdf.

37. Richard Florida and Gary J. Gates, *Technology and Tolerance: The Importance of Diversity to High-Technology Growth* (Washington, DC: Center on Urban & Metropolitan Policy, Brookings Institution, June 2001).

38. Meredith L. Weiss, "'We Know Who You Are. We'll Employ You': Non-Discrimination and Singapore's Bohemian Dreams," in *Sexual Orientation Discrimination: An International Perspective*, ed. M. V. Lee Badgett and Jeff Frank (New York: Routledge, 2007).

39. "Singapore: Thousands Turn Out in Support of LGBT," *Asian Correspondent*, July 2017, https://asiancorrespondent.com/2017/07/singapore-thousands-turn-support-lgbt-rights.

40. Marcus Noland, "Popular Attitudes, Globalization, and Risk," *International Finance* 8, no. 2 (2005): 199–229.

41. For example, see Ronald F. Inglehart, "Changing Values among Western Publics from 1970 to 2006," *West European Politics* 31, no. 1–2 (2008): 130–46, https://doi.org/10.1080/01402380701834747.

42. The Supreme Court of India decriminalized homosexuality with its *Navtej Singh Johar v. Union of India* ruling in 2018.

43. The contribution of the cost of homophobia to explain the between-country comparisons would be smaller when using the 132 country study findings. The global figure mentioned earlier of $2,065 per right on average is 18 percent of average GDP per capita, $11,579, for the 132 countries. See Badgett, Waaldijk, and Rodgers, "The Relationship between LGBT Inclusion and Economic Development."

CHAPTER 6: A WAY FORWARD

1. The rainbow flag was designed in 1978 by Gilbert Baker. Gilbert Baker, *Rainbow Warrior: My Life in Color* (Chicago: Chicago Review Press, 2019). Many LGBT organizational logos and report covers use some form of a rainbow, if not the flag itself.

2. This story is presented with permission and is based on presentations made at the Salzburg Global Seminar and on an interview with the author.

3. Roselyn Odoyo, *Outsider Citizen: Landscape Analysis of the Human Rights of Sex Workers and LGBTI People in Ethiopia* (Nairobi: UHAI EASHRI, 2015).

4. Odoyo, *Outsider Citizen.*

5. Dennis Altman and Jonathan Symons, *Queer Wars* (Cambridge, UK: Polity, 2016); Cynthia Burack, *Because We Are Human: Contesting US Support for Gender and Sexuality Human Rights Abroad* (Albany: State University of New York Press, 2018).

6. Badgett, Waaldijk, and Rodgers, "Relationship between LGBT Inclusion and Economic Development."

7. Andrew Kohut et al., "The Global Divide on Homosexuality," Pew Research Center, June 4, 2013, http://www.pewglobal.org/2013/06/04/the-global -divide-on-homosexuality.

8. Tom W. Smith, Jaesok Son, and Jibum Kim, *Public Attitudes Towards Homosexuality and Gay Rights Across Time and Countries* (Chicago: NORC/ Williams Institute UCLA School of Law, November 2014), https://williams institute.law.ucla.edu/wp-content/uploads/public-attitudes-nov-2014.pdf.

9. Andrew R. Flores and Andrew Park, *Polarized Progress: Social Acceptance of LGBT People in 141 Countries, 1981 to 2014* (Los Angeles: Williams Institute, UCLA School of Law, 2018), https://williamsinstitute.law.ucla.edu /wp-content/uploads/Polarized-Progress-April-2018.pdf. They estimated the index in years for which no relevant survey questions were asked in a given country.

10. Katie Rogers, "Trump's Celebration of L.G.B.T. Rights Is Met with Criticism," *New York Times*, June 1, 2019, https://www.nytimes.com/2019/06 /01/us/politics/trump-lgbt-rights.html.

11. Mariana Simões, "Brazil's Polarizing New President, Jair Bolsonaro, in His Own Words," *New York Times*, October 28, 2018, https://www.nytimes .com/2018/10/28/world/americas/brazil-president-jair-bolsonaro-quotes.html.

12. Tom Phillips and Anna Jean Kaiser, "Brazil Must Not Become a 'Gay Tourism Paradise,' Says Bolsonaro," *Guardian*, April 25, 2019, https://www .theguardian.com/world/2019/apr/26/bolsonaro-accused-of-inciting-hatred -with-gay-paradise-comment; Morgan Gstalter, "Brazil's New President Removes LGBT Concerns from Human Rights Ministry," *Hill*, January 2, 2019, https://thehill.com/policy/international/human-rights/423594-brazils-new -president-removes-lgbt-concerns-from-human.

13. Rahul Rao, "Staying Positivist in the Fight Against Homophobia," *Sexuality Policy Watch Newsletter*, no. 14 (July 3, 2014); Andil Gosine, "Rescue, and Real Love: Same-Sex Desire in International Development," in *Routledge Handbook of Queer Development Studies*, ed. Corinne L. Mason (New York: Routledge, 2018). I have also had many conversations and informal debates with human rights activists on these issues.

14. For an account of a recent debate, see Marc Parry, "Shackles and Dollars," *Chronicle Review*, Chronicle of Higher Education, December 8, 2016, https://www.chronicle.com/article/ShacklesDollars/238598.

15. Jeff Tyson, "At the World Bank, Turning Finance Ministers into Gay Rights Advocates," Devex (website), March 6, 2015, devex.com/news/at-the -world-bank-turning-finance-ministers-into-gay-rights-advocates-85633.

16. Kaushik Basu, "A Welcome Address on IDAHOT 2016," *Let's Talk Development*, blog, 2016, https://blogs.worldbankorg/developmenttalk /welcome-address-idahot-2016.

17. Aengus Carroll, *State-Sponsored Homophobia: A World Survey of Sexual Orientation Laws; Criminalisation, Protection and Recognition* (Geneva: ILGA, 2016).

18. Tracy McVeigh, Paul Harris, and Barbara Among, "Anti-Gay Bigots Plunge Africa into New Era of Hate Crimes," *Guardian*, December 12, 2009, https://www.theguardian.com/world/2009/dec/13/death-penalty-uganda -homosexuals.

19. Jeffrey Gettleman, "Ugandan Who Spoke Up for Gays Is Beaten to Death," *New York Times*, January 27, 2011, http://www.nytimes.com/2011/01 /28/world/africa/28uganda.html.

20. Gettleman, "Ugandan Who Spoke Up for Gays Is Beaten to Death."

21. New Humanitarian, "Briefing: Punitive Aid Cuts Disrupt Healthcare in Uganda," April 2, 2014, http://www.thenewhumanitarian.org/analysis /2014/04/02/briefing-punitive-aid-cuts-disrupt-healthcare-uganda#.

22. Stella Nyanzi, "The Paradoxical Geopolitics of Recriminalizing Homosexuality in Uganda: One of Three Ugly Sisters," *Sexuality Policy Watch Newsletter*, no. 14 (July 3, 2014), http://sxpolitics.org/article-nl14/9386#sthash .EFoePfBO.dpuf.

23. Yoweri Kaguta Museveni, "The Way Forward on Homosexuality: Should We Involve Uganda in Endless Wars with Our Trade Partners on Account of This?," Pan African Visions, October 4, 2014, https://www.

panafricanvisions.com/2014/way-forward-homosexuality-involve-uganda
-endless-wars-trade-partners-account/#.

24. Altman and Symons, *Queer Wars*; Javier Corrales, "The Expansion
of LGBT Rights in Latin America . . . and the Backlash," in *The Oxford
Handbook of Global LGBT and Sexual Diversity Politics*, ed. Michael Bosia,
Sandra M. McEvoy, and Momin Rahman (New York: Oxford University
Press, 2019).

25. For a good discussion of that process in the United States, see Burack,
Because We Are Human.

26. Badgett, Waaldijk, and Rodgers, "The Relationship between LGBT
Inclusion and Economic Development."

27. M. V. Lee Badgett, Laura E. Durso, and Alyssa Schneebaum, "New
Patterns of Poverty in the Lesbian, Gay, and Bisexual Community" (Los
Angeles: Williams Institute, UCLA School of Law, June 2013), http://williams
institute.law.ucla.edu/wp-content/uploads/LGB-Poverty-Update-Jun-2013
.pdf; Alyssa Schneebaum and M. V. Lee Badgett, "Poverty in US Lesbian and
Gay Couple Households," *Feminist Economics* 25, no. 1 (2019): 1–30, https://
doi.org/10.1080/13545701.2018.1441533; M. V. Lee Badgett, "Left Out? Lesbian,
Gay, and Bisexual Poverty in the U.S.," *Population Research and Policy Review*
37, no. 5 (2018): 667–702, https://doi.org/10.1007/s11113-018-9457-5; Sonya
Arreola et al., *Access to HIV Prevention and Treatment for Men Who Have Sex
with Men: Findings from the 2012 Global Men's Health and Rights Study* (Oakland, CA: Global Forum on MSM & HIV [MSMGF], 2012); Lori E. Ross et
al., "Bisexuality, Poverty and Mental Health: A Mixed Methods Analysis," *Social Science and Medicine* 156 (2016): 64–72, https://doi.org/10.1016/j.socscimed
.2016.03.009; Micro Rainbow International, *Poverty, Sexual Orientation and
Refugees in the UK* (London: Micro Rainbow International, October 2013),
https://microrainbow.org/wp-content/uploads/2013/10/MR_REPORT_UK
_digital-final-for-the-web-Reduced.pdf; S. C. Noah Uhrig, "Sexual Orienta-
tion and Poverty in the UK: A Review and Top-Line Findings from the UK
Household Longitudinal Study," *Journal of Research in Gender Studies* 5, no.
1 (2015): 23–72, http://search.proquest.com.ezp.waldenulibrary.org; Lucas
Paoli Itaborahy, *LGBT People Living in Poverty in Rio de Janeiro* (London:
Micro Rainbow International, June 2014); Rachana Chhoeurng, Yara Kong,
and Erin Power, *Poverty of LGBT People in Cambodia* (London: Micro Rainbow International, May 2016), https://mrifoundation.global/wp-content
/uploads/2017/12/CambodiaReportEN.pdf.

28. See Article IV, Section 10 of World Bank, "International Bank for
Reconstruction and Development Articles of Agreement," 2012, http://
pubdocs.worldbank.org/en/722361541184234501/IBRDArticlesOfAgreement
-English.pdf.

29. World Bank, *Inclusion Matters: The Foundation for Shared Prosperity*
(Washington, DC: World Bank, 2013).

30. Fabrice Houdart, personal communication, various dates; Tyson, "At the World Bank, Turning Finance Ministers into Gay Rights Advocates."

31. Jim Yong Kim, "The High Costs of Institutional Discrimination," *Washington Post*, Febrary 27, 2014, https://www.washingtonpost.com /opinions/jim-yong-kim-the-high-costs-of-institutional-discrimination /2014/02/27/8cd37ad0–9fc5–11e3-b8d8–94577ff66b28_story.html.

32. Danielle Douglas-Gabriel, "Here Is Why the World Bank Withheld Aid to Uganda," *Washington Post*, April 3, 2014, https://www.washingtonpost .com/news/wonk/wp/2014/04/03/here-is-why-the-world-bank-withheld-aid -to-uganda.

33. For example, see Amsterdam Network, The Amsterdam Network Guiding Principles (Version 1.0), 2013.

34. Civil Society Coalition on Human Rights & Constitutional Law, "Guidelines to National, Regional, and International Partners on How to Offer Support Now That the Anti-Homosexuality Law Has Been Assented To," Kampala, Uganda, March 3, 2014, http://www.ugandans4rights.org /attachments/article/428/14_03_03_CSCHRCL_guidelines_to_partners.pdf; New Humanitarian, "Briefing: Punitive Aid Cuts Disrupt Healthcare in Uganda."

35. See the World Bank's page on SOGI issues: https://www.worldbank .org/en/topic/sexual-orientation-and-gender-identity#1.

36. Clifton Cortez, telephone conversation with author, March 22, 2019.

37. World Bank, *Bank Directive: Addressing Risks and Impacts on Disadvantaged or Vulnerable Individuals or Groups* (August 4, 2016), https://policies .worldbank.org/sites/ppf3/PPFDocuments/e5562765a5534ea0b7877e1e775f 29d5.pdf.

38. World Bank, "ID Enabling Environment Assessment Guidance Note," October 2018, https://id4d.worldbank.org/sites/id4d.worldbank.org /files/2018-12/IDEEA%20Guidance%20Note%20-%20Consultation%20 Draft%20V11142018.pdf.

39. World Bank, *Identification for Development: Strategic Framework* (2016), http://pubdocs.worldbank.org/en/179901454620206363/Jan-2016 -ID4D-Strategic-Roadmap.pdf; Neelam Pandey, "In a First, Aadhar Recognises 1,600 Transgender Persons," *Hindustan Times*, August 27, 2013, https:// www.hindustantimes.com/delhi-news/in-a-first-aadhar-recognises-1–600 -transgender-persons/story-Geb68xqQ8KiVT1cyUeqLxL.html.

40. Burack, *Because We Are Human.*

41. See United Nations, "The Price of Exclusion," Free & Equal, https:// www.unfe.org/the-price-of-exclusion, accessed May 18, 2019.

42. UNESCO, *Out in the Open: Education Sector Responses to Violence Based on Sexual Orientation and Gender Identity/Expression* (Paris: UNESCO, 2016).

43. J. Lester Feder, "Homophobia Costs India an Estimated $31 Billion Annually—Should Development Institutions Care?," *BuzzFeed*, March 14, 2014, https://www.buzzfeednews.com/article/lesterfeder/homophobia-costs

-india-an-estimated-31-billion-annually-shou; Erik Lamontagne et al., "A Socioecological Measurement of Homophobia for All Countries and Its Public Health Impact," *European Journal of Public Health* 28, no. 5 (2018): 967–72, https://doi.org/10.1093/eurpub/cky023.

44. UN Office of the High Commissioner for Human Rights, *Tackling Discrimination Against Lesbian, Gay, Bi, Trans, & Intersex People: Standards of Conduct for Business* (New York: OHCHR, 2017).

45. See the UN Development Programme web page for this program, "Being LGBTI in Asia and the Pacific," http://www.asia-pacific.undp.org /content/rbap/en/home/programmes-and-initiatives/being-lgbt-in-asia.html, ongoing project begun in 2014.

46. See UN Development Programme (UNDP), "Measuring LGBTI Inclusion: Increasing Access to Data and Building the Evidence Base," June 2016; M. V. Lee Badgett and Randall Sell, *A Set of Proposed Indicators for the LGBTI Inclusion Index* (New York: UNDP, 2018). For more on the SDGs and how they could address inclusion of LGBTI people, see Elizabeth Mills, "'Leave No One Behind': Gender, Sexuality and the Sustainable Development Goals," *IDS Evidence Report*, Sexuality, Poverty and Law, no. 145 (October 2015), https://opendocs.ids.ac.uk/opendocs/bitstream/handle /123456789/7104/ER154_LeaveNoOneBehindGenderSexualityandtheSDGs.pdf; Jeffrey O'Malley and Andreas Holzinger, "Sexual and Gender Minorities and the Sustainable Development Goals," United Nations Development Programme, 2018, https://www.undp.org/content/dam/undp/library/HIV -AIDS/Key%20populations/SDGs_SexualAndGenderMinorities.pdf; Andrew Park and Lucas Ramon Mendos, *For All: The Sustainable Development Goals and LGBTI People* (Stockholm: RFSL Förbundet, 2019), https://doi .org/10.13140/RG.2.2.23989.73447.

47. Burack, *Because We Are Human*; US Department of State, "Global Equality Fund," March 18, 2019, https://www.state.gov/global-equality-fund.

48. Andrew Wallace, Ben Francisco Maulbeck, and Lyle Matthew Kan, *2015–2016 Global Resources Report: Government and Philanthropic Support for Lesbian, Gay, Bisexual, Transgender, and Intersex Communities* (New York: Funders for LGBTQ Issues and Global Philanthropy Project, April 2018), https://lgbtfunders.org/wp-content/uploads/2018/04/2015-2016_Global _Resources_Report.pdf.

49. USAID, "LGBT Vision for Action: Promoting and Supporting the Inclusion of Lesbian, Gay, Bisexual, and Transgender Individuals," 2014, https://www.usaid.gov/sites/default/files/documents/1861/LGBT_Vision _For_Action_May2014.pdf; USAID, "Nondiscrimination for Beneficiaries: Frequently Asked Questions," December 23, 2016, https://www.usaid.gov /what-we-do/democracy-human-rights-and-governance/protecting-human -rights/nondiscrimination-faq.

50. Other original partners included the Astraea Lesbian Foundation for Justice; the Arcus Foundation; Gay & Lesbian Victory Fund; the Williams

Institute; the Swedish Federation for Lesbian, Gay, Bisexual, Transgender, and Queer Rights (RFSL); and the National Gay & Lesbian Chamber of Commerce. USAID, "The LGBTI Global Development Partnership," fact sheet, USAID, https://www.usaid.gov/sites/default/files/documents/2496/LGBTI_Global_Development_Partnership_Fact_Sheet_Final_160622.pdf.

51. Anthony Cotton, Aline Magnoni, Derek Simon, and Brett Tolman, *Suggested Approaches for Integrating Inclusive Development Across the Program Cycle and in Mission Operations* (Washington, DC: USAID, 2018), https://usaidlearninglab.org/sites/default/files/resource/files/additional_help_for_ads_201_inclusive_development_180726_final_r.pdf.

52. Javier Corrales, "Understanding the Uneven Spread of LGBT Rights in Latin America and the Caribbean," *Journal of Research in Gender Studies* 7, no. 1 (2017): 52–82, https://doi.org/10.22381/JRGS7120172.

53. One expression of this principle comes from the Amsterdam Network that started the global conferences. Amsterdam Network, "Amsterdam Network Guiding Principles (Version 1.0)."

54. Annika Nilsson and Jessica Rothman, *Evaluation of the Sida Supported RFSL Projects: "LGBT Voices" and "Rainbow Leaders"* (Stockholm: Sida, 2017), https://www.sida.se/contentassets/a09863bdac41467ea541a12e2160caf5/22051.pdf.

55. Civil Society Coalition on Human Rights & Constitutional Law, "Guidelines to National, Regional, and International Partners on How to Offer Support."

56. Jon Miller, personal email communication with author, June 2, 2019.

57. Reuters, "Kenya Losing Over Sh100 Billion Annually in LGBT Discrimination, Firms Say," *Standard Digital*, February 27, 2019, https://www.standardmedia.co.ke/article/2001314601/gay-discrimination-costs-kenya-over-sh100-billion.

CHAPTER 7: STRATEGIES FOR REALIZING THE GAINS FROM LGBT (AND LGBTI) EQUALITY

1. Movement Advancement Project, *2018 National Movement Report: A Financial Overview of Leading Organizations in the LGBT Movement* (Boulder, CO: Movement Advancement Project, 2018), http://www.lgbtmap.org/file/SAR-2018-National-FINAL.pdf.

2. The figures on the global picture in this section include intersex organizations, too, and come from Wallace, Maulbeck, and Kan, *2015–2016 Global Resources Report*. However, the data on funding is missing from UNDP and the UK government, and it is partial for the US government. Given the size of most country-level contributions, it seems unlikely that including those would significantly change the patterns described here.

3. Wallace, Maulbeck, and Kan, *2015–2016 Global Resources Report*, 64.

4. Wallace, Maulbeck, and Kan, *2015–2016 Global Resources Report*, 9.

5. There's little included on issues related to families, particularly parenting laws and marriage equality, mainly (I think) because of concerns about

backlash in some countries and about stacking the index in favor of the high-income countries with marriage equality.

6. See Tilcsik, "Pride and Prejudice"; Marieka Klawitter, "Multilevel Analysis of the Effects of Antidiscrimination Policies on Earnings by Sexual Orientation," *Journal of Policy Analysis and Management* 30, no. 2 (2011): 334–58, https://doi.org/10.1002/pam.20563; Amanda K. Baumle and Dudley L. Poston Jr., "The Economic Cost of Homosexuality: Multilevel Analyses," *Social Forces* 89, no. 3 (2011): 1005–32; Michael E. Martell, "Do ENDAs End Discrimination for Behaviorally Gay Men?," *Journal of Labor Research* 34, no. 2 (November 13, 2012): 147–69, https://doi.org/10.1007/s12122–012–9154–9; Ian Burn, "Not All Laws Are Created Equal: Legal Differences in State Non-Discrimination Laws and the Impact of LGBT Employment Protections," *Journal of Labor Research* 39, no. 4 (2018): 462–97, doi.org/10.1007/s12122–018–9272–0.

7. Charles Kenny and Dev Patel, "Norms and Reform: Legalizing Homosexuality Improves Attitudes," working paper, Center for Global Development, 2017, https://doi.org/10.2139/ssrn.3062911.

8. Tarik Abou-Chadi and Ryan Finnigan, "Rights for Same-Sex Couples and Public Attitudes Toward Gays and Lesbians in Europe," *Comparative Political Studies*, 2018, doi.org/10.1177/0010414018797947; Cevat G. Aksoy et al., "Do Laws Shape Attitudes? Evidence from Same-Sex Relationship Recognition Policies in Europe," Discussion Paper Series, IZA Institute of Labor Economics, Bonn, August 2018. See also Andrew R. Flores and Scott Barclay, "Backlash, Consensus, Legitimacy, or Polarization: The Effect of Same-Sex Marriage Policy on Mass Attitudes," *Political Research Quarterly* 69, no. 1 (2016): 43–56, https://doi.org/10.1177/1065912915621175.

9. US Chamber of Commerce Foundation, *Business Success and Growth Through LGBT-Inclusive Culture* (Washington, DC: US Chamber of Commerce Foundation, 2019), 28, https://www.uschamberfoundation.org/sites/default/files/Business-Success-Growth-LGBT-Inclusive-Culture-FINAL-WEB.pdf.

10. Perry v. Schwarzenegger, 704 F. Supp. 2d 921 (N.D. Cal. 2010).

11. Wallace, Maulbeck, and Kan, *2015–2016 Global Resources Report*, 24.

12. M. V. Lee Badgett and Philip Crehan, "Developing Actionable Research Priorities for LGBTI Inclusion," *Journal of Research in Gender Studies* 7, no. 1 (2017): 218–47, https://doi.org/10.22381/jrgs7120178.

13. Institute of Medicine, *Health of Lesbian, Gay, Bisexual, and Transgender People*.

14. Stephenie R. Chaudoir, Katie Wang, and John E. Pachankis, "What Reduces Sexual Minority Stress? A Review of the Intervention 'Toolkit,'" *Journal of Social Issues* 73, no. 3 (2017): 586–617, https://doi.org/10.1111/josi.12233.

15. Chhoeurng, Kong, and Power, *Poverty of LGBT People in Cambodia*; Micro Rainbow International, *Poverty, Sexual Orientation and Refugees in the UK*; Itaborahy, *LGBT People Living in Poverty in Rio de Janeiro*.

16. US Chamber of Commerce Foundation, *Business Success and Growth Through LGBT-Inclusive Culture*, 33.

17. Examples exist of networks coming together to work on important practical questions about how to collect data on sexual orientation and gender identity on large-scale surveys. See Sexual Minority Assessment Research Team, *Best Practices for Asking Questions about Sexual Orientation on Surveys* (Los Angeles: Williams Institute, UCLA School of Law, 2009), http://williams institute.law.ucla.edu/wp-content/uploads/SMART-FINAL-Nov-2009.pdf; Gender Identity in US Surveillance Group (GenIUSS), *Best Practices for Asking Questions to Identify Transgender and Other Gender Minority Respondents on Population-Based Surveys* (Los Angeles: Williams Institute, UCLA School of Law, September 2014), https://williamsinstitute.law.ucla.edu/wp-content /uploads/geniuss-report-sep-2014.pdf.

18. UN Development Programme, *Being LGBTI in China*, 40.

19. Burack, *Because We Are Human.*

20. Danny Lee and Phila Siu, "Hong Kong's Airport Authority Joins MTR Corp in Reversing Ban on Cathay Pacific Same-Sex Ad After LGBT Outcry," *South China Morning Post*, May 21, 2019, https://www.scmp.com /news/hong-kong/transport/article/3011055/hong-kongs-mtr-corp-buckles -under-lgbt-criticism-and.

21. "GDP Indicators 2019," *Statistics Times*, http://statisticstimes.com /economy/gdp-indicators-2019.php.

22. World Bank, "Gross Domestic Product 2018," https://databank.world bank.org/data/download/GDP.pdf.

INDEX

ABOUT THE AUTHOR

M. V. Lee Badgett has studied the economics of LGBT life for more than twenty-five years. She is a professor of economics and the former director of the School of Public Policy at the University of Massachusetts Amherst. She is also a Williams Distinguished Scholar at the Williams Institute for Sexual Orientation and Gender Identity Law & Public Policy (UCLA School of Law), where she was a cofounder and the first research director. Badgett received a PhD in economics from the University of California, Berkeley, in 1990, and earned a BA in economics from the University of Chicago in 1982. She has also taught at Yale University and the University of Maryland.

Badgett's first book, *Money, Myths, and Change,* debunked the myth of gay affluence and showed economic inequalities based on sexual orientation. She has testified on her work before the US Congress, many state legislatures, and in California's Proposition 8 trial. Badgett has appeared on many radio shows and in several publications, including the *Wall Street Journal, New York Times, Los Angeles Times,* and *Washington Post.* In 2008 *Curve* magazine named her one of the twenty most powerful lesbians in academia, and she has appeared on the *Advocate* magazine's "Our Best and Brightest Activists" list and in *Out* magazine's "Out 100." Her most recent book, *The Public Professor,* draws on her experiences in the public eye and shows scholars how to be more engaged and influential in public debates.

With the publication of her book *When Gay People Get Married*, which demonstrated that marriage by same-sex couples did not harm the institution of marriage in the Netherlands, she has branched out to study the global situation for LGBT people. As a consultant to the World Bank, she developed an innovative and widely cited model of the cost of homophobia in India. She has worked closely with the United Nations Development Programme on the creation of a global LGBTI Inclusion Index. The US State Department twice selected her for its speakers program, sending her on international speaking tours. Badgett is a fellow of the Salzburg Global Seminar's LGBT Forum and has spoken about her research at the OECD, USAID, Asian Development Bank, Inter-American Development Bank, Australian Parliament, and many other locations around the world.